INTRODUCTION

The Merthyr Tydfil Historical Society was formed in 1972 to preserve the past, protect the present and propagate the future. In 1976 the Society published a series of lectures under the title: "Merthyr Historian". The favourable reception of this publication encourages us to offer a further series of lectures to the public as Volume Two of the Merthyr Historian.

The lectures, which cover a variety of topics, have been arranged in four groups:

Industrial History

Living Conditions

Aspects of Social History

Sources towards a History of Merthyr Tydfil.

Readers of the earlier volume will meet several authors who contributed to that volume and again supplied articles for Volume Two.

Mr. Robert V. Barnes writes a fascinating article covering the history of the railways of the whole of Wales. Mr. John Owen, who combines technical expertise of all aspects of iron and steel production with a thorough knowledge of Merthyr's industrial past, writes about the fifty years up to World War I. He also contributes a unique description of the locomotives of the Dowlais Works, which is not only of general interest but will also appeal to railway enthusiasts everywhere. Mr. Owen also provided the illustrations for his articles, selected from his vast collection of photographs. Miss Margaret S. Taylor describes the life and work of another of Merthyr's famous sons and daughters, namely Thomas Stephens. Joseph Gross describes the many difficulties and final success in providing Merthyr with an adequate supply of water and efficient drainage. In a second article he traces the history of the hospitals in Merthyr.

New contributors include Mr. Leo Davies, who uses his wide knowledge of Merthyr's bridges to describe the Iron Bridge of 1800. Mrs. Diane Green draws on her extensive research into the domestic architecture of Merthyr. She also kindly supplied the illustrations for her article. Mr. Jeremy K. Knight writes a scholarly article on the early christian era in South Wales. Mr. Huw Williams and Mr. Alun Morgan deal with conditions of life during the General Strike and the great depression following it. Mr. Williams also contributes a survey of sources available to those who wish to explore Merthyr's fascinating history further. We are grateful to all the authors who made their lectures freely available for this publication.

We also wish to thank Mr. Idris Farr, who kindly provided the drawings of the Iron Bridge and the now demolished "Triangle". These drawings appear on the front and back covers of the book. We are also grateful to the Planning Department of the Merthyr Tydfil Borough Council for kindly supplying another illustration of the Iron Bridge (Illustration 54).

We further wish to express our thanks to Mr. T. Whitney, Chief Librarian, Mr. M. Harris, Librarian and all members of the staffs of the Merthyr Libraries and Museum for their unfailing help and support. We are also grateful to Mr. John Gross for his great help with many of the photographs.

JOSEPH GROSS, *Editor*,
Yr Hafod, Heol Y Mynydd
Cefn Coed, Merthyr Tydfil
Mid. Glam.

MERTHYR HISTORIAN

VOLUME TWO

MERTHYR TYDFIL HISTORICAL SOCIETY
SOUTH WALES
1978

First Edition 1978

© MERTHYR TYDFIL HISTORICAL SOCIETY
ISBN 0 9504845 1 2

THE STARLING PRESS LTD.
PRINTERS & PUBLISHERS
RISCA NEWPORT GWENT
GREAT BRITAIN

PHOTOGRAPHS

Reproduction of some of these photographs has been impaired due to age. They are included however since it is important to have them as historical records. The reader is requested to make allowances when bearing this in mind, since the Printers have attempted to overcome this difficulty. Blurred images and variations in tone are due to faulty photographs and are not the product of printing inadequacies.

CONTENTS

LIST OF ILLUSTRATIONS

I. INDUSTRIAL HISTORY

1. ROBERT V. BARNES

THE RAILWAY AGE IN WALES

The Industrial Revolution in the second half of the eighteenth century drew attention to the desperate need for improved means of communication. Initially this gave rise to the canal age, and for large bulk commodities the coming of the canal represented a tremendous step forward in terms of cost and ease of transport. The geography of Wales, however, meant that the canal was strictly limited in its usefulness. As I have indicated elsewhere, the geographical nature of South Wales restricted canals to the valleys and largely prevented any major linking with the fairly comprehensive English network. The railway was able to overcome many of these difficulties, and, in addition, provide a rapid, efficient and reasonably cheap means of transport.

Communications in Wales around 1760 were virtually non-existent. Professor A. H. Dodd, in his book "The Industrial Revolution in North Wales" describes the following situation,

> "If travellers about to cross the Welsh border no longer had need to go in bands, well armed and fortified beforehand by prayers for safety from highwaymen, it needed a measure of courage to encounter 'a Welsh journey'."

He goes on to explain that since Roman times roads had not been made but had merely developed and he quotes contemporary sources as asserting that there were " but few travellable roads in the whole district". Some turnpike trusts had been set up on parts of the principal mail routes, but apart from these travel was hard and perilous.

It was into conditions like this that the Railway Age in Wales was born. Its birth was long and protracted and not, indeed, without attempts by those with vested interests in the countryside, to smother the infant before it had had time to develop.

Railways developed largely as a result of three factors : firstly in their earliest and most primitive forms they provided the means of conveying mineral traffic from mine and quarry, iron works and copper works, to canal or port. I described in detail in the last lecture I gave to this Society the way in which Merthyr Tydfil became the cradle of the Railway Age in Wales with the development of primitive feeder tramroads in the area at the beginning of the nineteenth century and the important experiment of Trevithick at Penydarren. Tramroads were developing elsewhere in Wales during the second half of the eighteenth century and the early years of the nineteenth. Around the towns of Neath and Swansea wooden plateways had appeared as early as the 1750's. In North Wales, to meet the requirements of the slate quarries, primitive tramways had been developed around Port Dinor-

9

wic, Penrhyn, and further south around Port Madoc. On the Welsh border similar developments were taking place around the estuary of the Dee, whilst in Mid-Wales the famous Hay Railway was built during the first decade of the nineteenth century. In this context, therefore, primitive railways met a peculiarly local need. Their very crudeness meant that they were often a less satisfactory second choice than a canal, necessitated often on grounds of economy or geography, or both. As such, these developments represented the first faltering steps of the Railway Age in Wales. Yet as the railway developed, as it became more sophisticated and reliable, so it established itself in Wales, as elsewhere in the British Isles, as one of the most dynamic forces in the rapid rise of an industrial society, and brought about changes more rapid and more revolutionary in society than those witnessed during the whole of the preceding millenium.

If the first reason for the development of railways in Wales was peculiarly local, the second reason was exactly the opposite. The Railway Age proper came to Wales as a result of the desire by the British government to establish more efficient transport links with Ireland. In North Wales the line to Holyhead eventually provided an important communication artery from London to Ireland, whilst the South Wales Main line, also provided a fast connection between London and Ireland via Milford Haven. Indeed, in the first flush of the railway mania of the 1830's, grandiose proposals had been put forward for a railway through the mountains of Central Wales and Porthdinlleyn on the Lleyn peninsula which would afford a new and shorter embarkation point for Ireland than Holyhead. The cost and the engineering were formidable and so the scheme was abortive but it foreshadowed grand schemes yet to emerge, like the Manchester & Milford Railway project, doomed to a similar fate, and also aimed at conquering the great fastnesses of Wales.

The third factor to influence the Railway Age in Wales was also the last chronologically. This was the desire, again by local communities to obtain railway communication. The success of the railway had already been amply demonstrated, both in North and South Wales where the main lines had already appeared and throughout England. This led to a feeling that the prosperity of an area and the obtaining of a railway were somehow inextricably linked and the result was the promotion of innumerable railway schemes to link even the remotest parts of Wales to the main railway network of the country. It is these schemes which form the basis of this lecture, for it is they which resulted in the railway network of Wales prior to the savage axing of Dr. Beeching in the 1960's—that railway network, which for all its faults and idiosyncrasies, served Wales well in the pre-motor age—that railway network which gave to Wales the numerous little independent companies and branches each proud of its independence and its achievements, each distinctive in its livery, its locomotives. and its lines, yet each contributing effectively to the quality of life, and to the society of its own particular part of the principality.

No account of the Railway Age in Wales would be complete without reference to two important facts. In the first place, all the railway development which took place in Wales, took place as a result of private enterprise. Often finance was raised locally to promote railways, in other cases lines were financed by the big London railway companies. It is no small tribute to the enthusiasm of Victorian Wales for railways nor of the confidence placed in railways as an investment, that this finance was forthcoming. In some cases this confidence proved unfounded and money was lost or no dividend declared. In others, like the industrial railway companies of South Wales such as the Taff Vale and the Rhymney, a high level of dividend to shareholders was sustained and large profits made.

The second fact is the actual feat of construction involved in bringing the railway into Wales. It must be remembered that all the Welsh railways were constructed in the pre-mechanized age. They were the result of navvy labour to make cuttings, embankments and tunnels. They involved significant civil engineering features — the Chepstow bridge, the Landore viaduct and the Cockett tunnel on the South Wales main line, the Britannia tubular bridge, the Conway suspension bridge and the work at Penmaenmawr high above the shoreline on the North Wales main line, and features like the Crumlin, Barmouth, Walnut Tree, Hengoed, Cefn Coed and Porthkerry viaducts on other lines as well as remarkable tunnels like Wenvoe, Rhondda, and Festiniog, and cuttings like Talerddig. The Railway Age in Wales stands as a tribute to industry and engineering skill, to enterpise and endurance.

I propose to deal with the Railway Age in Wales geographically, dividing the Principality with South, Central, and North. Within each geographical area I propose briefly to treat the subject chronologically in order to give in outline, a picture of how railways developed, flourished and declined in Wales between 1830 and the present day. I have to confess to only giving the most cursory coverage to the dawn of the Railway Age in Wales in the development of tramroads between 1750 and 1820. This would be a study in itself. For myself, I have chosen to concentrate on the Railway Age proper from 1830 to the present day—or the death of Huskisson to the axe of Beeching.

When I addressed you last time I dealt in some detail with the history of the railways of Merthyr and its associated valleys. I do not propose to go over that ground again in detail but merely to trace it in outline to set it in its context of the wider history of the Railway Age in Wales.

South Wales was the scene of many early railway developments. One of the earliest was the Oystermouth Railway, which, built originally as a tramroad by Act of Parliament obtained in 1804 as a substitute for a canal, developed later in the century into a standard gauge railway as the now famous Mumbles Railway. It lays claim to having been the first passenger railway in the world and operated for some five miles from Rutland Street in Swansea along the shores of Swansea Bay to the village of Oystermouth, and later, by an extension opened in 1898, to Mumbles

Pier. There was also a short mineral branch from Blackpill three miles from Swansea to feed coal mines in the Clyne Valley. During its long history the Mumbles Railway developed from horse working to steam traction in 1877 and to electrification in 1929. It was finally abandoned in 1960 and has subsequently been completely removed.

The Taff Vale Railway lays claim to being the first railway proper in South Wales. Incorporated by Act of Parliament in 1836 it extended from Merthyr in the north down the valley of the Taff to Cardiff with a later extension to Cogan Pill or Penarth. It paralleled the Glamorgan Canal, and eventually developed into a vital and important transport artery for the coal and iron trade of South Wales. Its long arms spread out like tentacles into every crevice of the valleys of Glamorgan. The Aberdare Valley was opened up in 1846, and in 1851 an incline opened from Merthyr to Dowlais. The opening up of coal mines in the Rhondda Valley during the 1840's led to the construction of the branch to Ferndale in 1856 and subsequently to Maerdy in the Rhondda Fach. The Rhondda Fawr was developed also in 1856 when the branch to Treherbert was opened. Rivalries developed between the Taff Vale and its neighbour the Rhymney Railway, and the latter finally pioneered its own direct line into Cardiff through Caerphilly Mountain to avoid the congestion experienced in the lower reaches of the Taff Valley on the approach to Cardiff. In its later years, the Taff Vale developed tentacles deep into the heart of the rural Vale of Glamorgan with a view to reaching the coast at another point—Aberthaw. Its railway lines from the Rhondda to Llantrisant and on to Cowbridge were opened in 1865, whilst a further extension through St. Mary Church to Aberthaw was opened in 1892. Economically not very successful, by 1930 they were already contracting, though the lines to Llantrisant and Cowbridge survived as rural branches until 1952.

Both the Taff Vale and the Rhymney were essentially mineral lines serving a densely populated area of South Wales. Largely unencumbered with long rural arms, like the Brecon & Merthyr and the Neath & Brecon, they paid handsome dividends to their shareholders until the grouping of 1923 when they became part of the Great Western Railway System.

The main line into South Wales was first mooted during the 1830's. However the first firm proposal was placed before Parliament in 1844 as a bill to connect the G.W.R. at Gloucester with Fishguard and thence to Ireland by package steamer. A branch was proposed from the main line at Whitland to the town of Pembroke. In 1846 an Act was passed and work begun on the project as the South Wales Railway Company.

The depression of the late 1840's put paid to the more grandiose plans for a new harbour at Fishguard and the line was diverted to the existing harbour at New Milford or Neyland as it was later called via the county town of Haverfordwest. Similarly the branch to Pembroke was dropped and it was left to two local companies, the North Pembrokeshire Railway through Maenclochog & Rosebush to develop a line to Fishguard, and the Tenby & Pembroke to develop a line eventually linking these two places to Whitland.

The engineer for the South Wales Railway was Isambard Kingdom Brunel, and the line was constructed to his famous broad gauge of 7 foot. It was opened from Chepstow to Swansea by mid 1850, including the first Landore viaduct near Swansea, which was a lattice work wooden structure. Chepstow bridge was opened in 1852 completing the link with the G.W.R. at Gloucester. By 1856 the Neyland terminus had been reached. The branch from Pembroke to Whitland was opened by the local company in 1866, and, having been built to the standard gauge presented break of gauge problems at Whitland eventually forcing the South Wales Railway to convert one of its two tracks from Carmarthen to Whitland from broad to narrow gauge. Eventually the G.W.R. attempt to maintain the broad gauge was abandoned and it disappeared from South Wales in 1872.

Later, again as a result of local initiative a branch line was constructed from Whitland for 14 miles up the Taf Valley to Crymmych Arms in 1869 and extended for a further 11 miles to Cardigan in 1886. From the outset it was worked by the G.W.R. and absorbed completely in 1890. Always a minor rural branch and subjected from the outset to the G.W.R.'s own 'bus competition from Carmarthen & Newcastle Emlyn, the Cardigan branch survived until the Beeching era in 1962. A short branch from Johnston (Pembs.) to Milford Haven was opened in 1863 and now serves as the terminus of the main West Wales line from Swansea.

The branch-line from Clynderwen to Maenclochog, Rosebush and later Fishguard is a classic example of local tenacity and initiative succeeding in bringing a railway to a remote rural part of West Wales. It owed its origins in 1871 to the initiative of Edward Cropper a local quarry owner with quarries at Maenclochog and Rosebush some eight miles fom the South Wales main line at Narberth Road (later Clynderwen) station. Later, when the quarries fell into decay, local initiative tried, rather unsuccessfully to develop Rosebush as a spa in the foothills of the Prescelli's and in 1878 a proposal was put forward to extend the line to Fishguard via Puncheston and Letterston. After long delays and numerous changes of name the line finally reached Fishguard in 1897 by this rather circuitous single-line route. Exhausted by the effort the local company sold out to the G.W.R. in 1898 which immediately promoted a new direct line from Clarbeston Road to Fishguard, a project which was completed with the opening of a new harbour at Fishguard in 1906. Henceforth the North Pembrokeshire line became just another rural branch line and passenger services were withdrawn in 1937. The line was finally closed and lifted for most of its length in 1952.

A railway project envisaged in the grand style of the railway mania of the mid-nineteenth century was the Manchester and Milford Railway. This was an age of fierce competition, with all the major companies vying with each other for traffic and influence. A grand scheme was envisaged for a railway linking the great manufacturing centre of Man-

13

chester with the Atlantic harbour of Milford Haven. This was to be accomplished by running powers over existing railways like the Mid-Wales, the Cambrian and L.N.W.R. in the North, and the South Wales Railway in the South, and by the construction of a completely new line from a junction with the Carmarthen and Cardigan Railway at Pencader to a junction with the Mid-Wales Railway near Llangurig in the Rhayader area of Central Wales. In total it would involve 207 miles of railway from Manchester to Milford. Sad to say the early euphoria soon evaporated and the Manchester & Milford Railway ended up with a line 27 miles from Pencader to Strata Florida high in the Cardiganshire hills. Money and enthusiasm ran out, and the company finally constructed a deviation line from Strata Florida into Aberystwyth where it arrived in 1867 to share a station as the poor relation of the more prestigious Cambrian. The M. & M. was absorbed by the G.W.R. in 1914 and the passenger service from Carmarthen to Aberystwyth withdrawn in 1965. The former M. & M. platform at Aberystwyth is now used for Vale of Rheidol trains.

Railways in the Carmarthen town area seemed characterized by early dreams of grandeur which were later tempered by the harsh realism of finance. The Carmarthen & Cardigan Railway incorporated in 1834, never reached the latter place and ended its life as a G.W.R. branch to Llandysul and Newcastle Emlyn, losing its passenger services in 1952 but surviving for freight until 1972. A second branch from Lampeter on the M. & M. to Aberayron began life as a more grandiose scheme for an alternative route to Aberystwyth. It was opened in 1911 but was even by that date subject to road competition and was closed to passengers in 1951.

Before leaving South Wales, mention must be made of two other minor railways of the area. The Burry Port and Gwendraeth Valley Railway traced its origins back to the middle years of the eighteenth century to the construction of Kymers Canal from Kidwelly into the Gwendraeth Valley. Feeder tramways were constructed from an early date and by 1873 a railway had not only replaced the canal, but had also been constructed from the new harbour at Burry Port to the anthracite coal mining area of the Gwendraeth Valley, terminating at Cwmmawr. A more ambitious project to extend the line to Llanarthney in the Towy Valley never came to fruition. Passenger services were introduced officially during the early years of the present century when a fatal accident revealed the illicit carriage of passengers earlier. The low clearance under some of the overbridges, a legacy from the canal along which the railway ran, necessitated the use of special passenger rolling stock and locomotives. The passenger service ceased in 1953, but the opening of new anthracite pits in the area gave a new lease of life to the line as a mineral railway and it still serves this function today, as does its neighbour, the Mynydd Mawr railway from Llanelli.

The Llanelli and Mynydd Mawr Railway was a late comer on the railway scene and was not completed until the 1880's. It was single line throughout and had no signalling. It operated for coal and goods only,

14

and apart from a daily colliers' train carried no passenger traffic. A proposal to introduce a passenger service with G.W.R. assistance in 1920 failed because of the primitive working conditions. Like the Gwendraeth Valley line it has survived largely because of the development of anthracite mining at Cynheidre near Cross Hands.

Our survey of the railways of South Wales has been necessarily brief and there have been many omissions. The industrial lines of the Swansea area demand detailed treatment as too do the railway developments centred around Port Talbot and Bridgend. Independent concerns like the South Wales Mineral Railway with its rope-worked incline at Briton Ferry, and its tunnelling into the Afan Valley at Pontrhydyfen to reach its terminus at Glyncorrwg are fascinating studies in themselves. Similarly activity in the Llynfi Valley around Maesteg and in the Garw, Ogmore and Gilfach Valleys radiating from Bridgend and Tondu demand attention from the serious student of railway history as well as from the industrial archaeologist. The vision and magnitude of local enterprise right at the end of the nineteenth century resulting in the construction of the Rhondda and Swansea Bay Railway from Treherbert at the top of the Rhondda through the almost two mile tunnel to Blaengwynfi at the top of the Afan valley and thence to Port Talbot and Swansea is a tribute to the railway builders of Victorian Britain, whilst the relationship between railway and dock enterprises is exemplified in South Wales by the Duffryn Llynfi and Porthcawl (1825), the Llanelli Railway & Docks Co. (1828), the Barry Railways (1884) and the Port Talbot Railway & Docks Co. (1897).

I propose, however, to leave detailed consideration of these to another time, and to move into Central Wales to trace developments there. These developments centred upon two areas. To the south the county town of Brecon was the centre of some early railway developments and became the focal point for some of the most scenic and interesting railways in Wales.

The earliest railway into Brecon was the Hay Railway. Incorporating the Talyllyn tunnel constructed in 1812, the Hay Railway, engineered by John Hodgkinson was opened between Brecon and Hay-on-Wye in 1816 and extended to Eardisley in 1818. Horse worked, it was built to a gauge of 3 ft. 6 ins. and served as a feeder to the Breconshire Canal. It was later acquired in 1860 by the Brecon & Merthyr Railway Company, and, after broadening the bore of the Talyllyn tunnel, was used as the route of that railway from Talyllyn into Brecon.

The 1850's and 60's was a time of intense railway activity around the town of Brecon. It is strange that railways clamoured in from all directions, but none reached Brecon by the geographically obvious and more direct route from Abergavenny via Crickhowell. The Brecon and Merthyr reached Brecon by 1870 and provided a through route from Newport. The Mid-Wales Railway had opened its line from Moat Lane Junction via Builth and Three Cocks Junctions to Talyllyn in 1864, and by an arrangement with the B. & M. enjoyed running powers over the line from Talyllyn into Brecon. A battle royal had taken place

15

around Builth for access to Llandovery, and the Mid-Wales had had to accept defeat by the Central Wales Railway and content itself with its rather circuitous line to Brecon instead. In 1888 it became part of the Cambrian Railways.

During the same period the Hereford, Hay and Brecon Railway arrived on the scene with the construction of its line from Hereford to Three Cocks Junction from where it enjoyed running powers over the Mid-Wales and the B. & M. into Brecon. The Neath & Brecon, another local concern opened its line in 1867 from Neath Riverside Station through to Dulais Valley to Coelbren Junction where the Swansea Vale Railway joined it, and thence over the bleak moorlands through Craig-y-Nos (Penwyllt) and Cray, into the rich farming area around Devynock and Sennybridge station and on to Brecon to make an end on junction with the other companies. In the 1880's the Midland Railway Company absorbed the Hereford, Hay & Brecon and the Swansea Valley line, and by running powers over the Neath and Brecon from Brecon to Coelbren was able to run a through service from Birmingham and Worcester into Swansea (St. Thomas). This service ended in 1930, though the Neath and Brecon service survived, albeit in skeletal form until 1962. All lines to Brecon were finally closed to passengers in 1963 and the last tenuous freight link from Merthyr lifted in 1964. It is pleasing to note that the tourist industry has led to the re-opening of part of the B. & M. from Pontsticill to Talybont-on-Usk as a narrow gauge line.

In central Wales proper, the Railway Age was dominated by two major companies. The Central Wales Railway, ultimately absorbed by the L.N.W.R. promoted and built a line from Shrewsbury to Swansea with branches from Llandeilo to Carmarthen and Pontardulais to Llanelli. This line served the popular spa towns of Llandrindod Wells, Llanwrtyd Wells, Llangammarch Wells, and, from Builth Road, Builth Wells. It came about as a result of the amalgamation of a number of local projects, the earliest of which was the Llanelli Railway of 1828 which by the early 1840's had reached Llandeilo as well as constructing a branch from Pantyffynon up the Amman Valley.

The Knighton Railway, promoted locally, to build a line from the Shrewsbury and Hereford line at Craven Arms to Knighton, was opened in 1861. It was followed in 1865 by the Central Wales Railway from Knighton to Llandrindod, and in 1868, after the long struggle about access to Llandovery with the Mid-Wales, extended to the latter town as the Central Wales Extension Railway. At Llandovery it met end on with the Vale of Towy Railway which had been opened in 1858 from Llandeilo to Llandovery and leased to the Llanelli Railway to work. In 1884 the L.N.W.R. absorbed all the Central Wales Companies, and when, in 1889 the G.W.R. absorbed the Llanelli Railway, the Vale of Towy line became joint Branches from Swansea (Victoria) to Pontardulais and Llandeilo to Carmarthen had been opened in the mid 1860's and these were quickly absorbed by the L.N.W.R. allowing through working from Shrewsbury to Swansea after 1868. In 1964 the lines from

16

Swansea to Pontardulais and from Llandeilo to Carmarthen were closed and abandoned, and through working diverted via Llanelli.

The other railway system to dominate central Wales was the Cambrian. Its official title was the Cambrian Railways and the plural form of the noun was a reflection of its development from a number of independent concerns.

Central Wales featured early on in the nineteenth century in rather grandiose schemes. In 1836 a proposal was put forward as a result of the report of the Irish Railway Commission on the need for better communication with Ireland, for a line through Central Wales. Its author was C. B. Vignoles, and his proposal was for a line from Shrewsbury via Llangollen, Bala and Dolgellau to the coast and thence northwards to Porthdinlleyn on the north coast of the Lleyn peninsula which was thought a better point of embarkation for Ireland than Holyhead on the stage-coach route.

Even the great Brunel became interested in Porthdinlleyn and proposed a broad-gauge line from Worcester via Ludlow, Craven Arms, Montgomery, crossing the Severn by a 170 ft. high viaduct at Newtown, and thence via Talerddig to Dinas Mawddwy and under Cader Idris to the coast before proceeding via the Vignoles route to Porthdinlleyn. George Stephenson's easier route along the North Wales coast and across Anglesey to Holyhead was soon preferred, however and the incorporation of the Chester and Holyhead Railway Company in 1844 meant the end of all proposals for railways to Porthdinlleyn.

The failure of either Vignoles' or Brunel's grand schemes to materialise had aroused the inhabitants of Central Wales to the advantages of railways. The L.N.W.R. entered the arena next with a proposal for a line from Shrewsbury through Welshpool and Machynlleth to Aberystwyth. Although less grandiose than anything previously proposed, it would still have been an important rail artery. However, from the outset the proposal ran into problems. Originally it was proposed to route the line via Llanidloes but later this was dropped and the line was to by-pass that town. So incensed were the inhabitants that they immediately promoted their own railway project from Llandiloes to Newtown. The irony of the situation was that the larger L.N.W.R. proposal was thrown out by parliament whereas the Llanidloes to Newtown scheme was adopted. The result was that the railway first came to Mid-Wales not through any grandiose scheme to Ireland, not even through any major scheme to Aberystwyth, but rather through an independent local scheme, completely isolated from the rest of the railway system of Britain, between Llanidloes and Newtown in Montgomeryshire.

So often however, it is from little acorns that large oak trees grow, and it was as the result of a series of locally promoted railway schemes that the Cambrian Railways finally emerged. David Davies of Llandinam and his partner at that time, Thomas Savin enter the scene as railway contractors. They were responsible for building the Llanidloes to Newtown line (opened 1859), the Oswestry to Welshpool line (opened 1860) and finally for linking the two between Welshpool and Newtown

17

in 1861. In addition there were three branches on the Oswestry/Newtown section from Llynclys to Porthywaun (1860), Abermule to Kerry (1861) and Llanymynech to Llanfyllin (1861).

The next step was the construction of the line westwards from Newtown towards Machynlleth. This was developed as another independent concern and was opened from Moat Lane Junction to Machynlleth in 1863. It involved the tremendous engineering feat in Talerddig Cutting. Severe weather delayed the work and the partnership between Davies and Savin was dissolved at this time causing further delays. David Davies was responsible for finishing the line, which, when it was built incorporated the biggest rock cutting in the world with a depth of 120 ft. Some of the navvies working on the cutting are reported to have found gold.

Finally the system was extended to the North East with the construction of the Oswestry, Ellesmere and Whitchurch Railway opened in 1864. It was in that year that the four independent companies amalgamated to create the Cambrian Railways.

Meanwhile Davies' erstwhile partner Thomas Savin had been heavily involved in the Aberystwyth and Welsh Coast Railway. This was opened in stages after Savin had experienced considerable financial difficulties. Machynlleth to Borth was opened in 1863 as also was the isolated section from Aberdovey to Llwyngwril. In 1864 the line was extended in the south from Borth to Aberystwyth and in 1865 the northern line was extended from Llwyngwril to Barmouth Junction (later Morfa Mawddach) and part of the Dolgellau branch from the junction to Penmaenpool was also completed. It was not until 1867 that the line over the Dovey estuary from Dovey Junction to Aberdovey was completed, and also the famous viaduct over the Mawddach from Barmouth Junction to Barmouth, which allowed the completion of the line northwards to Pwllheli. In 1868 the Dolgellau branch was completed and a junction made with the G.W.R. line from Ruabon through Llangollen, Corwen and Bala Junction which had been completed in stages between 1859 and 1868 as a series of local enterprises operated by the G.W.R. and finally absorbed by them in 1877.

The main Cambrian Railways system was completed in 1888 when the formerly independent Mid-Wales Railway from Moat Lane Junction to Brecon via Three Cocks and Talyllyn was absorbed into it. This line had been opened in 1864 and has been dealt with earlier in that part of the lecture tracing the development of railways around Brecon. Subsequently some short branches were added to the system : Cemaes Road to Dinas Mawddwy, built as the Mawddwy Railway in 1867 and absorbed by the Cambrian in 1911; the Van Railway from Caersws to Van opened in 1873 and worked by the Cambrian from 1896. Wrexham to Ellesmere, opened in 1895; Tanat Valley, opened in 1904; Vale of Rheidol narrow gauge, opened 1902 and absorbed by the Cambrian in 1913 and the Welshpool and Llanfair narrow gauge opened in 1904. These last two survive, the former as British Rail's only steam operated line, and the latter as one of a number of preserved narrow gauge lines in North and Mid-Wales. In addition the Cambrian operated the Elan Valley Railway between 1895 and 1906 which had been built to make possible the construction of the Dams associated with the Birmingham Corporation Water Works.

What survives of these railways of Central and Mid-Wales? The Central Wales line from Swansea through Llanelli and Llandrindod Wells to Shrewsbury still operates for passengers. The Cambrian main line from Shrewsbury to Aberystwyth survives, as also does the Cambrian Coast line from Dovey Junction to Pwllheli. With the exception of the Vale of Rheidol, and the preserved Talyllyn Festiniog and Welshpool and Llanfair, all other railways in Mid-Wales have gone. Even the little independent railways of the Welsh border, the "Potts" from Shrewsbury to Llanymynech, and the infamous Bishops Castle from Craven Arms have succumbed to the advance of the motor age, whilst the rural branches from Leominster to Kington, Presteigne and New Radnor were early casualties of the decline of railways. Those lines which survive, do so with the aid of substantial government and local authority grants and are the subject of constant attack by those who feel they are an expensive luxury.

Let me, in conclusion, turn to North Wales, and sketch briefly how the Railway Age came to that area. We saw earlier how the grandiose schemes of Vignoles and Brunel were ousted by Stephenson's North Wales Coast route proposal. This was brought about as the Chester & Holyhead Railway, incorporated in 1844 with an authorized capital of £2,000,000. Robert Stephenson was the engineer and the line was opened from Chester to Bangor in 1848. Later in the same year the line across Anglesey from Llanfair P.G. to Holyhead was also completed. The famous tubular bridge across the Menai Straits was opened in March 1850, the same year in which the South Wales Railway reached Swansea. In 1856 the Chester and Holyhead Railway was taken over by the L.N.W.R.

At Chester General Station the line connected with the Chester and Crewe and the Shrewsbury and Chester Railways authorized in 1837 and 1847 respectively. It crossed the Dee by a viaduct built in 1846 for the Shrewsbury and Chester Railway of cast iron girders—the longest bridge of its type at that time. In 1847 one of these girders collapsed under the weight of a Shrewsbury train and the whole train, except for the locomotive and tender plunged into the river. Five deaths resulted from the accident.

Along the course of the main line various branches were constructed. Rhyl to Denbigh was opened in 1858 and extended in 1860 to Corwen via Ruthin to meet the Ruabon/Barmouth line. The branch from Mold to Denbigh was opened in 1869, the same year in which a short branch from Prestatyn to Disserth was also opened. The branch from Holywell Junction to Holywell Town was a late arrival on the railway scene being added in 1912.

Another group of branches radiated from Llandudno Junction. The St. George's Harbour Railway to Llandudno was opened in 1858 and the

Conway & Llanrwst Railway incorporated in 1860 opened its line in 1863, was absorbed by the L.N.W.R. in 1867 and extended to Bettws-y-Coed in 1868. In 1879 after earlier plans for a narrow gauge line had failed, a standard gauge line was constructed from Bettws-y-Coed to Blaenau Ffestiniog incorporating the Ffestiniog tunnel which at 3,726 yds. long is the eighth longest in the British Isles. Strange to say, work was well advanced on the tunnel before the decision to change from narrow to standard gauge was taken and the reboring of the tunnel through the exceptionally hard rock greatly added to the cost of the line.

From Bangor, the L.N.W.R. opened its branch to Bethesda in 1884, a competitor to the earlier mineral only Penrhyn railway.

On Anglesey itself there were two branches from the main line. The first, originally planned as a loop line from Gaerwen, through Amlwch and back to Valley, eventually became a branch to Amlwch opened in 1867 by the Anglesey Central Railway and absorbed by the L.N.W.R. in 1876. The second was the branch from Holland Arms to Red Wharf Bay opened in 1909. It was an early casualty, losing its passenger service in 1930 and being closed completely in 1950.

The ancient town of Caernarfon was served by three separate railway companies, initially isolated from each other and eventually joined together by a fourth concern. The Bangor & Caernarfon Railway opened its line from Menai Bridge to Caernarfon in 1853; the Caernarfonshire Railway, was authorized to construct its line from Caernarfon to Afonwen on the Cambrian Coast line in 1862. It incorporated in part of its course the old Nantlle Railway, a 3 ft 6in. gauge line opened in 1828 between Caernarfon and Nantlle. The Llanberis branch from Caernarfon was opened in 1869 and absorbed by the L.N.W.R. in 1870, when the three lines were joined together to share a single station at Caernarfon and operated throughout by the L.N.W.R. Closure has been complete, the last section to survive being the branch from Menai Bridge to Caernarfon.

In conclusion, mention must be made of the extensive narrow gauge railway system of North West Wales. It developed because of the demand for slate from the industrial towns of South Wales, the Midlands and the North. The inaccessibility of the slate valleys dictated narrow gauge railways as the most economical and effective means of transporting slate, and these developed in and around Portmadoc in the north west and Caernarfon in the north quite extensively.

The Ffestiniog Railway is perhaps the best known. Opened in 1836 and incorporating in its course part of an earlier tramroad of 1807 across the Cob, it was horseworked until 1863 when steam was introduced. Built to the 1 ft. $11\frac{1}{2}$ in. gauge it ceased operations in 1946 but was reopened by a preservation society in 1955 and is presently engaged in constructing an alternative route into Blaenau to bypass a section of the original route flooded as part of a hydro-electric scheme.

Associated with the Ffestiniog and linked physically to it at Portmadoc was the Welsh Highland Railway. Brought about as a result of a linking of the North Wales Narrow Gauge Railway opened in 1881 and the Croesor tramway of 1863, the Welsh Highland was opened throughout from Portmadoc to Dinas Junction on the Caernarfon Afonwen line in 1922. It passed through the magnificent scenery of Snowdonia and the village of Beddgelert. Unfortunately it was too early for the tourist industry of the present day and ceased to function in 1937, being dismantled in 1941.

Also in the area of Portmadoc was the Gorseddau Tramway. Built originally before 1845 to a gauge of 3 ft., it was converted to 1 ft. 11½ in. to make it compatible with its neighbours and was closed and dismantled between 1885 and 1895. On the other side of Snowdon, Britain's only rack railway, the 2 ft. 7½ in. Snowdon Mountain line from Llanberis was built in 1896 as a tourist attraction and survives as such.

Further down the Merionethshire coastline the Talyllyn is also worthy of mention. It ran from Towyn to Abergynolwyn where it served slate quarries. It opened in 1865 and began carrying passengers in the following year. Built to the 2 ft. 3 in. gauge it followed the course of an earlier tramroad to Aberdyfi but the advent of the Cambrian coast railway made the Aberdyfi extension unnecessary and the line was brought to a new terminus at Towyn Kings adjacent to the main line where there were interchange sidings. Passenger traffic was permitted only after the lines were moved under the bridges to create greater clearance, and one side of the carriages permanently sealed off. Operated until 1910 by the Abergynolwyn Slate Quarry Company which was controlled by the Lancashire Magnate William McConnell, it passed in that year into the hands of Henry Hadyn Jones. Jones was at that time Liberal candidate for Merioneth, which seat he won in 1910, and as a gesture to the area which was experiencing mounting unemployment he agreed to keep both the quarries and the railway open. The quarries, however, were eventually forced to close in 1946, largely due to the effects of poor quarrying earlier and the depression in the slate industry, but Sir Henry Hadyn Jones vowed that as long as he lived the railway would continue to operate and he kept this promise until his death in 1950. Two passenger trains a week had operated, although the line was extremely run down and had not made returns to the railway clearing house since 1910. In July, 1950 Sir Henry died, but his last instructions were that the railway should be kept going until October. In that month a preservation society was formed and the line reopened for the summer season in 1951 and has continued ever since.

There can be no doubt that only the person of Sir Henry Hadyn Jones saved the Talyllyn from the fate of its neighbour the Corris. The Corris originated in 1858. It too was built to the 2 ft. 3 in. gauge and extended from Aberllefenni to the harbour of Derwenlas on the south shore of the Dovey estuary. It passed through Machynlleth on its 11 mile course. In 1864 the section south of Machynlleth was abandoned as this had been rendered redundant by the coming of the Cambrian and in 1878 steam locomotives were introduced. Passenger trains only ran officially after parliamentary sanction in 1883. In 1930 the Corris was taken over by the G.W.R. and passenger services suspended. Flooding near Machynlleth in 1948 brought about final closure.

Finally just a brief word about the Fairbourne Railway. Now a 15 in. gauge tourist attraction, it started life as a 2 ft. gauge horse tramway in 1890 to ply between Fairbourne station and the Barmouth Ferry. It was developed essentially to attract holidaymakers by the firm of Solomon Andrews and Co. of Cardiff who also developed the Pwllheli & Llanbedrog tramway in 1896. The latter was a 3 ft. 6 in. gauge line, four miles long and was closed and lifted in 1927. In 1916 the Fairbourne was converted to the miniature 15 in. gauge and eked out a precarious existence between the wars. In 1940 it closed and was severely damaged from artillery practice activity during the second world war. It reopened in 1948 and has continued ever since.

The Railway Age in Wales has probably brought about the greatest changes in the principality since the geological activity which threw up the mountains and the glacial activity which incised the deep valleys. Not only were its effects seen on the geography of Wales in great viaducts, huge cuttings, cliff ledges and tunnels, but it had profound social effects on the people of Wales. It brought remote communities within easier reach of large towns, and within reach of the world outside Wales. It facilitated emigration from the countryside and immigration into Wales from other parts of Britain. Of itself it created a new source of employment, and did much to stem the rapid depopulation of parts of rural Wales by creating jobs in these areas.

The Railway Age was the steam age. Its high noon was undoubtedly the last quarter of the nineteenth century and the first decade of the present one. The railways served Britain well in the Great War, but they emerged in a very weak and exhausted condition and were already beginning to feel the cold draught of road competition. The Railway Age was characterized by the rivalry and pride of the different companies each with its characteristic livery and idiosyncrasies. It marked a distinct period in the social history not only of Wales but of Britain as a whole and the tremendous opposition with which closure proposals were met was indicative that railways had worked their way into the affections of the people in a way which the motor bus or even the motor car has never succeeded in doing.

2. JOHN A. OWEN

MERTHYR TYDFIL INDUSTRIAL DEVELOPMENT 1870-1918
(*Illustrations 1 to 15*)

Introduction

By the year 1870 the industrial base of the Merthyr district had a distinctly shaky look. The monolithic iron trade which in the middle of the century looked likely to last forever was crumbling, with once great companies moving rapidly to oblivion.

Penydarren closed in 1859, Plymouth changed hands in 1862 and by 1880 was closed, Cyfarthfa closed in 1875 for iron manufacture and did not reopen as a steel works until 1884, the original verve and entrepreneurial drive had gone, it was absorbed by GKN and Co. Ltd. in 1902 and shut in 1910, to be briefly resuscitated in 1915 for the First World War effort, only to be finally closed in 1919.

It was the giant Dowlais Works that lasted longest as a metaliferous manufacturing entity. It took the traumatic change from iron making to steel production in its stride, whilst continuing to make good profits. At the same time by investing capital judiciously over many years in updating its plant the Works products remained competitive in the face of fierce worldwide competition.

Although the demise of the ironworks in general signalled the rise of the coal industry throughout the district. Not only did the traditional works exploit their coal holdings to a great degree, but specialised coal companies sunk large pits in the Taff Valley, at Merthyr Vale and Treharris. These collieries proved to be amongst the most productive and profitable in the whole South Wales coalfield.

The Merthyr Four Feet steam coal represented by the "Four Feet" from Castle pit, Dyffryn Pits and Merthyr Vale was taken as the standard of excellence and perfection of smokeless steam coals, by which all other steam coals were gauged. All the best varieties were called "Merthyr Steam Coals".

With the change in the industrial structure of the area the relationship between employers and work men also changed, it entered a more bitter, violent and warring phase. With the men combining into better organised combinations, which led to strong unions by the turn of the century. There were strikes throughout the period in 1871 lasting eleven weeks, the great strikes of 1874/75 and 1898 lasting six months, the bitter one in 1912. All for improved wages and a stabilisation of working arrangements. Out of the strife evolved the sliding scale agreement on wage payments controlled by the price of coal. The first one was signed on 11th December, 1875. The chairmanship of the joint committee from 1880 to 1899 was held by the Merthyr industrialist, Sir W. T. Lewis, and in that time nine agreements were signed.

Out of the continual disagreements, in 1898, the South Wales Miners'

Federation was formed, the first universal miners union in the coalfield. During the whole period, the coal producers experienced periods of booms and slumps, due mainly to over-production for export demand, but the general trend was an increasing output for all local pits to a peak tonnage of over 3,000,000 tons in 1913. When the Great War started in 1914, the pits came under full government control, profits and wages were regulated on a national basis. This state of affairs existed until 1921 when all coal holdings were returned to private ownership.

Thus the Merthyr District throughout the period had changed its industries and absorbed technological advances like a chameleon to retain its cohesive, corporate identity.

Plymouth Works/Collieries (1870-1918)

Anthony Hill, the guiding genius of the Plymouth Iron Works for 36 years, died in 1862, and since there was no one of his line to carry on his trade the whole business was sold for £250,000 to Messrs. Hankey, Fothergill and Bateman.

The Works consisted of the following departments in 1870.

Duffryn Iron Works
Blast Furnaces, Nos. 5, 6, 7, 8 and 10.
Speculation Engine House.
Refineries.
Fitting-up Shops.
Boiler/Smith Shops.
Eolus Engine House.
Two sets of Boilers and stacks.

The Water Wheel Pit
Housing two blast wheels (breast driven), driven by water from the Plymouth feeder.
Limestone Sheds.
Stables.

Pentrebach Forges
Puddling Furnaces.
Re-heating Furnaces.
Rolling Mills.
Boiler Plants.

The Plymouth Works
Blast Furnaces, Nos. 1, 2, 3, 4 and 9.
Blast Engines.
Coke Ovens.
2 large Water Wheels.

When the Works were purchased from the Hill family the leading figure and dominant force of the business was Richard Fothergill, who owned Iron Works at Abernant and Llwydcoed in the Aberdare Valley. In 1865 he had been elected the first President of the "Aberdare" Coal Association, founded by Sir W. T. Lewis, but later in the troubled times of 1872/74 it was re-organised and called the "South Wales and Monmouthshire Coalowners Association". Its main aim was to protect the interests of the colliery proprietors, although it proved of incalculable benefit in matters relating to the whole coalfield and gave stability to the trade.

RUINS OF PENYDARREN IRONWORKS 1880
(looking towards Merthyr Tydfil)
(See John A. Owen, Section 2)

MERTHYR VALE COLLIERY 1885
Sunk by John Nixon in 1875 for the Company Messrs Nixon Taylor & Cory. The viewer
was George Brown who was in charge of the sinking with a depth of over 400 yards.
left of photo—Nixonville   foreground—Gas Works   background—Merthyr Vale Colliery
(See John A. Owen, Section 2)

CYFARTHFA STEELWORKS 1890
Rolling mill No. 1 (Roughing rolls) Cogging mill has 8 repeating furnaces.
36 ins. mill driven by geared set of horizontal reversing engines 42 ins. dist x 5 ft. stroke
with rolls having 6 ins. lift controls by balancing rams and steam screwing down gear.
Ingots are cogged to a bloom 7 ins. square.   (See John A. Owen, Section 2)

HILLS PLYMOUTH CO. – ABERCANAID COLLIERY 1893
Note–Building in the foreground houses electric haulage and lighting plant machinery.
(See John A. Owen, Section 2)

CRAWSHAYS BROS., CYFARTHFA 1895
Castle pit looking south down the Taff Valley. The second from the left wagon has the
following inscription: Crawshay Bros., Cyfarthfa, Smokeless.

also the cage house has a square stone set in   RC
the wall with the following inscription: 1869

330 yards deep, first coal raised in 1866 sale-coal colliery
(See John A. Owen, Section 2)

HILL'S PLYMOUTH COLLIERIES, MERTHYR TYDFIL
Coal Wagon 1906   (See John A. Owen, Section 2)

"GOAT MILL" ENTRANCE TO G.K.N. CO. LTD. WORKS AT
DOWLAIS—On 27th June, 1912.
For the visit of the King George V and Queen Mary to Guest Keen
and Nettlefolds Co. Ltd.   (See John A. Owen, Section 2)

DOWLAIS IRON Co.
Colliery shaft "North Pit" Tunnel Colliery (Up cast fan) 1895
Showing "Waddle" Fan Ventilation System which ventilated the
South Pit and Long Work Pit, Cwmbargoed.
(See John A. Owen, Section 2)

JULY 9, 1906
Blowing Engine House building and foundation of "A" Blast furnace
(See John A. Owen, Section 2)

MARCH 1908
Blowing   Engine House, Boilers for Engine in front. A Blast Furnace, Pump House
in front of Furnace and return water pump.   (See John A. Owen, Section 2)

MERTHYR VALE COLLIERY 1910 (Nixon's Navigation Colliery, Aberfan)
(See John A. Owen, Section 2)

1913–PLYMOUTH COLLIERY, MERTHYR TYDFIL
(See John A. Owen, Section 2)

CRAWSHAY BROS. CYFARTHFA STEEL WORKS, MERTHYR TYDFIL
Coal Wagon.　(See John A. Owen, Section 2)

DEEP NAVIGATION COLLIERY, TREHARRIS
(See John A. Owen, Section 2)

COLLIERY, TREHARRIS
(See John A. Owen, Section 2)

He was also in 1868 elected the junior M.P. for Merthyr Tydfil, the senior being Henry Richard. His contemporaries said of him "that he made a first class politician but sacrificed his position of a successful ironmaster", and in that statement lay a key to the rapid decline of the great Plymouth Iron Works.

When the Iron Works were re-organised by the new partnership from the stagnation which marked the end of Anthony Hill's reign, the first big step taken was to introduce hot blast blowing techniques on the furnaces to produce bulk iron cheaper. Richard Fothergill then made a fatal miscalculation, he geared the Plymouth Iron Works to enter the mass production rail-manufacture business to challenge Dowlais and Cyfarthfa. He abandoned the high class, cold blast pig iron, merchant bars, iron cables and rod iron markets which Plymouth had always dominated. In doing this he sealed the decline for the Iron Works which led to its closure by 1880. Other traumatic forces were also at work, namely indifferent Management, due to Richard Fothergill's political duties and the terrific impact of the steel age both Bessemer and Siemens' methods which developed throughout the difficult strike torn years of the 1870's. The iron works never really recovered from the 1874/75 coal strike which crippled its business. These instances coupled to the evolution of the metal melting trade with the huge capital investment needed to keep abreast of business and economic production was another crucial factor for decline. Although to his credit he did make a significant impact on the coal side of the business which was considerable at that time, also for all South Wales when he and Lord Swansea advertised and lobbied all government and industrial users regarding the superiority of Welsh Steam Coal, especially to the Board of Admiralty for firing Royal Navy ships.

They both promoted the crucial trials of Welsh Steam Coal which gave it prominence and proved its superiority over coals from the North of England and Scotland.

When Richard Fothergill retired, in great financial trouble, the ironmaking era at Plymouth was ended. Sir W. T. Lewis (later Lord Merthyr) made a strong effort to acquire and restart the Works for the benefit of the district, but after a very short period this proved unsuccessful and the concern was dismantled.

Adjacent to the old Duffryn site an effort was made in September 1882 to start a wire works by a Mr. D. Williams of the Taff Vale Brewery, Merthyr, and others, but the venture did not last many months and closed.

Richard Fothergill died in Tenby in June 1902, aged 81 years, he had retired there after the financial collapse of his industrial enterprises in 1880 both in Merthyr and Aberdare.

Thus in 1880 the Plymouth Iron Works ceased as a manufacturing enterprise but the seeds of evolution had already been well laid. The coal producing capacity of the Plymouth mineral estate, which had been well established for at least 50 years, was to be fully exploited for great profit.

25

In 1880 the Hankey family obtained control of the whole Plymouth industrial complex, closed the iron business down but expanded the coal mining operations. Therefore, in 1882 the company changed its structure when it was taken possession of under a mortgage of the executors of the late Mr. Thomas Alers Hankey, who lost no time in arranging a thorough development of the mineral property.

Mr. F. A. Hankey one of the executors, and chairman of an important banking firm extended a great deal of his expertise and energy in developing the new coal business. He entrusted the management of the collieries to Mr. Thomas Henry Bailey of the firm of Messrs. S. and J. Bailey, Civil and Mining Engineers, Birmingham, whilst at the same time appointing Messrs. Adams and Wilson, Cardiff, sole agents for the sale and shipment of Plymouth coal. Under the new management and production restructuring the collieries were extensively enlarged and modernised.

In 1886 the gross tonnage of coal raised was 337,819 tons, whilst in 1887 it amounted to 326,722 tons.

Moreover in 1890 the whole concern without any change of ownership was converted into a limited liability company under the title of *Hills Plymouth Company Limited*. The company's activities were all centred $1\frac{1}{2}$ miles south of Merthyr Tydfil and consisted of the following pits and levels.

South Duffryn No. 1, 2 and 3 pits

This colliery was very productive, mining best quality low volatile dry steam coal it was worked on the long wall stall method and had a timber head frame carrying the winding sheaves.

The 3 shafts were (oval) No. 2 South, No. 1 North, Monte shaft, the deepest sinking being 270 yards.

Until the 1870's furnaces at the pit bottom were the only means of ventilation. New winding engines were fitted to No 1 pit in 1885 and No 2 pit in 1890.

North Duffryn Colliery

No. 1 pit north, sank to the nine feet coal at 162 yards.

No. 2 pit south, sank to the lower four feet coal at 213 yards, this pit was later used as a ventilating upcast shaft for the south Duffryn Colliery.

Graig No. 1 Colliery

No. 1 pit north, sunk to ironstone vein at 151 yards, lower four feet at 142 yards.

No. 2 pit used for pumping.

Graig No. 2 Colliery

No. 1 pit north sunk to lower four feet coal at 182 yards.

No. 2 pit, pumping, sunk to nine feet coal at 128 yards.

Tai Bach Colliery
   Sunk to nine feet coal at 150 yards.

Abercanaid Colliery
   No. 1 pit, sunk to lower four feet coal at 150 yards.
   No. 2 pit, sunk to seven feet coal at 131 yards (Furnace Pit).
   No. 3 pit, sunk to nine feet coal at 60 yards.
   Pen-Cae-Bach Pit sunk 91 yards.
   Glyn Mil No. 1 Pit.
   Glyn Mil No. 2 Pit.

Forge Level.
Saron Level.
Brazil Level.

South Duffryn Level (above ground haulage for underground work).

   By 1890/1893 the pits both on the surface and underground were lighted by electricity, also it was used for pumping and haulage, this was a very advanced technology for the time. The generators, dynamos and engines being erected on the surface of the workings. At the Abercanaid Pit the new motive power was also used to drive the underground haulage which was based upon the "Main and Tail" principle which was generally adopted throughout South Wales at the time. The application of electric drive to this haulage was the only successful one of its kind in the country. It was also reported that the outbuildings of the colliery and village was also lighted by electricity. The whole colliery enterprise was entirely self-contained to the detail of building their own coal wagons and trams together with at the time mechanical workshops containing apparatus for welding by electricity.
   The Plymouth coal was one of the best smokeless steam fuels raised in the whole country. Extensively used by the Royal Navy, leading steamship companies and railways both at home and abroad, with vast quantities being shipped to coaling bunker stations all over the world up until after the First World War. The analysis of the Plymouth Collieries Smokeless steam upper four feet and nine feet coal was :—

Carbon	... ...	86.98
Hydrogen	... ...	4.39
Oxygen	... ...	1.72
Nitrogen	... ...	1.07
Sulphur	... ...	0.80
Ash	... ...	3.97
Moisture	... ...	1.07
		100.00

In 1892 the collieries raised 342,936 gross tons of coal. Whilst in 1893 the annual output of all the coal holdings was 403,833 tons with 2,500 men being employed. Not only was the company a key employer in the district but the general manager, Thomas Henry Bailey, also took a keen interest in the Merthyr Tydfil Urban District Council, he was a councillor for the collieries district and chairman of the M.T.U.D.C. being elected to that office on 31st December, 1894. He was also a member of the board of Guardians and a man of deep religious beliefs. In 1895 the collieries raised 353,000 gross tons of coal, whilst in 1896 the output decreased to 280,959 tons. In August 1896 William Walker Hood succeeded Thomas Bailey as general manager of the Plymouth Collieries. He was the son of Archibald Hood a large colliery owner (The Glamorgan Coal Co.) of the Rhondda Valley.

When he took over the management of the firm it was rated at £12,103 per annum held leases of 2,500 acres of mineral district in the Parish of Merthyr Tydfil, they raised 281,000 tons of coal for the year employing 2,500 men whilst paying in wages £160,000. At this point in time the Hankeys were still the major shareholders in the Company. In 1902 W. Walker Hood resigned his position as agent and general manager of the company to take over his father's business in the Rhondda. He was succeeded in turn by Mr. W. W. Green, Collieries manager, Pentrebach. On 25th September, 1902, Abercanaid Pit was closed due to its uneconomic productive capacity. The amount in wages paid in 1902 by the Plymouth Collieries being £285,215 with over 3,000 men employed.

The business was still wholly owned by the Hankey family, with Norman F. Hankey the resident director of the Company the mineral tract was then 2,409 acres, employing over 2,000 men with the rateable value at £10,851.10.0d.

Although the company had gone through a very difficult period from 1898/1903 with the 22 week colliery strike of 1898 and the rationalisation of the whole company with pit closures and modernisation, during that period of time the business lost £115,000, but from the investment at the turn of the century the company went on to the high water mark of the South Wales coalfield of 1913 very profitably. Hills Plymouth Co. Ltd. produced 567,895 tons of coal in 1911. Then with the outbreak of the first world war the coal outputs continued as never before with 3,000 men still employed and coal wanted on a national basis. Although during 1915 the companies main mineral leases expired, but were successfully renegotiated, so that in 1920 the Plymouth Collieries were in a healthy state with the main concentration centred on two very productive collieries, South Duffryn No. 1 and 2 pits and Graig No. 1 and 2 pits employing 2,400 men.

Cyfarthfa Works and Collieries (1870-1918)

In 1870 the iron works employed 2,000 men, whilst at the extensive colliery operation a further 3,000 men were employed.

This once great ironworks was also in decline, it needed modernisation to all its production plant, in all a massive injection of capital was re-

28

quired. At this date no decision was made at Cyfarthfa as to whether they should follow the Dowlais lead and convert to steelmaking, but the sale coal collieries of the company were proving very profitable with production increasing as was the coal business throughout South Wales.

The collieries/levels of Cyfarthfa, under their engineer/agent the Kirkhouse family, had been estabilshed like the other ironworks from the 1820's and had evolved from levels and balance pits like Winchfawr, Gethin No. 1, Gethin No. 2 and Cwm pits, to the large modern styled collieries. The sale coal side of the business was really established with the sinking of Castle pit in 1866/1869 it was a huge undertaking, sunk in a stone quarry above Troedyrhiw, 333 yards deep, the shape of the shaft was oval 22' 8" long x 12' 0" wide with a brattice dividing the window parts from the pumps. The pit was fitted with a huge pump which was highly regarded by all engineers at the time, the stroke was 8' 0" at the pump end, but 13' 4" at the crank end, the piston of the steam engine driving it was 68" dia. and pressure of steam at the boilers 40 lbs./sq. in., the dia. of fly wheel being 26' and weighed 37 tons.

The winding engine had 36" dia. cylinders x 4' 6" stroke, with a steam pressure of 45 lbs./sq. in., winding drums 12' 0" dia.

The cages were double decker to wind 2 trams at once, each loaded with coal weighing 31 cwt.

To reach this large colliery and provide transportation for its coal the private railroad to the Gethin pits were extended down to Troedyrhiw, so that Castle pit was serviced by a quick efficient means of communication to Merthyr, where it was then exported all over the world. Later a direct junction was made from the colliery to the G.W.R. and joint R.R. railway when that line was constructed, it passed within a stone's throw of the pit.

Some other named collieries/levels belonging to Cyfarthfa at the time were :—

Pwll Tasker Pit—sunk to 9' 0" seam, 50 yards deep.

Glyndyrus Levels.

Pwll Patch Pit—sunk to 3'/4' seams of coal (also served as an interconnecting level between Cwm Pit and Glyndyrus workings).

Level Cwm—mined 4' 0" seam.

Coedcae Pit.

Waun Level—mined to yard coal—2' 9" seam and 4' 0".

Colliers Row Level—mined 6' 0" seam.

Colliers Row Pit (Pwll Bach) sunk to Bute and 9' 0" seam.

Lefal Pound drift, mined Bute and 9' 0" seams.

Canal Level, mined Bute and 9' 0" seams.

Ynysfach Drift Mine.

Rhydycar Pits—sunk to Gellideg seam.

Roblings Pit—sunk to Bute lower 2' 9" seam, 7' 0" seam and Gellideg coal 100 yards deep.

Cwm Du Pit.

Lefal Berni—mined Bute and lower 2′ 9″.

Also too many other level/drift workings to mention.

The "Merthyr Telegraph" newspaper was faithfully recording the progress of the Merthyr District businesses and was expounding their predicament in the decline of iron generally and the vigorous rise of the coal trade.

At Cyfarthfa the general malaise of the company was further exacerbated during the 1860's by Robert Crawshay's illnesses and inability to manage the works properly, especially with the difficulties of the declining iron trade. The firms' troubles were so apparent that Robert's father William Crawshay considered selling the whole concern for £400,000.

In November of 1872 Robert Crawshay started negotiations for the sale of Cyfarthfa Works. Various valuations of the concern ranged from £800,000 to £1,050,000 with some dubious people bidding for it, so inconclusive was the projects of a sale that by December of 1873 all enquiries were cancelled by the family.

At this juncture William Thompson Crawshay, the son of Robert developed a keen interest in the Works, this made his father only consider selling on the most stringent conditions. Therefore, more deals for sale were being arranged in early 1874 with Robert Crawshay prepared to reduce the asking price by a considerable amount, provided the money was paid in cash on completion of sale contracts.

One reason the sale was being pushed vigorously was the greatly increased activity of the trade unions and their refusal to consent to a wage reduction, this compelled the Crawshays to close the works on 10th April, 1874, like most of the iron and coal businesses in South Wales and the great strike started.

Robert Crawshay appeared to be more intractable in regard to the men's demands than the other ironmasters in the area over the question of issuing dismissal notices and insisting on a 20% wage reduction instead of the general 10% reduction.

R. T. Crawshay wrote in a letter dated 7th May, 1874, "I hear for a certainty that the forge coal colliers will not work on the reduction of 20%, until the notices in the other works are out. Also that the enginemen will not work, so there will be no blast. And again the furnace men themselves will not work on the 20%. I have therefore this last hour given orders to commence blowing out all my blast furnaces. I have no orders of any kind and cannot obtain any at a price which would save my losing money unless a 20% reduction took place and it would be sheer folly to stock iron at present prices".

Conditions throughout South Wales were very bad due to the strike, there was great hardship and suffering with a general lock-out during the early months of 1875, the Merthyr district suffered greatly.

The strike ended in May, 1875, but Cyfarthfa ironworks did not start operations again until 1879.

On May 18th, 1879, Robert Thompson Crawshay died at Cyfarthfa

Castle aged 62 years. In his Will he left the Works to his three sons, William Thompson, Robert Thompson and Richard Fredrick Crawshay, who carried on the business under the style of *Crawshay Brothers and Co.*

These three brothers saw the great change-over at Cyfarthfa from ironmaking to steel production. Although only W. T. Crawshay was resident at the Works and he moved to Caversham Park the family seat, sometime before 1890.

It was very apparent when the Brothers took control of the business that the bulk iron trade for inland works in South Wales was largely dead. If the works were to continue to trade profitably they would either have to spend a large amount of capital on the ironworks or invest in a steel plant as at Dowlais and Ebbw Vale.

In order that the great expenditure of capital could be justified and as an incentive to invest the money needed, they approached Sir William Thomas Lewis, the mining adviser to the freeholders of the Cyfarthfa estates and he agreed to arrange a new lease on the properties on modified terms to the existing leases. On condition that the works expend £150,000 in constructing a new steel works capable of producing 50,000 tons of finished steel per year, production to commence on or before 25th March, 1884.

To this end Mr. Edward Williams was appointed consulting engineer for the whole project, he was one of the leading authorities on steelworks construction and manufacture in the whole world. He was a Dowlais trained Engineer/Manager who had moved to Middlesbrough where he managed the largest works in the country Bolckow Vaughan. He later had his own extensive works at Low Moor and was known as the Northern Iron King. All the plans for the new works were prepared to his own design and he personally superintended the construction.

The new works were initially completed in May, 1884, when two of the blast furnaces were lit. At this time the collieries were continuing very successful in production and profits, in 1886 total coal raised from the collieries was 203,593 tons and in 1887, 216,407 tons.

When the transformation work was nearing completion another Dowlais trained engineer/manager was appointed to run the new undertaking, namely, William Evans, who was appointed general manager of the steelworks and collieries. The previous manager Mr. William Jones who had a distinguished career at Cyfarthfa retired when the new works were completed.

William Evans had left Dowlais to work at Rhymney and later very successfully in the North of England, therefore, it was considered by the Crawshays he was the best man to run the new Cyfarthfa.

Their choice was fully justified in that he piloted the works through its commissioning period and the difficult years of the late 19th century very successfully. This far sighted engineer not only ensured the new technologies made profits for the concern but constantly introduced new innovations to keep costs/expenses to a minimum whilst running all sections of the plant economically. He also introduced electric power into the works during the 1890's as a replacement for steam on the main machinery drives. His salary could only be described as fabulous £3,500 p.a., $2\frac{1}{2}\%$ commission on dividends, Directors fees, Rent, House and Coal free.

The rebirth of the works in 1884 placed such a financial strain on the Crawshay Brothers that they were forced in 1890 to form a limited company, the date of incorporation was 30th July, 1890, and the new company was named Crawshay Brothers, Cyfarthfa Limited.

The aims of the new company were very broadly based and a complete diversification from what they had carried out before, not only were they iron and steel manufacturers but still major coal owners, also brick-makers, patent fuel proprietors as well as chemical manufacturers, distillers, gas makers and the whole gamut of manufacturing fancy.

Alas it never happened, they still clung to their very narrow production base of steel and coal. This fact ultimately led to the closure of all iron and steel making at Cyfarthfa. Prior to this the new capital of the reformed business was £600,000, in £10-shares, with not less than three directors or more than six. The Crawshay Brothers were the first directors at a salary of £1,000 per annum.

In 1892 total coal raised was 322,404 tons and in 1893, 357,596 tons, for 1895 the total coal raised in the collieries was 377,525 tons whilst in 1896 it increased to 427,815 tons.

The Steelworks 1897

The model equipped works of May 1884 had by 1897 evolved to its final form of plant and manufacture, in that it was a fully integrated steelworks catering exclusively to the mass production of steel rails of all sizes and shapes producing annually 75,000 ton of finished steel, employing 4,000 men and paying in wages £220,000 per annum. It consisted of the following main areas.

Blast Furnaces

Five furnaces 70′ 0″ high, iron cased, closed top (cup and cone), bosh diameter 18′ 0″. The last furnace was constructed large enough to have a modified bosh of 20′ 0″ dia. if required. The internal capacity of each furnace being 12,000/13,000 cubic feet of burden, averaging 800 tons of iron melted each per week. All the furnaces were hand charged, the manual skip charges being lifted to the furnace charging platforms by vertical and inclined plane haulages.

Blast was supplied by three vertical direct acting condensing blowing engines, made by J. C. Stevenson, Preston. Each having a steam cylinder 33″ dia., blowing cylinder 72″ dia. x 4′ 5″ stroke. Also three direct acting vertical condensing engines by Davey Bros., Sheffield, steam cylinder 44″ dia., air cylinder 96″ dia. x 5′ 0″ stroke. The pressure of blast $5\frac{1}{2}$/6 lbs./sq. in., six copper tuyeres to each furnace equi-distanced around the shell. The furnaces were served by 15 Cowper hot blast stoves.

Bessemer Steel Plant

Consisted of four acid converters of 10 tons capacity each, two casting pits 72' 0" centres, each served by a casting crane. The pressure of blast being 25 lbs./sq. in. and was supplied by two blowing engines, both vertical condensing. The Spiegel cupolas were situated adjacent to the converters.

Rolling Mills

There were 6/7 mills at Cyfarthfa, two of which, the old rail mills were called the Pandy and Castle, had been reconstructed on the most modern standards of the time and were renumbered 1 and 2 steel mills. They, together with a merchant bar and guide mills formed a vast integrated rolling and cooling complex adjacent to the Bessemer steel plant covering 12 acres of ground.

The reconstructed mills were served by 8 reheating furnaces and soaking pits, a 26" cogging/universal mill for besides supplying the rail mill with blooms it could also roll sections, slabs and billets of various sizes. Also attached to the mills was mechanical manipulators for turning the blooms between passes.

The normal bloom rolled in the cogging plant was 7" square which when cut by the shears was long enough to roll into 2/3/4 lengths of rails as required of 30'—40'—60' long.

The rail finishing plant was housed in a large building with 3, 60' 0" x 120' 0" long bays, in the area were straightening presses, ending machines, drills, punching and testing apparatus.

Steel Sleeper Plant

This consisted of a steam lever shears for cutting hot billets to lengths of sleepers required also a patent heating furnace together with a hydraulic sleeper press and two hydraulic punching machines.

All the structural iron/steelwork for the plant and buildings structures was made at the Cyfarthfa Works.

Moreover, there were also contained in the Works all the ancillary support activities to maintain a large heavy steel plant in production. Namely, quarries, coke ovens—180 coppee ovens producing 2,000 tons of coke per week. Brick yards—capable of making 20,000 bricks per day of all types, red, fire bricks, stoppers for ladles, Bessemer blowing nozzles, hot blast stove regenerator linings all made by hand/mechanical means.

Engineering Shops

Fitting, Pattern, Boiler, Smiths, Carpenters and Wagon Shops together with the iron steel and brass foundries.

The total estimated mechanical horse power for plant in the works was 29,136, such was the manufacturing entity called Cyfarthfa nearly at the end of its great productive life.

The Crawshays persistence in maintaining their traditional manufacturing role in limited heavy steel i.e. rails, sleepers, etc., was by the year 1900 working against them, the new steel plant had worked well, but world markets were getting so competitive in relation to production costs that the inland location of Merthyr in a fiercely cut-throat business was a millstone to the works. The final curtain of the Crawshay control of the business came on 8th March, 1902, when Guest Keen and Nettlefolds Co. Ltd., of Dowlais announced that they had acquired the share capital of Cyfarthfa.

The Cyfarthfa manager William Evans became general manager of the new integrated works at Merthyr and Dowlais. At the time the works employed 4,200 men and wages paid per annum averaged £325,000.

This act was almost the end of Cyfarthfa Works as a great manufacturing business, as no more investment was made in up-dating processes, in fact no great money had been injected into the Works since the 1880's.

It was decided that Dowlais in 1905 would receive all the capital investment for new blast furnaces etc., and that the Cyfarthfa Works would be allowed to quietly run-down. To this end all iron production from the furnaces was stopped by 1910, with the Works allowed to idle. In 1911 the Cyfarthfa collieries continued to prosper greatly and produced 484,435 tons of saleable coal. Although in 1915 the furnaces and mills were re-commissioned with government grants by the ministry of munitions employing some 800 men to produce shell steel for the First World War armies. But in 1918 the works were once again allowed to idle, when the government subsidy ended especially in the face of a crippling post war slump. So much so that on 28th August, 1919, the last blast furnace was finally stopped and 300 men were added to the list of Merthyr unemployed. With the demise of Cyfarthfa, a once great manufacturing entity which challenged and conquered many industrial frontiers, but lost many social encounters, Merthyr's Industrial Empire was crumbling at a frantic pace, although without its presence, Merthyr Tydfil, Wales and Britain would not have been as great and the industrial development of the late 18th century early 19th century would have been severely retarded.

The Cyfarthfa collieries in 1920 were still a very successful and profitable operation with two very large undertakings in Castle Pit employing 1,534 men and Gethin Pit employing 805 men and eight other small colliery/drift workings employing some 605 colliers in total. These coal mining operations would continue into the mid/end of the 1920's, although the Cyfarthfa leases expired in 1924.

Dowlais Iron and Steel Works (1870-1918)

In 1870 the Dowlais Iron Company was run by the two trustees named in Sir Joseph John Guest's Will, they were George Thomas Clarke and H. A. Bruce (Lord Aberdare). G. T. Clarke was the resident managing trustee, living in Dowlais House and directing all the commercial policy of the company in markets, products and capital, whilst the Works and collieries were ruled by William Menelaus the general manager. These

34

two men proved to be a fantastically successful partnership, in that during their stewardship of the business vast profits were made and steel/coal was produced in the most economic and efficient way possible.

The Works were starting the transition period from exclusively manufacturing iron components to producing steel sections and rails. Although the Dowlais Bessemer steelworks was in its infancy, consisting of 6 acid steel converters, each of 5 tons capacity. Otherwise the rest of the business was still iron dominated, the 17 blast furnaces each made approximately 174 tons of iron per week which could be equated to 2,500/3,000 tons of iron per week from the furnace capacity. The company employed 5,000 people in the works and 4,000 in the collieries.

Such was the eminent position of Dowlais in the trade that the newly formed Iron and Steel Institute of Britain visited the Works in the summer of 1870 and toured the plant extensively, noting with particular interest William Menelaus experiments to perfect a practical rotary puddling machine, but this was one of the brilliant engineers projects that did not come to fruition, although it took the steel age to stop him.

Coupled with the acid Bessemer converters at the Works in 1871 he installed Siemens-Martin open hearth steel furnaces and from this date, both production systems were sued side by side, although 80% of all bulk steel production was made by the Bessemer process.

A significant factor that was prophetic even in 1871 was that out of a total profit of £174,565 for the year, the steel plant contributed £54,102 or 30% of the whole.

Another by-product of the merging steel age was the final demise of the Dowlais ironstone mining operation. During the early 1870's they stopped mining iron ore locally and closed nearly all the levels. The local ore had been used less throughout the previous 30 years but with the advent of acid Bessemer practice it became completely unsuitable, because the blackband ironstone, contained a high percentage of phosphorous and sulphur.

From the early 1800's Dowlais had increasingly imported Cumberland hematite ore from Whitehaven, also ores were experimented with from Spain and Cuba. Therefore, when the need for vast tonnages of pure hematite ore arose with the steelmaking process, Dowlais in 1873, decided to open mines/quarries in Spain to control this vital basic raw material. To this end Dowlais together with the Consett Iron Co. and others, formed the Orconera Iron Ore Co. Ltd. of Bilbao.

The capital of the company was £200,000 in 20 shares of £10,000 each. The mines were situated in the mountains of the province of Vizcaya, near Bilbao, at an elevation of 1,200 feet above sea level, with the ore being transported down the mountainside by a series of inclined plane haulages to the companies wharf at Luchana on the river Nervioh, where 3 shipping berths provided for its export. It was first received in bulk at the Dowlais furnaces in August, 1876. Later in 1896 the company leased a further group of iron mines at Obregon in the province of Santander and in 1919 purchased the property of the San Salvator Mining Co. adjoining those of Obregon. This venture was the start of the immigration of Spanish workers to the Dowlais works and their colony at Penywern.

Through the early years of the 1870's the business prospered, with vast quantities of iron rails exported all over Britain and the world. Also the sale—coal side of the enterprise was expanded rapidly. The tunnel pits which had originally been started in 1859, but stopped to concentrate on Fochriw, were restarted sinking in 1869, with the first production coal being raised in the South pit (338 yards) in August 1874. The first coal raised from the North pit in April 1876, the total cost of sinking and mechanical plant was approximately £62,000. Also in 1874 to further increase coal production Bedlinog Colliery was sunk and after many difficulties was completed in 1886. Production coal was first raised from No. 1 pit (582 yards) in June, 1881, and from No. 2 pit (580 yards), in June, 1883. The total cost of sinking and machinery being approximately £131,000. Then in 1878 Nantwen Colliery was started and completed in 1883 (85 yards). This pit supplied all the bituminous coal produced by the company together with No. 8 Colly Level.

Coupled to the importation of Spanish iron ore was the completion of the Rhymney Railway and Great Western Railway joint railroad up the Taff Bargoed valley on the 10th January, 1876. Thus Dowlais had a direct link to the sea ports of Newport and Cardiff and no longer had to rely on the Taff Vale Railway incline to Dowlais Works or the Brecon and Merthyr Railway with their indirect routes to the seaboard. Although Dowlais had constructed its own private railway down to Bedlinog " The Colly line" in 1865, this was to connect the new coal leases and levels (the Colly levels No. 1 to 8) to the Dowlais Works.

The new railroad incorporated the Dowlais railway and enabled the company to have exclusive running powers over it for their colliery engines and CWBS to take their colliers to work at Bedlinog and Nantwen Pits. Also during the 1870's Menelaus started to rebuild completely the Works blast furnaces, from the old type fire brick/iron banded "small" types, to the iron cased "cupola" closed top, semi-mechanically (hydraulic materials hoist) charged furnaces. The Dowlais pattern, pipe hot blast stoves were superceded by the more efficient Whitewell and Cowper stoves. The new type of furnaces were 60/70′ high, 18′ 0″ dia. of bosh, 9′ 0″ bell opening and 14,000 cubic capacity, the average weekly make of iron was 260 tons each in 1877.

To illustrate the significant trend in business, in March 1877, the Works had orders for 15,180 tons of wrought iron rails at £5.6.11d. per ton but had 28,810 tons of steel rails to roll at £7 per ton. The universal acceptance of steel components was well underway, for the year 1877 the steelworks alone made a profit of £76,335.

In 1880 Sir Ifor Bertie Guest, the owner of the Dowlais Iron Co. was created Lord Wimborne, but still undisputed leaders of the business were G. T. Clarke and W. Menelaus.

In 1882, with William Menelaus' health failing, Edward Pritchard Martin, returned to Dowlais to act as assistant general manager. He was the son of George Martin who had been collieries agent for 60 years, and had started his career in Dowlais. Afer learning his trade he left and very successfully managed other concerns. Whilst manager at Blaenavon he befriended Sidney Thomas and his cousin Percy Gilchrist whose experiments on the dephosphorization of steel, led successfully to the "Basic" steel process, which gave great reward to the two inventors and Edward Martin both academically and monetarily. When William Menelaus died in 1882, Edward Martin assumed his role as general manager of the business.

From 1851 Menelaus had been a key figure in the rebirth of Dowlais, from the drama of the lease renewal, the death of Sir J. J. Guest and the transition of the firm from iron manufacturers to steel makers. In all, he had always striven to make the concern economic and profitable, installing mechanical plant wherever possible to lighten the arduous labours of workmen in the industry. A keen protagonist of apprentice training and enlightened industrial management, he had through his efforts brought the name of Dowlais before all the leading manufacturers in the world, to become synonymous with new development, techniques and innovations in the iron and steel industry.

When E. P. Martin assumed control of the works he concentrated his immediate energies on continuing the development of the Blast furnace plant, this was the area where the greatest economies could be achieved with new furnaces melting iron cheaper, to offset some of the high cost of ore freightage.

As an expansion, in 1879 Menelaus had erected 3 tin plate mills to absorb some of the spare iron capacity in the works, but this diversification never really came to anything, so in 1883, Martin dismantled them. Although he did plan to erect as a small expansion of products a colliers' tyre-mill but this also came to nothing. Instead, in 1885, to broaden the base of products, he designed and constructed new mechanical plant for making steel sleepers. The idea had first been thought of by Mr. F. W. Webb of the L.N.W. Railway, their eminent locomotive engineer. Martin adopted the idea and made steel sleepers from rolled tin bar, pressing them into the desired shape hydraulically. The finishing operation was pickling the sleepers in hot tar or creosote. India first created the demand for this product, but soon all the colonial countries had turned to steel railway sleepers, and Dowlais, as ever, with admirable foresight was able to participate greatly in the trade. In 1884 the pits raised 980,000 tons whilst in 1886 they raised 1,025,236 gross tons of coal and in 1887 the total coal production was 846,638 tons.

In 1889 the up-dating of steelworks plant was continuing with the installation of two new Siemens-Martin open hearth furnaces, double the size of any furnace that was then in operation. They were 25 tons capacity and with the new facility the scope of steelmaking ability was greatly increased.

At the time Dowlais employed 5,500 persons in the works, the collieries raised 985,606 gross tons of coal, 4,232 tons of Welsh Mine was obtained from shallow drift workings and used as a mixture with the imported iron ore for special types of iron. The make of finished iron

37

was reduced to 16,373 tons, 131,327 tons of finished steel was made and 9,888 tons of steel blooms produced.

With all successful operations at Dowlais proving very profitable, seeds had been sown two years earlier in 1887 that would grow into plants that one day would make Dowlais redundant. G. T. Clarke and E. P. Martin in 1887 started planning a steel-making complex adjacent to the Bute Docks at Cardiff to obviate the long haulage of raw materials up the hill to Dowlais, and the long return journey for finished products. Thus effectively cutting costs and enabling the companies products to challenge for orders on a world market which was starting to be dominated by the Krupps of Germany.

With the new works at Cardiff it was questionable whether it was prudent to keep Dowlais as a manufacturing entity, but Lord Wimborne was resolutely opposed to the cessation of steelmaking on the old site, because of the dependence of the community on the works.

The first iron was made at Cardiff on 4th February, 1891, by the blowing-in of No. 1 and 2 blast furnaces, whose capacity was over 1,000 tons of hot metal per week. The steelworks and plate mill commenced operations on 12th September, 1895. The melting shop consisted of six Siemens-Martin open hearth furnaces each of 35/40 tons capacity, hand charged, producing acid quality steel. The rolling mill consisted of one 36″ slabbing mill and one 32″ plate mill the latter equipped with roughing and finishing rolls. The capacity of this mill complex was in excess of 1,500 tons of steel plates per week.

When the new steelworks was planned by E. P. Martin and G. T. Clarke they not only built it to obtain more economically viable products, but to broaden their manufacturing base in that the variety of finished products could be considerably expanded. The new works would add to the mainly Dowlais rail/tin bar production, by producing mild steel ships' plates and structural steel sections.

Whilst the new works was being constructed at Cardiff, Dowlais was still a profitable monolith. In 1892, George Thomas Clarke retired as managing trustee of the Dowlais Iron Co. On that day Dowlais lost another of her giants, a man of letters who was a superb businessman, he took a keen interest in all the local activities, the Merthyr School Board, The Board of Guardians, etc. and was the guiding light of the famous Dowlais schools.

During his "reign" at Dowlais great profits had been made, from 1810 to 1891 the company made a nett profit of £4,814,265 or an average of £58,710 per year. New technical processes and innovations made the record half of the century the most profitable, when he was chief controller. For the 46 years up to 1855, the average yearly nett profit had been £33,951 but for the following 36 years was £90,347.

After his retirement Lord Wimborne the owner of the concern came more into the picture and took up the reins of policy making with E. P. Martin.

Commensurate with building the new steelworks at Cardiff a new colliery was started to be sunk in 1890 at Abercynon to supply coking coal for the new works. The sinking was under the direction of H. W. Martin and John Vaughan. In 1896 after tremendous difficulties especially with water (up to 12,000 gallons per hour), the "two-feet-nine coal" was won at 650 yards. Two shafts were sunk to the "nine-feet coal" at a depth of 740 yards, the deepest sinkings in Wales then, the final cost of sinking and machining being in excess of £270,000.

In 1893 the Dowlais coal holdings raised a total tonnage of 849,696 tons and in 1894 increased the tonnage of coal raised to 985,609 tons.

Although on 10th January, 1893, the No. 1 and 2 shafts of Penydarren Pits stopped raising coal, the company shut the colliery down with its coal worked out for economical production, only 8 men were employed after this date carrying out pumping operations and repairs.

E. P. Martin in 1897 became the president of the Iron and Steel Institute and on Thursday, 5th August, the Institute visited the Dowlais Works. At this time, the Works consisted mainly of the following departments.

Blast Furnaces

Six working Nos. 1, 3, 9, 10, 11 and 19 and five idle Nos. 8, 14, 15, 16 and 18.

Blast Engines

Nos. 1, 2, 3 and 8, blast pressure 4 lbs.

Bessemer Steelworks

There were two bessemer steel plants, one consisted of 4 converters each of 10 tons and the new ones constructed in 1895, alongside the "goat mill" consisting of 2 converters each of 15 tons. Also two new 120 tons each, hot metal mixers.

Siemens-Martin Steelworks

Two open hearth furnaces of 25 tons each and 6 furnaces of 12 tons each.

Cogging Mills

"A"	$37\frac{1}{4}''$ centres	1500 HP	for tin bar.
"B"	$37''$ centres	1500 HP	for steel blooms.
"C"	$37\frac{1}{4}''$ centres	2500 HP	for steel blooms.

Rolling Mills

Goat Mill "Right"—For rails, 2 high reversing,
25" centres, 3000 HP.

Goat Mill "Left" —For rails, 3 high non-reversing,
23" centres, 1200 HP.

Tin Bar Mill and Billets—3 high non-reversing,
23″ centres 1200 HP.

Big Mill—Light rails, bars, etc., 2 high non-reversing,
20″ centres, 400 HP.

All the straightening, drilling, ending machines, cold saws etc., were worked by electrical power and the lighting of the main parts of the works. The generating station consisted of one compound engine 13″ x 23″ x 2′ 0″ stroke, working pressure 140 lbs., the dynamo generated 150 HP at 230 volts.

Coal Washing Machine
Coppee and Lhurig's patent, for washing 1,000 tons of coal per day.

Coke Oven
224 Coppee and 130 Welsh type.

Ifor Works
One forge with 19 puddling furnaces, one light plate mill of 22″ centres and two 12″ merchant bar mills together with locomotive, fitting, boiler, carpenters, wagon, pattern shops, brass, iron and steel foundries.

On 27th September, 1899, the Dowlais Iron Steel and Coal Co. Ltd. was formed and registered with a capital of £1,100,000 to take over Lord Wimborne's industrial properties.

The new Directors were :—

> Rt. Hon. Lord Wimborne (Chairman).
> Hon. Edward Viscount Duncannon C.B. (Vice-Chairman).
> Rt. Hon. Lord De Ramsey.
> Hon. Ivor Guest.
> Edward Pritchard Martin.
> Fredrick Gordon.

The first board meeting was held on 20th October, 1899. At this time all the affairs of the old Dowlais Iron Co. were wound up.

The new company was formed as being the prelude to either a complete sale or a merger with a similarly orientated business. The whole Dowlais works was still a very profitable concern and would be sold as such, the nett profit for the half year ending 30th September, 1899, was £132,500. But there were serious problems looming on the horizon, in water supplies for the works processes, Iron Ore supplies from Spain and growing labour troubles, in that the men were actively campaigning for better wages and working conditions.

The demise of the Dowlais Iron Co., came quickly after the new enterprise was formed, with a meeting of directors held at Wimborne House on Friday, 11th May, 1900, Mr. Arthur Keen and E. Windsor Richards

LOCO No. 1 1859 "SAMSON" — Builder Kitson & Son of Leeds (No. 701/59)

(See John A. Owen, Section 3)

LOCO No. 14 1878 "PEACOCK No. 1"
Builder Beyer Peacock & Co.   Photo taken in steelworks, September 1905
(See John A. Owen, Section 3)

LOCO No. 17 "BEDLINOG"
Photo taken Thursday, 12 July, 1934. Dan Davies on footplate (foreman of wagon shop). Sharp Stewart & Co. 1883—works No. 3141/83—saddle tank 140 PSI—Inside cylinders 16 ins. dia. by 24 ins.   (See John A. Owen, Section 3)

LOCO No. 24, 1887 "CLYDE"
Builder –Clyde Locomotive Co. of Glasgow   (See John A. Owen, Section 3)

LOCO No. 25 "GWERNLLWYN" 1889
Builder–Kitson & Co.   Photo taken about 1900–driver on right David Jones of Caeharris–fireman on left M. Richards   (See John A. Owen, Section 3)

COLLIERS CWB 1890

i.e. Workmen's carriage   (See John A. Owen, Section 3)

LOCO No. 30 1890 "DOWLAIS"

Builder – Andrew Barclay & Son   Photo taken 1912

(See John A. Owen, Section 3)

LOCO No. 37 1902
Builder–Hudswell Clarke & Co. Works No. 626/02 Saddle tank 160 PSI
Driver on left Dai Probert (See John A. Owen, Section 3)

LOCO No. 38 1906 "ARTHUR KEEN"
First loco built at Dowlais Iron Works. Loco superintendent George Robson, formerly
with GWR at Swindon. (See John A. Owen, Section 3)

LOCO No. 41 "SANDYFORD"

Built Dowlais Loco Shop 1908 (No. 4/08). Designed by Loco superintendent George Robson

(See John A. Owen, Section 3)

ACCIDENT IN 1910

Loco "Kingfisher" & "Colliers Cwb" at Cwmbargoed. Water main burst and washed railroads away.

(See John A. Owen, Section 3)

LOCO No. 46 1920 – The ninth loco built at Dowlais and the last.

(See John A. Owen, Section 3)

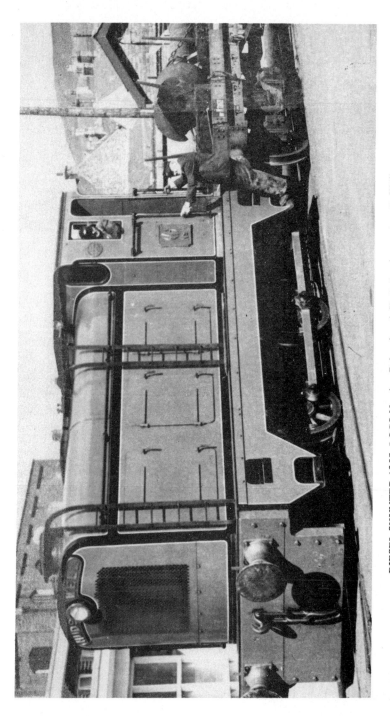

DIESEL SHUNTER 1957, LOCO No. 1 — Driver in cab K. C. Lewis, on stops B. Williams.
Hudswell Clarke & Co. Ltd. built 1955 works No. D984. Load on wagon articulated head for driving Morgan Mill, Cardiff Steelworks
(See John A. Owen, Section 3)

attended. Then in July, 1900, Messrs. Guest Keen and Co. published a prospectus for the new company stating a capital of £2,000,000. The new business was officially registered on 28th August, 1901, and amalgamated the iron steel, colliery and engineering aspects of both concerns, the chairman of the company was Arthur Keen.

Following closely on this industrial manoeuvre the last link of the chain was forged. In 1902 Guest Keen and Co. further merged with the firm of Nettlefolds Ltd.; they were the largest producers of wood screws in the world, with works in Birmingham and Newport. The name was officially changed on 7th June, 1902, and was quoted with a capital of £3,000,000, Arthur Keen was again the chairman of the new Guest Keen and Nettlefolds Co. Ltd.

Also in 1902, the last act was being played at Cyfarthfa Works when Guest, Keen and Co. acquired the share capital of Crawshay Brothers Ltd. Thus in 1902 the two remaining Iron and Steel Works in the district were under the same rule, although Cyfarthfa, due to economic business pressures, would close within the next decade. William Evans the Cyfarthfa Manager became the general manager of both concerns at a salary of £1,300 p.a.

At Dowlais, excluding the collieries, the workforce was approximately 4,000 persons, with the furnaces producing 4,000 tons of iron weekly, but the works were trying hard to reduce the cost per ton of steel produced. New Blast Furnaces were being planned to the latest American pattern, with fully automatic charging equipment, the first in Britain. Work commenced on the new complex on 10th July, 1905, and was under the consultancy of David E. Roberts a Dowlais trained engineer. With the new furnaces being built and the mills modified with labour saving devices, the company were consciously fighting their now isolated manufacturing position in the hills, to combat the long costly lines of haulage, iron ore in and finished steel products out.

The new Blast Furnaces were completed in 1909, when the two "Yankee" furnaces lettered "A and B" were commissioned, the first cast from "A" furnace was made on 12th November, 1909. They were of the following size, 80′ 0″ high, 20′ 0″ bosh dia. Blast temperature 1000/1400°C. The storage bunkers for limestone, coke, iron ore, etc. were 360′ 0″ long x 47′ 0″ wide, 50′ 0″ high with a storage capacity of 371,000 cu. ft. The total cost of the complete new work was in excess of £250,000.

In 1910 the Dowlais Colliery holdings were still very successful, profitable and a huge coal producing complex.

They consisted of the Fochriw and Bedlinog steam coal takings and Nantwen, Bituminous takings, with the following pits producing.

Fochriw No. 1 Pit

Mining 1,900 tons of coal weekly, from the Upper two feet nine and upper four feet seams.

41

Fochriw No. 2 Pit

Mining 3,900 tons of coal weekly, from the Big Coal, Red Coal and Rhas Las seams.

South Tunnel Pit

Mining 2,200 tons of coal weekly, from the little Vein seam, Rhas Las and Red coal seams.

Long Work Pit (Cwmbargoed)

Mining 700 tons of coal weekly from the Black Vein and Top Coal seam.

New Black Vein Drift (Trecatti)

Mined 600 tons weekly, from the coal of its name. In 1910 the estimated reserves of unworked coal in the Fochriw area was 13,000,000 tons for all seams.

Bedlinog No. 1 Pit

Mined 4,300 tons of coal weekly, from the Rhas Las and Little Vein seams.

Bedlinog No. 2 Pit

Mined 3,000 tons of coal weekly from the Rhas Las and Little Vein seams. The estimated reserves of unworked coal in the Bedlinog area in 1910 was over 3,500,000 tons.

Nantwen Pit and No. 8 Level

Mined 2,900 tons of coal weekly, from the Brithdir bituminous seam, the whole output of bituminous coal for Dowlais was produced from this pit. The estimated reserves of unworked coal in this colliery area in 1910 was 1,700,000 tons. The total coal produced from the colliery holdings in 1909 was 1,143,759 tons.

At this time the pits were in a fairly healthy position and by investing approximately £23,000 in the various collieries they would increase production by about 20%. A startling fact was that about 10% of the gross output of the pits went in firing their steam boilers, so a fair proportion of the proposed expenditure was to make the boiler plants more economical.

On 27th June, 1912, King George V and Queen Mary visited the Dowlais Steelworks and toured the main manufacturing areas of the plant which consisted of :—

Blast Furnaces

"A" and No. 11 in blast, "B" and No. 3 under repair.

Bessemer Steel Plant

Two 15 ton converters, three 10′ 0″ dia. cupolas, rated at 120 tons per day. The average output was 450 tons of ingots daily. Two 120 tons hot metal mixers. Each ingot cast was 18 tons, consisting of 5 ingots, 5′ 0″ high x 20″ sq. at top x 22″ sq. at bottom, weighing 3 tons 10 cwt. each.

Goat Mill

Length of rail rolled from each ingot was 232′ 0″ each finished length of rail being 45′ 0″ long. The make per day of 12 hours was 450 tons.

Sleeper Mill

The average daily make was 2,100 steel sleepers.

Sole Plate Mill

The average daily make was 9,500 components.

Fishplate Mill

The average make per 12 hour day was 40 tons.

Siemens Steel Plant

Consisted of two 25 tons open hearth furnaces.

Dowlais for the year ending 31st December, 1911, raised from its collieries 1,132,836 tons of coal, melted through the blast furnaces 175,181 tons of iron and manufactured 163,250 tons of steel.

The royal visitors had a tremendous welcome throughout the district, which was decorated overall for the occasion especially in and around the works, with two famous triumphial arches erected for the visit. The coal arch leading to Dowlais House where they entered the works and the steel Goat Mill gate where they left the works at the end of the tour. The steel arch was decorated with a complete array of components made by all the skilled trades in the works.

Dowlais was still prosperous in 1913, after the injection of capital over the previous decade, but despite the fact that it formed part of a steel combine with large financial resources it had many inherent weaknesses, which in the next decade became obvious and ominous, namely.

1. An isolated "hill" location, with long and costly lines of communications for importing raw materials (500,000 tons of iron ore yearly) and exporting its finished products.

2. Specialised export trading dependent on world market conditions and events (for its railroad furniture).

3. The concentration on traditional "heavy" steel production—rails, fishplates, steel sleepers, tin bar and light sections (colliery arches), in which manufacturing costs, as against raw materials and transportation costs, brought for smaller profits in added value.

4. Lastly, the benefits of improved blast furnace design and operations reducing the cost per ton of iron produced in relation to coal and coke utilisation were dwarfed into insignificance when one realised that two tons of iron-ore still had to be imported into the Works via long lines of costly haulage, for every ton of finished steel produced. Ore freightage to Dowlais was about $3\frac{1}{2}\%$ of the selling

price of rails and about 5% of the tin bar. The journey back to the docks exporting the finished products added another 2% to rail prices.

In 1914 another boom was at hand in producing steel and coal for the war effort. At the outbreak of war the Dowlais works employed 4,500 men whilst at the collieries 8,315 men worked and in the previous 12 months had produced 1,794,444 tons of coal.

At the end of hostilities in 1918 the steelworks employed 3,395 persons, paying out £482,141 in wages, whilst the collieries produced a total of 1,353,067 tons of coal.

Moreover, Dowlais Works had prospered greatly through it, so much so that the GKN and Co. Ltd., combine doubled the number of shares by a bonus issue. In subsequent events the firm was over-capitalised, having to carry the burden of extra dividends, thus only sowing the seeds for future disaster.

Nixon's Navigation Co. Ltd.,
Merthyr Vale Colliery (1870-1918)

John Nixon the founder of the company was born at Barlow near Newcastle, Durham, in 1815. He first came to Wales in 1840 when he undertook for Lord Bute a survey of the mineral property at Dowlais prior to negotiations for the renewal of the Dowlais lease in 1848. He made a great impression with Lord Bute due to his skill and finesse in doing the survey but he refused employment in South Wales and took a job in France for an English company.

Although this venture lasted no time and having been a champion of Welsh steam coal since the Dowlais Survey days, he lost no time in selling that product into France, establishing a market and investing in large stocks. After that venture he obtained leases on the Werfa property in Aberdare, from Lord Bute, where he proved the famous four foot seam of coal.

From this enterprise he went from strength to strength with his partners Taylor and William Cory, by sinking, Nixon's Navigation Pit at Aberdare, this was a gigantic undertaking in sinking deeper than had been ever done before.

It took seven years of operations before the coal was won, with the colliery being fitted with the most modern plant available.

From the Aberdare Valley he moved his attention to the Taff Valley and started sinking Merthyr Vale Colliery on 23rd August, 1869. After 5½ years on 1st January, 1875, the four foot coal seam was won, it represented a tremendous achievement in overcoming great physical difficulties also the financial strain of the breaking-up of his business partnership with Taylor and Cory.

The two shafts were completed to 495 yards and 493 yards which was below the nine feet seam, the main workings of the colliery were the four feet, six feet and nine feet seams of prime quality dry steam coal, the first production coal was raised on 4th December, 1875.

44

John Nixon was not only an industrial entrepeneur but a clever scientific colliery engineer of great inventive nature. He designed for his new pit special winding gear and ventilating systems, as well as re-organising the whole working arrangements for underground production. He substituted the very inefficient "pillar and stall" method of mining coal (traditional in South Wales) with the well proven North of England innovation, "longwall" method of mining. This change took great courage and determination to introduce into a very conservative, parochial working environment, also he introduced the double shift system of working at the same time. Together, these changes to the colliers' working arrangements and hours of work provoked a storm of opposition at the time, but with perseverance Nixon's arrangements proved fantastically successful.

This colliery was to prove one of the most productive in the whole coalfield mining the highest single tonnages for many years.

The head frames of the two shafts were rail and lattice structures, produced at John Nixon's foundry and workshops at Mountain Ash. The No. 1 winding engine had two cylinders, 83″ in diameter x 4′ 0″ stroke generating 1000 HP.

No. 2 winding engine also had two cylinders 50″ diameter x 6′ 0″ stroke, generating 800 HP.

The two air compressors at the pit head were 2 cylindered of 36″ and 40″ diameter respectively.

The ventilation was catered for by a Waddle fan 40′ 0″ diameter connected to Nixon's Patent ventilator consisting of 3 exhausting pistons, 50′ 0″ x 22′ 0″ capable of exhausting 400,000 cubic feet of air per minute.

The huge colliery could be described as a model industrial undertaking in any age, and certainly one of the finest in the world at the time. By 1880 the surrounding villages that had sprung up were consolidating and expanding rapidly, for instance, Merthyr Vale had a gas works, reading room, volunteer organisation and building clubs. In that year the pits were already employing 1,000 men, with the colliers underground using the clanny lamp to work by for production and the firemen using the Davy Safety Lamps.

Also in the same year a series of very advanced and interesting experiments were carried out at the colliery, when Colonel Grey and Major Bell, piped some of the exhausted atmosphere from underground, containing a high percentage of carbon monoxide (CO) to the surface and used the unstable waste product from the coal seams to illuminate the offices and colliery yard, also fire three sets of boilers, thereby saving 100 tons of coal weekly. This innovation was directly proportional to using waste blast furnace gas (also with high concentration of carbon monoxide) at the ironworks to fire boilers and hot blast stoves which had been in use since the 1850's.

In 1886 the Nixon collieries in the Aberdare/Merthyr valley raised a gross total coal tonnage of 714,642 tons, whilst in 1887 the Merthyr Vale pits alone raised a total coal tonnage of 333,841 tons.

The pits prospered under the vigorous management of John Nixon with ever increasing tonnages in 1892—420,228 gross tons of coal were produced. In 1893—430,309 gross tons of coal were mined.

In 1894 John Nixon retired as general manager of Nixon's Navigation Co. Ltd., and he was succeeded by his nephew Mr. H. E. Gray as head of the company. He spent his retirement in London and Brighton, a millionaire and when he died in 1899 he was buried at Mountain Ash.

In 1894 the manager of Merthyr Vale colliery was Major W. Bell, who was a councillor for Merthyr Vale ward of the M.T.U.D.C. J.P. for Glamorgan, Major 3rd V.B. Welsh Regiment and a Member of the Board of Guardians.

The production capacity of the colliery continued to grow throughout the 1890's in 1895—555,288 gross tons of coal were mined whilst in 1896 —588,917 gross tons were mined, at the time they employed approximately 2,500 colliers.

By the turn of the century in 1901 it was one of the biggest single coal undertakings in South Wales producing 750,000 tons for the year.

In 1902, 3,064 men were employed, raising 830,000 tons of coal and were paid some £268,000 in wages. The population of the Merthyr Vale ward was 13,000 inhabitants a far cry from the 200/300 in 1870, whilst the capital investment extended by the company in its operation at Merthyr Vale pits since 1869 was some £330,000. In 1906 the colliery raised 832,000 tons of coal for the year.

Like time itself the progress of the colliery was inexorable with vast tonnages being produced yearly with an average of 3,000 men continually employed, in 1911 the pits mined 610,849 tons of coal. With the impetus throughout the early years of the twentieth century, to the zenith of coal production of 1913 when some 3,250,000 tons were mined in the Borough of Merthyr Tydfil, through the first World War up to the hungry twenties. In 1920 the colliery employed 2,852 men whilst in 1924 the figure was 3,685 the highest ever.

In 1930 the No. 1 shaft was deepened to 542 yards and No. 2 shaft to 538 yards, to just below the Gellideg, the lowest seam in order to exploit this coal and the seven feet seam above it, to offset the diminishing reserves in the higher coal seams.

Ocean Coal Company Limited

Deep Navigation Colliery—Treharris (1870-1918)

The important mining village of Treharris is situated at the lower end of the parish of Merthyr Tydfil on the hillside above Quakers' Yard at an elevation of 350/400 feet above sea level.

It came into existence in the early 1870's as a direct result of coal prospecting on land belonging to Twynygraig, Pantannas and Cefn Forest farms. It is reported that in 1870 some strange, formally attired gentlemen appeared in the district where they made a casual survey of the above named farm lands and especially the Bargoed valley adjacent to Pontnewydd farm.

46

Some time later the district was sent into a state of turmoil when it was announced that a mining company was going to sink a pit on land belonging to Twyngarreg farm.

The company that was going to commence operations was headed by Mr. F. W. Harris as Chairman, and Messrs. Webster, Hill, Huckett and Judkins as Directors.

On Monday, 28th September, 1872, a level was opened near the Bargoed river. Binding coal was first obtained and was utilised by the navvy sinkers in their "Huts".

On the first Monday in February, 1873, the first sod was cut for the sinking of the colliery enterprise.

The business was known originally as Harris Navigation Pits, after the principal shareholder, who also gave his name to the village which grew up around them.

The two shafts were completed in May, 1878, and were the deepest at the time in South Wales being 760 yards to the nine feet seam, 200 yards deeper than any of the other collieries in the coalfield. The first coal was raised from No. 2 pit (North pit) in 1879. In 1881 the other shaft, No. 1 (South pit) was also raising coal in production quantities. A remarkable feature of the colliery was the installation in the South pit of a massive Cornish pumping engine supplied by the Perran Foundry Company of Truro, Cornwall. This engine had a 100" diameter cylinder x 11' 0" stroke and there were 8 lifts or stages to the pumping operation.

In 1886 the emerging business was consolidated and production tonnages of coal increased. For the year 343,033 gross tons were raised and 316,324 tons in 1887. In 1892 the total coal raised was 281,484 tons and in 1893—301,590 tons.

The declining coal production of the colliery heralded a business crisis for the Harris Navigation Company. Through mismanagement the concern was deep in debt even though the venture had cost to date in excess of £100,000. When rumours of the difficulties were made public, there was great distress in the district as it was thought the pits were to be closed.

This was not so. "The Ocean Coal Company Limited" (Treorchy), one of the giants of the South Wales coalfield, bought out the Harris company at a knock down price in the summer of 1893. The collieries were renamed "Deep Navigation" when the new company took control.

In 1895 the pits raised 436,813 gross tons of coal, in 1896—452,241 tons and in 1897—596,000 tons. At that date there were 2,500 men employed in the pits with a rateable value of £17,667.

The village of Treharris was fully developed as an urban area and had a thriving population of 7,000 persons.

By 1902 the Ocean Coal Company had further expended £600,000 on development work at the pits, introducing labour saving and highly mechanised plant to produce coal as economically as was possible. For the year they produced 327,000 gross tons of coal and employed 2,000 men, with the mineral leases covering 3,378 acres.

The whole modernisation of the mining operations from the purchase of the company up to 1902 had been masterminded by William Jenkins, who was Director of the business and General Manager of Treharris. He had been articled as a young engineer to W. S. Clarke, the Mineral Agent to the Marquis of Bute, where he had been a contemporary of Sir W. T. Lewis. In 1871 he had joined David Davies and Company (the Ocean Coal Company Limited) and ever since had seen the business expand at a colossal rate, into a lynch pin of South Wales industry.

The south and north shafts in 1902 were 768 yards deep intersecting the four feet seam at 693 yards, the six feet seam at 718 yards and the nine feet seam at 760 yards.

The road and workings were ventilated by a Schiele fan 14' 3" diameter producing a current of 230,000 cubic feet of air per minute. The roadways were watered by 2" mains from a height of 356' 0" to the pit bottom.

Then it was conveyed in $1\frac{1}{2}$" pipes to all headings and levels with $\frac{3}{4}$" taps placed every 40 yards.

The giant Cornish pump worked at 2 strokes per minute, delivering 435 gallons per minute.

The coal was hauled to the main roadways by horses, of which 150 were employed underground.

On the main roads all the haulage was carried out by compressed air engines, the power for which was generated by two Fowler air compressors of 2, 42" steam cylinders and 2, 45" cylinders x 6' 0" stroke.

The coal was raised in both shafts. The main haulage engines in the south pit had 20" diameter cylinders x 3' 0" stroke, fitted with drums 11' 0" over cheeks and 5' 0" over treads, and wire ropes of best plough steel $2\frac{1}{2}$" in circumference.

Each journey consisted of 34 loaded trams. The south pit was 17' 0" diameter and equipped with double-decked cages carrying 4 trams, 2 on each deck. At the pit bottom, a Key's patent creeper was used to raise the empties from the lower deck to the haulage level.

The winding engine was steam driven with 54" cylinders x 7' 0" stroke worked on a spiral drum increasing from 18' to 32' diameter by 14 coils.

The pit framing was made of wrought iron lattice work structure 81' 6" high carrying pulleys 20' 0" diameter. The cage speed was less than a minute to raise from the pit bottom to the surface.

The coal screening plant consisted of 4 tipplers arranged to transfer the coal from tram to screen with a minimum of breakage. When the coal reached the bottom of the screen, it passed onto travelling belts, alongside which workmen stood and picked out any dirt or foreign bodies. From the conveyor belts the cleaned large coal was loaded into railway wagons. The company was always progressive and prepared to spend capital to maintain economic production and increase efficiency and due to this policy kept the colliery in the forefront of the South Wales coal producers. In 1911 the gross output tonnage was 321,282 tons.

Another innovation at Treharris Deep Navigation Colliery was the pit head baths, built in 1916—a very progressive and far-thinking venture at that time. Prior to installation the company had selected a party of repesentatives from their various collieries to inspect the pit head baths in use at continental pits to recommend the best practice for the company to adopt. When constructed, they were the first baths in the South Wales coalfield and the Ocean Coal Company Limited were justifiably proud of them.

In 1920 there were 1,946 men working at the colliery employing the "Barry" or "Nottingham" system of coal cutting. This was the forerunner of the Longwall conveyor system of coal working, keeping the pits in the forefront of economic, profitable operation.

Bibliography—Principal References

1. The Crawshay Dynasty—John P. Addis, 1957.
2. South Wales Miners 1898-14—R. Page Arnot, 1967.
3. Merthyr Tydfil Incorporation Inquiries 1897 & 1903—J. G. E. Astle.
4. The Progress of Merthyr—J. G. E. Astle, 1897.
5. The Rhymney Railway—D. S. M. Barrie, 1952.
6. The Changing Economic Geography of the Merthyr Valley—D. G. R. Belshaw, 1955.
7. The Economic History of the British Iron & Steel Industry 1864-1939—D. L. Burn, 1940.
8. Cyfarthfa Iron and Steelworks 1897 Booklet.
9. Description of the Dowlais Works 1897 and 1912.
10. The Dowlais Iron Co. Papers, County Record Office, Cardiff.
11. A Descriptive Account of Merthyr Tydfil—Robinson, Son & Pike Brighton, 1893.
12. Historical Survey of Treharris and District—D. H. G. Davies.
13. The South Wales Coal Annuals 1903-1920—J. Davies and C. P. Hailey.
14. The Miners of South Wales—E. W. Evans, 1961.
15. Express Almanac and Year Book 1894, 1895, 1896, 1897, 1898, 1899.
16. Iron & Steel Institute Proceedings.
    1870—On Pumping and Winding Machinery at a Pit belonging to Mr. R. T. Crawshay, named the Castle Pit.
    1871—Visits to the Works of South Wales.
17. The South Wales Coal Industry 1841/1875—J. H. Morris & L. J. Williams, 1958.
18. Short History of the Dowlais Ironworks—J. A. Owen, 1973.
19. History of the Hamlet of Gellideg—F. J. Pedlar, 1930.
20. The Plymouth Ironworks and Collieries—Clive Thomas, 1974.
21. Changes in location of the South Wales Iron & Steel Industry, 1860/1930—D. G. Watts, 1968.
22. The History of Merthyr Tydfil—Charles Wilkins, 1908.

23. History of the Iron, Steel and Tinplate Trades—Charles Wilkins, 1903.
24. South Wales—Coal, Iron & Freight Statistics for 1873/1899—Tellefsen, Holst & Wills, Cardiff.
25. Analysis of British Coals and Coke—C. A. Selyer, 1907.
26. South Wales Coals—L. J. Davies, 1920.
27. Merthyr Express, May 24th, 1884.
Merthyr Express, December 9th, 1919.
28. South Wales News—28th August, 1919.
29. South Wales Coal Trade and Its Allied Industries—C. Wilkins, 1888.
30. 20th Annual Conference of the I.L.P.—Merthyr Tydfil, 1912.
31. South Wales Institute of Engineers Centenary Brochure 1857/1957.
32. A History of the Pioneers of the Welsh Coalfield—E. Phillips, 1925.
33. "Mabon" (William Abraham 1842-1922)—E. W. Evans, 1959.
34. Merthyr Politics.
The Making of a Working-Class Tradition edited by Glanmor Williams, 1966.
35. The progress of Merthyr.
"A Diamond Jubilee Review"—J. G. E. Astle, 1897.
36. Western Mail, 26th April, 1921.

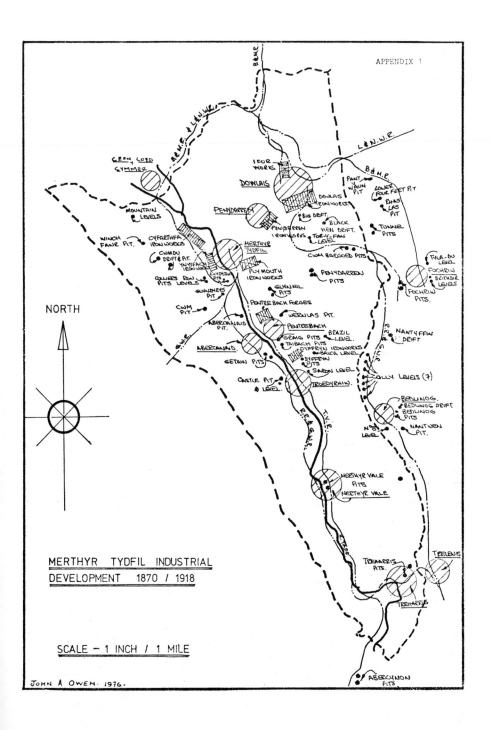

APPENDIX 1

B.&M.R.

B.&M.R. & L.&N.W.R.

L.&N.W.R.

B.&M.R.

GELLY CORD GYMMER

IFOR WORKS

DOWLAIS

PANT Y WAUN PIT

LOWER FOUR FEET PIT

RHAS LAS PIT

PENDARREN

DOWLAIS IRON WORKS

MOUNTAIN LEVELS

PENDARREN IRON WORKS

BIG DRIFT

BLACK VIEN DRIFT

TOR-Y-FAN LEVEL

TUNNEL PITS

WINCH FAWR PIT.

CYFARTHFA IRON WORKS

MERTHYR TYDFIL

CWM BARGOED PITS

TYLA-DU LEVEL

CWMDU DRIFT & PIT.

YNISFACH IRON WORKS

PLYMOUTH IRON WORKS

PENDARREN PITS

FOCHRIW

BRITHDIR LEVELS

COLLIERS ROW PITS LEVELS

GWAUNLLWYN PITS

GLYNHIL PITS

FOCHRIW PITS.

GLYNDYRYS PIT

CWM PIT.

PENTRE BACH FORGES

ABERCANAID PIT.

WERNLAS PIT.

PENTREBACH

BRAZIL LEVEL.

NANTYFFIN DRIFT

S.W.R.

ABERCANAID

GRAIG PITS

TAIBACH PITS

DYFFRYN IRONWORKS

BALCA LEVEL

DYFFRYN PITS

GETHIN PITS

SARON LEVEL

GOLLY LEVELS (7)

CASTLE PIT & LEVEL.

TROEDYRHIW.

BEDLINOG.

BEDLINOG DRIFT.

BEDLINOG PITS.

No 5 LEVEL

NANTWEN PIT.

R.&S.W.R.

T.V.R.

MERTHYR VALE PITS

MERTHYR VALE

R.&S.W.R.

TREHARRIS PITS

TRELEWIS

R. TAFF

TREHARRIS

NORTH

MERTHYR TYDFIL INDUSTRIAL
DEVELOPMENT 1870 / 1918

SCALE — 1 INCH / 1 MILE

ABERCYNON PITS

JOHN A OWEN. 1976.

APPENDIX 2.

NAME OF COLLIERY COMPANY.

— COAL OUTPUT IN TONS. —

YEAR	1870	1871	1872	1884	1886	1887	1889	1892	1893	1894	1895	1896	1897	1902	1903	1909	1911	1913	1918	1919
Miners Average Weekly Earnings	21/-	33/-	33/-	26/-	20/-	20/-	24/-	23/-	23/-	23/-	21/-	21/-	21/-	28/-	28/-	44/-	44/-		•	£4.15.6
Average Price per ton Large coal – Pithead				6/3	5/-	5/4	8/-	8/9	7/6	7/7	7/2	6/-	6/9	10/6	9/5	10/9	11/2			
Average Selling Price per ton Large coal.	9/3	10/6	15/-	9/10	8/5	8/-	10/6	11/7	9/9	10/8	9/7	9/2	9/3	13/7	12/10	13/9	14/9			
Ocean Coal Co. Ltd. Deep Navigation Treharris Pits					343,033	316,324		281,494	301,590	415,765	436,813	452,241	596,000	327,000			321,282		307,238	315,410
Nixon's Navigation Co. Ltd. Merthyr Vale Pits						333,841		420,224	430,309	525,864	555,288	588,917	561,351	750,000	830,000		610,849		441,968	451,149
Hills Plymouth Co. Ltd. Collieries	257,258	256,577	218,852	286,000	337,819	326,722		342,956	405,833	388,521	352,726	281,000	360,432						354,191	362,748
Cravely Brothers Oxfordfa Collieries	215,539	213,351	189,155		203,953	216,407		322,404	357,596	378,579	377,525	427,815	413,424			520,000	494,435		342,972	346,680
Dowlais Collieries																				
Fochriw				–	–	259,926			285,640	313,974	314,614	306,573			342,372	298,283		380,500	304,690	
Bedlinog				–	–	130,658			224,549	272,103	289,497	299,585			336,477	469,485		396,993	253,526	
Nantwen	–	–	–	–	–	143,562			140,000	177,606	179,169	165,087			100,762	440,642		147,952	158,360	
South Tunnel	–	–	–	–	–	131,100			108,374	124,594	137,354	139,758			154,567	138,309		139,339	105,592	
Cwmbargoed	–	–	–	–	–	721			77,045	80,533	76,374	78,465			71,521	39,195		57,514		
Black Vein Drift	–	–	–	–	–	–			74,089	16,799	16,273	22,932			16,148	38,045		4,017		
Abercanaid	–	–	–	–	–	–			–	–	–	4,610			406,346			671,137	550,844	
TOTAL	341,179	376,168	323,155	980,000	1,035,236	846,638	995,606		849,696	985,679	1,04,281	1,008,040			1,428,449		1,143,755	1,132,836	1,734,444	1,353,067

* Dowlais Collieries Only.

John A Owen

MERTHYR TYDFIL COLLIERY MANNING.

STATISTICS 1908 - 1920.

Name of Colliery	Type of Coal	Colliery Managers	1908	1909	1910	1911	1912	1913	1914	1915	1916	1917	1918	1919	1920
CRAWSHAY BROTHERS CYFARTHFA LTD.															
Canal Level	Steam	Matthew Truran	115	88	91		95	96	47	74	76	41	42	28	35
Castle Level	House Coal	W.T. Bowen D.Francis(1909)	95	101	115		114	128	116	135	97	80	81	81	102
Castle Pit	Steam	W.T. Bowen D.Francis(1909)	1075	1272	1286		1454	1361	1390	1281	1172	1226	1308	1330	1534
Gethin Pit	Steam	W.T. Bowen D.Francis(1909)	345	500	544		630	673	654	715	703	703	725	690	805
Colliers' Row	Steam	Matthew Truran	45	66	75		85	187	228	228	182	162	101	78	78
Coedcae Level	Steam	" "	20	12	13		10	-	-	-	-	-	-	-	-
Cwm Pit	Steam	" "	925	1040	966		802	39	40	-	-	-	38	40	95
Cwm Du Drift	Steam	" "	115	166	176		190	200	117	22	31	27	23	65	89
Mountain Levels	Steam	" "	55	57	66		78	146	176	239	176	155	134	120	120
Winch Fawr Level.	Steam	" "	20	37	44		31	11	14	12	14	20	24	24	24
Cwm Felin	Steam	" "	-	16	15		14	10	14	10	20	64	83	83	62
GUEST KEEN & NETTLEFOLDS CO. LTD.															
Bedlinog No.1	Steam	G.M. Evans	1080	1346	1483		2585	2327	2300	2300	1700	1590	1553	1553	1553
Bedlinog No.2	Steam	G.M. Evans	710	898	1070										
Old Black Vein Drift	Steam	Wm. Jones John Bevan	135	218	36		-	-	-	-	-	-	-	-	-
Cwmbargoed & Penydarren	Steam	W. Jones W. Davies	220	172	248		298	326	285	330	280	270	-	-	-
Abércynon No 1 and 2.	Steam	Bruce Jones T. Welsh Tudor Davies	2070	2502	2543		2694	2694	2694	2694	2400	2400	2430	2430	2430
Fochriw No.1.	Steam	J.H. Jones J. Bevan	525	547	582		624	709	714	750	650	630	560	560	560
Fochriw No.2.	Steam	J.H. Jones J.Bevan.	960	550	1138		1171	1250	1250	1250	1200	1160	1220	1220	1220
Nantwen and Dan y Deri	House & Coking	T, Bevan W.Jones.	365	363	378		380	380	380	400	400	430	420	420	420
South Tunnel	Steam	J.Bevan W. Jones W. Davies	465	542	616		654	741	741	700	560	540	540	540	540
New Black Vein Drift (Trecatti)	House		0	0	152		228	157	-	-	-	-	-	-	-
HILLS' PLYMOUTH CO. LTD.															
Balca Level	House Coke	Henry John	15	-	-		-	81	81	-	-	-	-	-	-
Brazil Level	House	Henry Thomas Alfred North	25	-	-		-	20	20	-	-	-	-	-	-
Glynmill	Steam	W.W.Green, J.M. Green D.L. Thomas	170	250	250		250	286	286	300	-	300	300	-	-
North Duffryn	Steam	" "	15	-	-		-	-	-	-	-	-	-	-	-
Penylan	Steam	" "	20	-	-		-	61	61	-	-	-	-	-	-
Seron	Coke	" "	90	150	150		150	-	-	-	-	-	-	-	-
South Dyffryn 1	Steam	" "	1200	1200	1200		1200	1860	1860	1250	1250	1250	1250	1300	1600
South Dyffryn 2	Steam	" "	395	300	300		300								
South Dyffryn Level.	Steam	" "	70	-	-		-	-	-	-	-	-	-	-	-
Taibach	Steam	" "	40	-	-		-	-	-	-	-	-	-	-	-
Graig No.1&2.	Steam	" "	150	500	500		500	534	534	450	450	450	450	800	800
Nantyrodyn	Steam	" "	-	-	-		-	36	36	-	-	-	-	-	-
NIXONS NAVIGATION CO. LTD.															
Merthyr Vale 1&2	Steam	T.Williams B.R. Edwards	3252	3387	3421		3300	3575	3424	3292	3292	2745	2745	2435	2852
OCEAN COAL CO. LTD.															
Treharris Deep Navigation	Steam	W.M. Jenkins W. Phillips	1765	1767	1913		1984	1880	1946	1946	1946	1946	1946	1946	1946
North & South Pits		Lewis Lewis													

JOHN A. OWEN. 1976.

PRODUCTION STATISTICS DOWLAIS WORKS.
1870 - 1884.

YEAR	WEEKS	PROFIT	BLAST FURNACES						PUDDLING FORGES (Puddled Bars)		ROLLING MILLS (Iron)		BESSEMER STEEL INGOTS		SIEMENS STEEL INGOTS		ROLLING MILLS (Steel)	
			IRON			SPIEGELEISEN												
			Make Statute Tons	Cost per Ton	Coal Yield	Make Statute Tons	Cost per Ton	Coal Yield	Make Statute Tons	Cost per Ton	Make Stat Tons	Cost per Ton	Make Stat Tons	Cost per Tons	Make Statute Tons	Cost per Tons	Make Statute Tons	Cost per ton
1870	54	197,756	165,719	2. 8,1,6.	37 - 31				124,364	3.14,2,6.	118,390	5.15,3,9.	21,179	6.17,11,8.			16,967	8,12,8
1871	51	165,840	158,728	2. 9,9,2.	36 - 56				115,477	3.15,10.	100,827	5.16,8,2.	25,958	6. 7,6,2.	581	6.11,9,3.	22,305	8. 3,8
1872	52	229,836	168,871	2.11,2,5.	37 - 21				121,165	3.17,9.	94,432	5. 2,9,5.	37,516	6,7. 0,3.	3,034	7. 3,3,4.	31,321	8,3,11
1873	53	190,513	126,042	3. 2,7,5.	39 - 26				81,264	4.16,5,9.	63,342	7.12,2,6.	28,246	7,8,1,3.	5,032	9,1, 5,4.	30,688	9,9, 7
1874	51	253,575	154,499	3.12,5,1.	41 - 97	2,243	6,16,3,1.		94,586	5,11,1,9.	77,864	8,13,7,7.	40,197	8,0,3,7.	10,579	7,17,5,2.	38,421	10,10,11
1875	52	49,129	114,784	3.11,6,7.	45 - 12	3,947	6. 4,6,3.		66,548	5. 5,0,8.	54,264	8, 5,9,5.	27,853	6,16,2,1.	8,944	7. 3,8,3.	31,810	9, 1,4
1876	53	45,712	142,043	3.1,11,8.	44 - 42	6,988	4. 7,6,3.		72,032	4. 6,2,5.	43,867	7. 2,2,1.	35,453	5.15,1,7.	14,175	5,14,8,7.	38,860	7. 9,5
1877	52	81,009	168,359	2.18,8,7.	44 -,47	10,612	3.16,9,3.	45 - 62	64,040	3.19,4,2.	48,738	6. 8,4,2.	54,660	4.15,7,5.	17,938	4.19,7,7.	63,257	6. 8,5
1878	52	68,144	173,364	2.13,8,2.	42 - 14	16,747	4. 1,8,4.	60 - 30	49,049	3. 6,4,1.	35,014	5.11,10,2.	70,403	4. 7,8,1.	19,049	4.10,1,1.	76,360	5,13,7
1879	52	94,010	178,803	2. 9,10,7.	40 - 20	19,567	3.14,4,3.	57 - 77	41,497	3. 5,0,7.	29,521	5. 7,2,3.	87,074	3.14,10.	17,787	3.18,11,4.	90,652	4.17,5
1880	52	143,872	152,508	2. 5,10,7.	40 - 56	22,032	3. 6,2.	58 - 3	34,530	3,2. 4,8.	53,609	5. 0,8,5.	83,460	3. 7,7,1.	18,629	3.12,6,7.	88,776	4. 9,7.
1881	53	139,030	172,342	2.11,8,8.	41 - 77	27,369	3.16,11,7.	63 - 57	43,569	3.13,6,1.	54,281	5.10,8,4.	101,132	3. 7,2,8,3.	18,685	3.16,5,5.	101,564	4.15,10
1882	52	192,441	186,234	2. 0,8,1.	42 - 56	25,163	4. 3,1,1.	77 - 66	42,433	3.12,11,8.	45,624	5.10,11,3.	113,433	3.12,11.	19,689	3.14,7,1.	105,505	4.19,4
1883	52	137,010	215,699	2. 9,4,2.	40 - 104	22,706	4. 2,3,8.	72 - 48	35,990	3.10,5,7.	36,614	5.10,11,3.	125,220	3.12,9,6.	18,799	4.17,2,9.	124,036	4,19,2
1884	52	70,775	191,467	2. 8,1,8.	40 - 111	13,650	4. 1,8,5.	60 - 65	32,865	3.13,6,4.	35,177	5.12,3,6.	118,919	3.12,1,2.	19,557	3.16,6,5.	121,397	4.19

John A. Owen.
28.2.76.

	DOWLAIS NUMBER & NAME	MAKER	WORKS NUMBER	DATE BUILT	TYPE	GAUGE	LOCO CLASS	CYLDER DIAMTER	STROKE	BOILER PRES'RE	WEIGHT	COST NEW	COMMENTS
1	"SUCCESS"	HEATH ABBEY IRON C°	—	1831/32	0-6-0	4' 2"/4' 4"	—	8½" OS	20"				GENERAL DUTIES DOWLAIS WORKS.
2	"PERSEVERANCE"	" " " "	—	1832	0-6-0	4' 2"/4' 4"	—	10½" OS	20"			£762	FITTED WITH RACK FOR WORKING ON PENYDARREN TRAMROAD.
3	"MOUNTAINEER"	" " " "	—	1833	0-6-0	4' 2"/4' 4"	—	8½" OS	20"	80 PSI.		£450	SPEED 7 M.P.H. H.P. 8½. GENERAL WORKS DUTIES.
4	—	" " " "	—	1833	0-4-0	4' 2"/4' 4"	—	8½" OS	20"				GENERAL WORKS DUTIES.
5	"JOHN WATT"	" " " "	—	1836	0-4-0	4' 2"/4' 4"	—	8½" OS			2T-0C	£500	RACK QUOTED FOR IN 1837 – £105 GENERAL WORKS DUTIES.
6	"YN-BAROD-ETTO"	" " " "	—	1837	0-4-0	4' 2"/4' 4"	—	8½" OS	20"			£420	GENERAL WORKS DUTIES.
7	"CHARLES JORDAN"	" " " "	—	1837/38	0-6-0	4' 2"/4' 4"	—	8½" OS	20"				GENERAL WORKS DUTIES.
8	"DOWLAIS"	" " " "	—	1838	0-6-0	4'-8½"	—	8½" OS	18"			£604	RACK FITTED. WORKED ON PENYDARREN TRAMROAD.
9	"COLLY"		—				—						NO INFORMATION. ONLY IN 1848 INVENTORY VALUE £200
10	"ENGLAND"		—				—						NO INFORMATION ONLY IN 1848 INVENTORY VALUE £100
11	"EXCAVATION."			1839	0-6-0	4'-8½"	—					£1,500	BOUGHT SECOND HAND IN APRIL 1844 FROM E. OLDHAM & SON FOR £500
12	"VOLCANO"			1840	0-6-0	4'-8½"	—					£1560	THE PAIR – CONTRACTORS LOCO'S FROM THE SWINDON JUNCTION RAILWAY.
13	—	SHARP BROS	687/51	1851	0-4-0	4'-8½"		IS		ST.		£1,350	GENERAL WORKS DUTIES
14	—	NEILSON & C°		1853	0-6-0	4'-8½"		10"		ST		£780	HAULING COAL TRAINS. CWMBARGOED TO DOWLAIS WORKS.
15	—	" "		1853	0-6-0	4'-8½"		10"		ST		£780	" " " "
16	—	" "		1853	0-6-0	4'-8½"		10"		ST		£780	" " " "
17	—	BEYER PEACOCK & C°	44/56	1856	0-4-0	4'-8½"				ST			GENERAL WORKS DUTIES
18	N°1 "SAMSON."	KITSON, THOMPSON & HEWITSON	701/59	1859	0-6-0	4'-8½"	"A"	16" IS	24"	140 P.T.		£2,200	MAIN LINE TRAFFIC IN WORKS.
19		MANNING, WARDLE & C°	29/61	1861	0-6-0	4'-8½"		11" IS	17"	140 ST			MINERAL TRAFFIC. TO DOWLAIS WORKS.
20		NEILSON & C°	813/63	1863	2-4-0 / 0-6-0	4'-8½"				ST			GENERAL WORKS DUTIES.
21	"MORLAIS"	MANNING, WARDLE & C°	75/63	1863	0-6-0	4'-8½"	"D"	14" IS.	18"	140 ST			IRON WORKS TRAFFIC & QUARRIES.
22		HUDSWELL, CLARKE, & C°	22/64	1864	0-4-0	4'-8½"		6½" OS	12"	ST	4T-10C		GENERAL WORKS DUTIES.
23	N°2 "TIR-Y-COLLY"	MANNING, WARDLE & C°	150/65	1865	0-6-0	4'-8½"	"B"	15" IS	22"	140 T	38 TON		ORIGINALLY HAULING COAL FROM FOCHRIW COLLIERY – LATTER AT SHEARS & COLD SAWS.
24	N°3 "KINGFISHER"	SHARP, STEWART & C°	1678/66	1866	0-6-0	4'-8½"	"A"	16¾" IS	24"	140 ST	38 TON		CWMBARGOED & FOCHRIW COLLIERIES.
25	N°4 "BARGOED"	MANNING WARDLE & C°		1866	0-6-0	4'-8½"	"B"	15" IS	22"	140 ST	32T 10C		ALL TRAFFIC OF WORKS AT LOWER BRANCH INCLINE.
26	N°5 "JOSHUA"	SHARP, STEWART & C°	1775/67	1867	0-6-0	4'-8½"	"A"	17" IS	24"	150 ST	43 TON		WEIGHING MATERIAL FOR SALE AT LOWER BRANCH INCLINE.
27	N°6 "PANT"	MANNING WARDLE & C°	269/68	1868	0-6-0	4'-8½"	"D"	13" IS	18"	140 ST	26 TON		WEIGHING MATERIAL FOR SALE.
28	"HAFOD"	MANNING, WARDLE & C°	275/69	1869	0-4-0	4'-8½"	"F"	10" OS	16"	140 ST			GENERAL WORKS DUTIES.
29	N°7	FLETCHER, JENNINGS & C°	84/69	1869	0-6-0	4'-8½"		IS		T			GENERAL WORKS DUTIES.
30	"GARTH"	MANNING, WARDLE & C°	312/70	1870	0-6-0	4'-8½"	"B"	15" IS	22"	140 ST			WORKED BETWEEN LOWER STEEL WORKS & IRON YARD.
31	N°8 "EHEDYDD"	KITSON & SON	1703/72	1872	0-6-0	4'-8½"	"A"	16/16½" IS.	24"	140 ST	40T-2C		BLAST FURNACE SLAG LADLES TO TIP.

	DOWLAIS NUMBER & NAME	MAKER	WORKS NUMBER	DATE BUILT	TYPE	GAUGE	LOCO CLASS	CYLDER DIAMTER	STROKE	BOILER PRES'RE	WEIGHT	COST NEW	COMMENTS
2	Nº9 "HEBOG"	KITSON & SON	1847/72	1872	0-6-0	4'-8½"	"A"	16"/17" IS	24"	140 ST	40T 2C		ATTENDING BLAST FURNACE GANTRIES.
3	Nº10 "EOS"	KITSON & SON	1846/72	1872	0-6-0	4'-8½"	"A"	16" IS	24"	160 ST	40T-0C		BLAST FURNACE SLAG LADLES TO TIP. IN APRIL 1917 SLID OVER TIP KILLING DRIVER
4	Nº11 "WHAUP"	HUDSWELL CLARK & Cº	141/73	1873	0-4-0	4'-8½"	"C"	13" OS	20"	140 ST	24T 0C		ATTENDING NAVVIES, MASONS & RAILROAD GANG.
5	Nº12 "MAVIS"	HUDSWELL CLARKE & Cº	137/73	1873	0-4-0	4'-8½"	"C"	13" IS	20"	140 ST	24T 0C		ATTENDING LIMESTONE TRAFFIC AT MORLAIS QUARRIES.
6	"PEEWIT"	HUDSWELL CLARKE & Cº	140/73	1873	0-4-0	4'-8½"	"C"	13" IS	20"	140 ST	24T 0C		ATTENDING LIMESTONE TRAFFIC AT MORLAIS QUARRIES.
7		JOHN FOWLER & Cº	2140/74	1874	0-4-0	4'-8½"	"C"	13"	20"	140 ST	23T 0C		ATTENDING LIMESTONE TRAFFIC AT MORLAIS QUARRIES
8		" " "	2141/74	1874	0-4-0	4'-8½"	"C"	13"	20"	140 ST	23T 0C		DITTO
9		" " "	2423/75	1875	0-4-0	4'-8½"	"C"	13"	20"	140 ST	23T 10C		DITTO.
10	Nº13 "BEYER Nº1"	BEYER PEACOCK & Cº LTD	1813/78	1878	0-4-0	4'-8½"	"F"	11"/10" IS	16"	120 ST	16T-0C	£950	ATTENDING TO COAL WASHERY AT STEEL WORKS.
11	Nº14 "PEACOCK Nº1"	" " " "	1814/78	1878	0-4-0	4'-8½"	"F"	11"/10" IS	16"	110 ST	16T 10C	£950	ATTENDING TO BOILERS & SOAKING PITS AT MILLS, ALSO TAKING ASHES TO TIP.
12	Nº15 "BEYER Nº2"	" " " "	1966/80	1880	0-4-0	4'-8½"	"E"	12" IS.	16"	120 ST	18T 0C	£1,090	ATTENDING NAVVIES, MASONS & RAILROAD GANG.
13	Nº16 "PEACOCK Nº2	" " " "	1967/80	1880	0-4-0	4'-8½"	"E"	12" IS.	16"	120 ST	18T 0C	£1,090	ATTENDING BESSEMER & SIEMENS CUPOLAS IN STEEL PLANT.
14	Nº17 "BEDLINOG"	SHARP STEWART & Cº	3141/83	1883	0-6-0	4'-8½"	"A"	16" IS	24"	140 ST	39T 0C	£1,800	ATTENDING BEDLINOG COLLIERY & LATER RAW MATERIAL STOCK BINS AT BLAST FURNACES
15	Nº18 "SWALLOW"	FLETCHER JENNINGS & Cº		1883	0-4-0	4'-8½"	"D"	14"/13 OS	18"	140 ST	20T-0C	£1,100	BRICKYARD TRAFFIC & SLURRY PONDS
16	Nº19 "MAGPIE"	PECKETT & SONS	424/83	1883	0-4-0	4'-8½"	"D"	14"	18"	140 ST	22T 0C	£1,300	BESSEMER & SIEMENS FURNACE SLAG TO SLAG REDUCTION PLANT.
47	Nº20 "BEYER Nº3"	BEYER PEACOCK & Cº	2374/83	1883	0-4-0	4'-8½"	"D"	13" IS	18"	150 ST	22T-0C	£1,300	TAKING HOT METAL FROM MIXER TO BESSEMER CONVERTERS.
48	Nº21 "PEACOCK Nº3"	" " "	2375/83	1883	0-4-0	4'-8½"	"D"	13 IS	18"	140 ST	22T 0C	£1,300	TAKING HOT METAL FROM MIXER TO BESSEMER CONVERTERS.
49	Nº22 "BEYER Nº4	" " "	2691/85	1885	0-4-0	4'-8½"	"F"	11" IS.	16"	115 ST	17T 0C	£925	ATTENDING NAVVIES, MASONS & RAILROAD GANG.
50	Nº23 "PEACOCK Nº4"	" " "	2871/87	1887	0-4-0	4'-8½"	"F"	11" IS	16"	120 ST	17T 0C	£800	TAKING ASHES FROM BOILERS & SOAKING PITS AT MILLS TO TIP.
51	Nº24 "CLYDE"	CLYDE LOCO WORKS	12/87	1887	0-6-0	4'-8½"	"A"	17½" IS	26"	180 ST	46T 0C	£1500	ATTENDING COAL WASHERY TRAFFIC & BRICKYARD
52	Nº22	SHARP STEWART & Cº	3450/88	1888	0-6-0	4'-8½"	"A"	16 IS	24"	140 ST	39T 0C		GENERAL DUTIES.
53	Nº25 "GWERNLLWYN"	KITSON & Cº	3210/89	1889	0-6-0	4'-8½"	"A"	17½" IS.	26	140 T	43T 10C	£1,800	ATTENDING RAIL BANK AT STEELWORKS.
54	Nº26 "BEYER Nº5"	BEYER PEACOCK & Cº	3086/89	1889	0-4-0	4'-8½"	"D"	14" IS	18"	130 ST	22T 0C	£1,150	ATTENDING COKE OVENS & TOP OF Nº11 BLAST FURNACE.
55	Nº27 "HUDSWELL CLARKE Nº4"	HUDSWELL CLARKE & Cº	322/89	1889	0-4-0	4'-8½"	"C"	14" OS	20"	160 ST	29T 5C	£1,000	ATTENDING COKE OVENS & TOP OF Nº11 BLAST FURNACE.
56	Nº28 "HUDSWELL CLARKE Nº5"	" " "	355/90	1890	0-4-0	4'-8½"	"C"	14" OS	20"	160 ST	29T 5C	£1090	ATTENDING BLAST FURNACE STOCK BINS.
57	Nº29 "FOCHRIW"	SHARP STEWART & Cº	3585/90	1890	0-4-0	4'-8½"	"A"	18"/17½" IS	26"	140 ST	45T 0C	£1,750	ATTENDING SOUTH TUNNEL, CWMBARGOED & FOCHRIW COLLIERIES.
58	Nº30 "DOWLAIS"	ANDREW BARCLAY & SONS	679/90	1890	0-4-0	4'-8½"	"C"	14"/13½" OS	22"/20"	140 ST	25T 0C		ALL IFOR WORKS TRAFFIC. BOUGHT SECOND HAND PONTYMISTER STEELWORKS.
59	Nº39	MANNING WARDLE & Cº		1892	0-4-0	4'-8½" 3'-0"	"H"	10" OS	15"	140 T	13T 10C		BESSEMER STEEL PLANT, INGOT MOULDS TO INGOT STRIPPER.
60	Nº16	KITSON & Cº	3603/95	1895	0-6-0	4'-8½"	"A"	17½ IS	26"	140 ST	44T 8C		PURCHASED FROM BUTE DOCKS RAILWAY GENERAL DUTIES.
61	Nº31 "PEACOCK Nº5"	BEYER PEACOCK & Cº	3881/97	1897	0-4-0	4'-8½"	"D"	14" IS	18"	140 ST	22T 0C		ATTENDING MERCHANT BAR MILLS IFOR WORKS.
62	Nº5	KITSON & Cº	3820/99	1899	0-6-0	4'-8½"	"A"	17½"	26"	140 ST	54T 8C		PURCHASED FROM TAFF VALE RAILWAY [illegible]

	DOWLAIS NUMBER & NAME	MAKER	WORKS NUMBER	DATE BUILT	TYPE	GAUGE	LOCO CLASS	CYLDER DIAMTER	STROKE	BOILER PRESRE	WEIGHT	COST NEW	COMMENTS
63	Nº6	KITSON & Cº	3816/99	1899	0-6-0	4'-8½"	"A"	17½ IS	26	140 ST	54T 8c		PURCHASED FROM TAFF VALE RAILWAY Cº GENERAL DUTIES.
64	Nº23	KITSON & Cº	3821/99	1899	0-6-0	4'-8½"	"A"	17½ IS	26	140 ST	54T 8c		PURCHASED FROM TAFF VALE RAILWAY Cº GENERAL DUTIES.
65	Nº15	KITSON & Cº	3872/99	1899	0-6-0	4'-8½"	"A"	17½" IS	26	140 ST	44T 8c		PURCHASED FROM CARDIFF RAILWAY Cº GENERAL DUTIES.
66	Nº32	L.N.W.R. Cº			2-4-0	4'-8½"	"B"	15¼" OS	20	120 T	26-14c		PURCHASED FROM GOLDEN VALLEY RAILWAY Cº (MONMOUTHSHIRE)
67	Nº33 "LADY CORNELIA"	PECKETT & SONS	834/00	1900	0-4-0	4'-8½"	"C"	14" OS	20"	150 ST	24T 0c	£1,175	ATTENDING MERCHANT BAR MILLS IFOR WORKS.
68	Nº34 "LORD WIMBORNE"	KITSON & Cº LTD	4020/01	1901	0-6-0	4'-8½"	"A"	17½" IS	26	150 ST	43T 4c	£2,125	ATTENDING BLAST FURNACES, PIG IRON TO STOCK.
69	Nº35 "HUDSWELL CLARKE Nº1"	HUDSWELL CLARKE & Cº	624/02	1902	0-4-0	3'-0"	"H"	9" OS	15"	160 ST	12T 10c	£695	BESSEMER STEEL PLANT. TAKING INGOTS FROM STRIPPER TO ROUGHING MILL
70	Nº36 "HUDSWELL CLARKE Nº2"	" " "	625/02	1902	0-4-0	3'-0"	"H"	9" OS	15"	160 ST	12T 10c	£695	BESSEMER STEEL PLANT. TAKING INGOTS FROM STRIPPER TO ROUGHING MILL
71	Nº37 "HUDSWELL CLARKE Nº3"	" " "	626/02	1902	0-4-0	3'-0"	"H"	9" OS	15"	160 ST	12T 10c	£695	BESSEMER STEEL PLANT. TAKING INGOT BOGIES TO STRIPPER.
72	Nº27	G.K.N. IFOR WORKS.		1903	0-4-2	4'-8½"	"C"	14" OS	20"	120 T	30T 10c		STEEL WORKS COKE OVENS & Nº11 FURNACE COMPLETE REBUILD OF Nº27.
73	Nº38 "ARTHUR KEEN"	G.K.N IFOR WORKS.	1/06	1906	0-6-0	4'-8½"	A1/A	18" IS	26"	180 T	55T 0c		WEIGHING ALL PURCHASE MATERIAL AT UPPER BRANCH.
74	Nº11 "GOWER"	AVONSIDE ENGINE Cº	1521/07	1907	0-4-0	4'-8½"							GENERAL WORKS DUTIES.
75	Nº7	G.K.N. IFOR WORKS	2/07	1907	0-4-0	4'-8½"	"C1"	17½" OS	22"	175 T	42T 0c		ATTENDING MORLAIS LIMESTONE QUARRIES & IFOR WORKS.
76	Nº40 "KING GEORGE V"	G.K.N. IFOR WORKS	3/07	1907	0-4-0	4'-8½"	"D"	14" IS	18"	190 T	35T 0c		TAKING HOT METAL FROM BLAST FURNACES TO METAL MIXER.
77	Nº41 "SANDYFORD"	G.K.N IFOR WORKS.	4/08	1908	0-6-0	4'-8½"	"A1"	19" IS	26"	180 T	57T 10c		ALL MAIN LINE TRAFFIC FROM UPPER TO LOWER WORKS - MOST POWERFUL LOCO AT WORKS
78	Nº42 "QUEEN MARY"	G.K.N. IFOR WORKS	5/09	1909	0-4-0	4'-8½"	"D"	14" IS	18"	200 T	35T 0c		TAKING HOT METAL FROM BLAST FURNACES TO METAL MIXER
79	Nº14	HUDSWELL CLARKE & Cº	888/09	1909	0-6-0	4'-8½"		15" IS	20"	ST			GENERAL DUTIES IFOR WORKS.
80	Nº43	G.K.N IFOR WORKS	6/12	1912	0-4-0	4'-8½"	"D"	14" IS	18"	200 T	35T 0c		ATTENDING BLAST FURNACE BUNKERS WITH RAW MATERIALS.
81	Nº44 "PANT"	G.K.N IFOR WORKS	7/15	1915	0-4-0 / 0-6-0	4'-8½"	"D"	14" IS	18"	200 T	35T 0c		ATTENDING FINISHED STEEL TRAFFIC
82	Nº45	G.K.N IFOR WORKS	8/17	1917	0-4-0	3'-0"	"H"	10½" OS	16"	200 T	13T 10c		BESSEMER STEEL PLANT. TAKING INGOT MOULDS TO STRIPPER.
83	Nº10	G.K.N. EAST MOORS.	2/19	1919	0-4-0	4'-8½"		15" OS	22"	ST	27T 0c		EX - EAST MOORS STEEL WORKS CARDIFF. GENERAL DUTIES. IFOR YAR[illegible]
84	Nº46	G.K.N. IFOR WORKS.	9/20	1920	0-4-0	4'-8½"	"D"	14" IS	18"	200 T	35T 0c		ATTENDING FINISHED STEEL TRAFFIC LAST LOCOMOTIVE MADE AT DOWLAIS.
85	"CAERLEON"	HUNSLET ENGINE Cº	1851/37	1937	0-4-0	4'-8½"	"D"	12" OS	20"	160 ST	22T 2c		GENERAL DUTIES IFOR WORKS
86	"SUSAN"	W. G. BAGNALL			0-4-0	4'-8½"		OS		ST			HIRED FROM I.C.I DOWLAIS. GENERAL DUTIES IFOR WORKS.
87	"JENNIFER"	W.G. BAGNALL	2667/42	1942	0-4-0	4'-8½"		OS		ST			PURCHASED FROM I.C.I DOWLAIS 1951 LAST STEAM LOCO AT DOWLAIS. SCRAPPED 1951
88	Nº1.	HUDSWELL, CLARKE & Cº	D 984	1955	0-4-0	4'-8½"		5½" IS	7¾"		30T 0c	£11,733	GARDNER DIESEL L.3 ENGINE - 4 CYLINDER GENERAL DUTIES IFOR WORKS.
89	Nº2.	" " "	D 1030	1957	0-4-0	4'-8½"		5½ IS	7¾"		30T 0c	£13,315	GARDNER DIESEL L.3 ENGINE - 4 CYLINDERS GENERAL DUTIES IFOR WORKS.
90	Nº3.	HUDSWELL, CLARKE & Cº	D 1246	1961	0-4-0	4'-8½"		5½" IS	7¾"		30T 0c	£10,000	GARDNER DIESEL L.3. ENGINE. 4 CYLINDERS GENERAL DUTIES IFOR WORKS.

3. JOHN A. OWEN

DOWLAIS WORKS—LOCOMOTIVES

(Illustrations 16 to 28)

The locomotives of the Dowlais Works covered the whole spectrum of industrial locomotion, when the industries of Britain were in full flood of the Industrial Revolution and became—Steam—Mobile.

Although South Wales generally lagged behind the rest of the country, considering that in February, 1804, on the Penydarren tramroad Richard Trevethick ran an engine on rails for the first time successfully and pointed the way ahead for mankind to take a step forward in civilisation. But these early experiments with steam engines petered out when the wayward Cornish genius took his talents elsewhere to try and further his work. There were no local engineers capable of filling the vacuum he left, therefore, the high pressure locomotive was developed in the North of England under the Stephenson's, Hackworth, Hedley, Ericsson etc.

It was not until 1831/32 that Dowlais purchased its first steam locomotives from the Neath Abbey Iron Works. This remarkable firm of engineers made locomotive, marine and pumping engines as well as iron related products. Dowlais sold them pig iron and as part of reciprocal trade started to purchase engines from them, although they did get quotations from Jones, Birmingham and Stephenson, Newcastle. Neath Abbey had only been in the locomotive business since 1829 when they supplied the Sirhowy Tramroad with an engine.

The Works at Dowlais needed more efficient internal/external transport due to the terrific expansion of the business. From the year 1815 when Josiah John Guest became managing partner it had grown from a struggling concern into a thriving, rapidly expanding entity, which by the late 1820's overtook the great Cyfarthfa Works in all aspects of trade.

The local raw materials had to be procured from an ever increasing radius from the works i.e. coal from Pantywaun and Cwmbargoed, ironstone from Carno, Dowlais Top and Mountain Hare, limestone from Morlais and Twyniau Gwynion, this necessitated a large integrated network of tramroads which could not adequately provide sufficient quantities of the basic raw materials with the slow, costly, small amounts that horse drawn transport provided. Also the importation of iron-ore from Whitehaven and elsewhere up the Glamorgan Canal and the export of their finished goods demanded a quicker, more powerful medium of transportation either from The Basin at Abercynon up the Penydarren Tramroad or from the Dowlais Canal-head at Pont-Store-House at Merthyr up the Dowlais Tramway.

Therefore, it was decided to purchase locomotives from the Neath Abbey Iron Co. Compared to the designs of the Stephenson's on the North East Coast, they were old fashioned but perfectly adequate for

51

their local use and purpose. Indeed the old bug-bear of poor plateway tracks to run on was to inhibit the local engines until the edge rail came into universal use locally in the 1840's.

The first two engines purchased were named "Success" and "Perseverance" both six wheelers with the latter being fitted with a rack attachment to assist its ascent from Merthyr, similarly other Dowlais locomotives were fitted with this refinement in later years.

Dowlais changed gauge in 1838, from 4' 2"/4' 4" plateway to 4' 8½" standard gauge, this was the introduction of the modern edge-rail-road into the district and paved the way for purchasing more powerful engines from English suppliers in the future.

The Works purchased approximately eight engines from Neath Abbey between the years 1831/1840 and apart from acquiring two secondhand tender, standard gauge engines in 1844 did not purchase any more until 1851.

This was due to the fact that the renewal of the Dowlais lease with Lord Bute was in doubt from 1840 to 1848, during this period large parts of the works and mechanical plant was allowed to run down as a possible prelude to a sale of the business.

When the lease was renewed in 1848 it represented a completely new phase of company operations. In that the coal holding had to be extensively developed to maintain the eighteen furnaces in coke, together with all the other manufacturing technologies expanding, requiring more space and hence quicker efficient transport.

Therefore, in 1853, Lady Charlotte Guest, started the campaign off when she ordered three large powerful locomotives from Neilsons of Glasgow for the coal traffic. Then in 1856 the new management team under the leadership of G. T. Clarke and William Menelaus completely reorganised the business in regard to minerals, manufacturing capability and markets. All this required powerful efficient locomotives and a good track, to this end from 1857 William Menelaus planned the purchase of new engines to keep pace with the expanding business. In 1857 there were only 11 locos in operation for the whole business, but from 1859 new machines were ordered from the largest builders, i.e. Kitson, Thompson and Hewitson, Leeds; Manning Wardle and Co., Leeds; Neilson and Co., Glasgow; Hudswell Clarke, Leeds; Beyer Peacock and Co., Manchester and Sharp Bros., Manchester. Apart from two small 0-4-0 locos in 1864/1869, fourteen large 0-6-0 engines were purchased from 1859/1872 to develop their coal holding at Fochriw, Cwmbargoed, South Tunnel and Colly Levels. Then between the years 1872/1887, sixteen, small general works locos were purchased to service the development in manufacture, especially the Bessemer Steel Plant which totally altered all industries, also some large 0-6-0 types again to cater for Bedlinog and Nantwen coal run.

Dowlais Built Locomotives

Dowlais continued to purchase new locomotives up until 1902, although from 1901 the large Dowlais engineering shops had started to rebuild as a trial their first complete loco in a special department at the Ifor Works. Also to direct the efforts they employed a locomotive engineer, namely George Robson, who had worked for the Taff Vale Railway and the G.W.R. to rebuild existing and design new locomotives.

Prior to this policy being adopted all the overhauling and rebuilding of works locomotives was subcontracted to Peckett and Son, Bristol.

The years up to 1906 were spent consolidating this vital activity, in that year George Robson designed and constructed his first complete locomotive in the Ifor Works, the first of nine engines built at the Dowlais Shops, namely "Arthur Keen".

The second locomotive built in 1907 was No. 7 a 0-4-0 which eventually went to Cardiff steelworks and worked up until the 1950's. Also in 1907 was built No. 40 "King George V", which together with No. 42 "Queen Mary" built in 1909 were personally named by their majesties on their visit to the Dowlais Works in June, 1912. The livery of the works locomotives at this time was smoke box, saddle, chimney and running plates glossy black; boiler and firebox medium green with black bands edged each side in yellow. Tanks, bunker sides and back, medium green with a broad black band having a finer yellow line between the black and the green.

Cab side sheets and roof bordered by a broad black band with a finer yellow line innermost. Dome and safety valve cover in the same green. Whistles polished brass as were the window framings.

Valves, underframe, guard irons and plates, step back plates green with yellow lining. The steps themselves were black and the sandboxes green unlined. Brake hangers and shoes unlined black, with the wheels painted green, black tyres and a yellow line between the black and the green buffer beams and stocks red bordered in black and lined in yellow.

All name, number and works plates had raised brass edges and raised brass characters on a black background. All the brass brightly polished.

Coupling rods, handrails, smokebox door handles and hinges, buffer heads and couplings together with the seating ring behind the smokebox door polished steel.

But in 1908 No. 41 "Sandyford" was built. It was the high water mark of Robson's design and motive power, the most powerful locomotive in the works. The works and collieries in this period were updating plant and machinery whilst the blast furnaces in the steelworks were being completely rebuilt to the most modern standards and size at that time. In 1912 No. 43 was built and in 1915 No. 44 "Pant". In that year a significant event happened. George Robson left the Dowlais Works. This first class engineer left behind as his testimonial the beautiful clear lined, powerful "Dowlais" locomotives, a man who completely understood the environment for which he was designing tractive effort for. The "Arthur Keen" locomotive had a round top firebox, but the "Sandyford" and the 0-4-0 T's had Belpaire fireboxes which rested on top of the frames, whilst the combination of inside cylinders and side tanks on small industrial locomotives was somewhat unusual. Although all George Robson's engines were of distinctive design, incorporating the

53

full main line railway companies innovations of style, engineering expertise and motive power. He also contributed another tremendous service to Dowlais. He had trained his successor David Hicks and established the well tried locomotive repair/build shops. Robson built seven completely new locomotives and rebuilt many more. When he left in February, 1915, the work carried on without a moment's hesitation. David Hicks built No. 45 a 3′ 0″ gauge, 0-4-0, Bessemer steelworks loco in 1917, a beautiful miniature engine faithfully reproduced to Robson's design.

With the works still booming after the 1914/18 war, David Hicks, in 1920 built what was to be the last completely new locomotive No. 46, a standard gauge 0-4-0.

From this date and until the steelworks closed in 1930 many locomotives were repaired and rebuilt, but no more were made complete. In all nine engines were constructed, surely a magnificent testimonial to the engineers and craftsmen at the Dowlais Works. One might say only nine locomotives do not constitute a great building programme, but when one considers that the works' business was iron, steel and coal and not locomotive engines, it puts the matter into true perspective.

From this date and up until the steelworks closed in 1930 only overhauls and some rebuilds were carried out in the Ifor Works Engineering Shops.

Throughout the 1930's some engines were transferred to Cardiff Works, but the majority were cut-up for scrap. In the 1940's about six second-hand engines were purchased from various sources until the last steam locomotive in the Works was "Jennifer" which stopped working in 1958 and was scrapped in 1959. When a total of three diesel shunters started service from 1955 to carry out all traffic duties in the remodelled works. These continued to operate until 1975 when all rail traffic was suspended in the plant.

Over the years from 1831 all the engines working at Dowlais had to be designed for the steep gradients both inside works areas and on the colliery rails, also the very sharp curves. Consequently terrific power had to be squeezed into squat short wheel based structures. For some of the larger six coupled locomotives the connecting rods had to be hinged to satisfy the demands of the track, which generally could be in very poor condition in places. Especially when the platelaying gang invariably had to replace defective rails with rejects or spare off-cuts from customers' orders it was possible to find four different types of rail in a 100 yard stretch from flat bottomed, bull head to bridge type. Nevertheless at any one time there was never enough locomotive power to satisfy all the needs of the vast Dowlais works empire from Nantwen Colliery in the south to Pantywaun Colliery in the north, through the great steel plants and furnaces of the lower works to the compact Ifor Works, the quarries of Morlais hill and onto the slag tips at Ifor and the great white tip. They were always overworked and pushed to their mechanical limits, but were lovingly cared for by their crews in a complete and utter devotion. Who knew their charges like children with a thorough knowledge of all their foibles and tantrums. When one speaks to old drivers and firemen and fitters who worked on them the pride, expertise and importance of their jobs becomes apparent immediately with a legion of stories and anecdotes about their charges.

Lastly the engineers through the years at Dowlais who were concerned with the locomotives in their purchase, repair and design. In the early years it appears everyone was connected with them, as one would have a new toy. The letters at the archives in Cardiff mention four men dealing with locos in the space of six years then throughout the 19th century the gradual specialisation of this facet of engineering under one man. Moreso, when George Robson was appointed locomotive superintendent in 1901/02 to design and construct engines as a matter of policy to suit all the peculiarities of Dowlais' requirements using the full technical resources in machines and skill available at the Ifor Works engineering shops. This he did with the greatest expertise and success.

Dowlais Works Locomotive Engineers

T. Gardiner C. Pearse A. Stephens J. T. Rastrick	1831/1840
S. Truran W. Menelaus	1840/1860
W. Jenkins W. Evans R. Evans E. Richards	1858 1880
D. Roberts D. Lewis J. Craig	1880/1902
G. Robson	1902/1915
D. Hicks	1915/1922
J. Jenkins P. Jones	1922/1952
J. J. Jones	1952/1965
C. M. Heath	1965/1969
E. D. Hughes	1969

The named engines represented, sentiments, areas of the district, birds, people and royalty in both Welsh and English, in all a very colourful addition to the turmoil of industry they worked in.

This short precis is very incomplete and the following facts and figures give no flesh to the bones, no colour to the scene but they do give a small appreciation of what once was and on reflection the everyday, dirty, sometimes gleaming steam locomotives shine through time as a romantic symbol of what never was, except in one's imagination.

References

1. Canals of South Wales and The Border—C. Hadfield, 1967.
2. Details of Dowlais Built Locomotives—BSC Dowlais, Drawing Office.
3. Dowlais Iron Co. Papers—County Record Office, Cardiff.
4. G.K.N. Rules and Regulations (Booklet). To be observed by all persons connected with or working on the Company's Railways. 1906 & 1919.
5. Hereford Times, 4th August, 1832.
6. Iron In The Making—Dowlais Iron Co. Letters 1782-1860—M. Elsas, 1960.
7. Model Railway Construction. Vol. 24 No. 281—September, 1957. Locomotives of the South Wales Railways—L. T. Jones.
8. Steam on the Penydarren—M. J. T. Lewis, 1975.
9. Stone Blocks and Iron Rails—B. Baxter, 1966.
10. The Cambrian, 18th August, 1832.
11. The Short History of the Dowlais Iron Works 1759-1970—J. A. Owen.

4. DIANE GREEN

HOUSING IN MERTHYR TYDFIL

(Illustrations 29 to 42)

According to Prof. Asa Briggs every age has its "shock city", which points to the future. In 1750 it was Merthyr Tydfil, in 1830 Manchester, in 1890 Chicago. The city of the 1970's is Los Angeles, whose freeways show clearly that the cities of the future must bow to the needs of the motor car.

Is Merthyr Tydfil then merely an historic fact, a shock city which no longer even raises an eyebrow? Many eminent historians have proved Merthyr to have been famous in the past, but little has been written about the town of the last one hundred years.

Merthyr still has much to offer; it is an industrial town for industrial people, and it is the story of these people, their homes and environments that interests me. Houses of past, present and future, Merthyr has them all. From tiny cottages built for the iron workers to futuristic glass and steel for present day captains of industry, we in Merthyr can still see domestic dwellings which span the centuries.

Let us hope that even if most of our past is demolished, which sadly seems likely, something worthwhile will rise from the rubble and it will not be merely a site for the slums of the 21st century.

Early housing in Merthyr

The name Merthyr Tydfil[1] comes from "Martyr Tudvil" who was, it is said, put to death on the site now occupied by the old parish church. Tudvil was one of the many children of Brychan Brycheiniog and was directly related to most Welsh and several European Saints.

By 1830, the hamlet had become a town, whose centre moved from the Parish Church to the Old Market, a site now occupied by a shopping precinct. The earliest houses were built near the river. Stonemasons were employed and as a result, timber joints were kept to a minimum. Stonework was placed over doors and windows and neat circular stone staircases led to the upper floors. A few of these houses can be seen today at Georgetown. One particular house there is built of both pennant and river stone. It has been suggested that the pennant stone was "lifted" illegally from nearby Heolgerrig, but became difficult to acquire, so river stone from the Taff was used to complete the dwelling. The Triangle, Pentrebach, is one of the earliest examples of purpose built dwellings for the iron workers and their families. A feature of these early houses were the plain slabs of stone which formed the lintels above doors and windows. Photographic examples are to be found in pictures showing "Under the Arches". This style later disappeared as lintels were made first of ornamented stone and later of bricks.

Three storey houses were quite common. The idea behind this type of dwelling was that the ground floor could be used by a young couple and the two upper floors by a family. When the family grew up and left home, the parents would change accommodation with the couple who by now had a family of their own[2]. This practice was discontinued when the police obtained court orders to convert two inferior dwellings into one decent house.

Another type was the "outshot" dwelling. This was a two storey building consisting of one upper and one lower room. A second ground floor room, usually the parental bedroom, was built behind the main room and the distinctive feature was the roof at the back sloped down, almost to floor level, covering both lower rooms.

The most famous, or perhaps I should say infamous house at this time was the back-to-back. This could merely mean, as in present day Morgantown, that houses shared a common back yard, or the houses could be joined at roof level, rather like siamese twins, or at its worst, the houses were joined at the apex of the roof. This was the most disturbing type, for 'tho the front bedrooms of each dwelling were ventilated by windows, the backrooms which shared a common wall were virtually unventilated. A grill was usually inserted in the wall which allowed a passage of stale air, household smells and noise to percolate between dwellings. The extreme width of the chimneys in houses in Aberdare Road and Castle Square suggest that these originally were back to backs.

Of course we have to mention the dismal cellars of China and Pont-storehouse, where the beds never got cold. Three men, each on a different shift, rented a bed for eight hours apiece.

Different styles abounded, Yorkshire Cottages built by Crawshay's men, Spanish bungalows for the men from Bilbao, Victorian terraces around the Quar and later semi-detached and terraced villas in the Walk and West Grove. There were too the big houses of the ironmasters, Cyfarthfa, Penydarren, Dowlais and Pentrebach, more of which one can learn elsewhere[3].

Following the Housing of the Working Classes Act 1890, the Council took over the role formerly performed by the Iron Masters and building speculators, that of housing the workers.

In 1891 the town had 11,267 houses. By 1893 this had increased to 11,600[4].

The earliest examples of council houses are at Penydarren, Council Street and Urban Street, built in 1902. These are two storey, single fronted dwellings built of stone.

This then was Merthyr at the turn of the century. Strip and ribbon development abounded. Houses were built onto houses already built onto houses. If you saw a place you built over it. "Hell with the lid off" was a fair description of the slums of old Merthyr. The appalling conditions were however about to improve. Government legislation combined with the imagination of several people was about to change the Merthyr of the 19th century.

Housing in the 20th Century

The first decade of this century saw little change in the development of Penydarren. Ribbon development continued, the old "courts" behind the High Street still existed; some larger villas had been built, but these followed the trend and were terraced in rows.

In 1912 a group of Penydarren people met for a discussion. They were, in the main professional people, teachers, solicitors and the like, married with young families and living in rented accommodation. They were excited by an idea made possible by government legislation, that of forming an Association and building their own homes. This had already been done in Penydarren, but being well travelled folk, they wanted a different type of home, not like the existing streets, but with gardens, like the Dutch and German workers were building : ideal family houses, not too big, but with three large bedrooms and best of all, real gardens at back and front. This type of housing was originally the dream of a man named Ebenezer Howard, an inventor who also worked for Gurneys, the official Parliamentary reporters. His concern was not for architects, but for people. He looked through binoculars, not microscopes.[5]

Howard wished to combine the virtues of living in the country, the fresh air, trees and grass, with the advantages of the town, nearness to work, piped water supply and electricity. He succeeded, and so Letchworth, Welwyn and Hampstead were built. The style of these houses was very much a vernacular style. While Victorian architects were casting about trying to find a style that they could call the modern style,[6] Thackeray's novels, set in the time of Queen Anne, sparked off an interest in anything said to be in the "Queen Anne" style. This was found to be ideal. It was a reaction against High Victorian Gothic and came to be known as the English Free Style. Many schools in Merthyr were built in this style. One of the best known exponents was Richard Norman Shaw. He did not invent the style, but he made it shine. This style was a combination of 17th century English domestic architecture with early Dutch features added.[7] Perhaps the most famous of Shaw's work is New Scotland Yard on the Embankment at London, though equally important is Bedford Park in the same city. The following was penned by a poet in 1881. The narrator is supposed to be J. T. Carr, the creator of Bedford Park :

" T'is a village I'll erect with Norman Shaw's assistance
Where men may lead a chaste, correct, aesthetical existence."[8]

This was directed at William Morris who maintained that aesthetics for the common man was a must, for one could change a man by surrounding him with beauty. Unfortunately the poor were unable to afford William Morris' beauty. An interesting point here is that a Dowlais girl, Annie Rees, did in fact reside in Bedford Park for many years.

I seem to have come a long way from Penydarren, but in fact the group of home builders were aware of all the facts now placed before you and saw no reason why Merthyr should not have its "Garden Village". They

59

formed themselves into the "Merthyr Tydfil Garden Village Association". Two of the members were Richard Davies and his wife Jessie Starr Davies. It is to two of their sons, Frank and Arthur Davies, that I am indebted for all the information of the association and its fate.

The group was headed by Prof. Jeavons, Lecturer in Economics at the University of Wales, who was also a member of the Cardiff Housing Reform Group. While at a meeting of the latter, Prof. Jeavons met the guest speaker, a London man, on honeymoon in Chepstow. This was to be a most important meeting, for the speaker was A. Hugh Mottram, junior Partner of Barry Parker and Raymond Unwin.

The Merthyr Tydfil Garden Village Association had discussed building houses similar to those built at Hagen in Holland by Lauweriks, but when A. Hugh Mottram accepted their invitation to address them, they delayed making a decision.

Parker and Unwin were the architects involved with Howard on the Garden City Schemes. They had worked with M. H. Baillie-Scott at Hampstead and Norman Shaw at Bedford Park. A. Hugh Mottram offered to design fourteen houses for the Association and they joyfully accepted. They pooled their capital and borrowed money from a bank, enough to buy a piece of land from Dan Davies, a local farmer and built fourteen semi-detached houses above Penydarren. Each member had to pay 5% on share capital and 4% on loan capital until the total loan was paid off.

With immense pride they instructed A. Hugh Mottram to draw up the plans and selected the designs. The first stone was laid with great ceremony by Lord Wimborne in late 1913. Garden City was off the ground, a dream about to be realized, but tragedy was around the corner. The Great War began. Building restarted after the winter was halted for the duration of the war. The houses were roofless, so no one could move in. Not only were they paying off the loan, but they also had to pay for their existing accommodation. What was even worse was the fact that a time clause stood in the contract. If the houses were unfinished after three years, both homes and land reverted to Dan Davies and this in fact was what happened. Not only did the Association lose everything, but they still had to pay off the bank.

Seymour Berry, later Lord Buckland heard of their plight and did one of his characteristic good turns. It is said that he paid off the loan. I am unable to find documented evidence of this, but the memory of the deed lives on in the minds of those he helped. For the M.T.G.V.A. the dream became a nightmare, but for those who finally lived in "Garden City" when the council took over, it was a dream come true. Space, good planning, a place to breathe, how different from the courts and huddled streets of the previous century.

Hy Brasail

In 1912 another Merthyr dream was realized. About two miles as the crow flies from Garden City was an old welsh farmhouse known as "The Cottage" Vaynor. "The Cottage" was owned by John Herbert James,

Barrister at Law and son of Charles Herbert James, former M.P. for Merthyr. J. H. James was a lover of travel. Throughout his life he wintered in Italy. He decided to extend the Cottage to house his collection of art, books and objects d'art. Two stories are told of his reasons for building the type of extension he did. Firstly that he fell in love with a beautiful Italian Contessa and built an Italian wing as a replica of her home and secondly, being a keen astronomer, he needed a tower and being also a lover of Tuscan architecture combined the two and built the house we know today.

The house survives very much as it was. Mr. and Mrs. W. Bowen appreciate and take great pride in their home. The mounting block used by J. H. James was not thrown away but set into the lawn. The only surviving original window, consisting of 30 small panes of glass, has been moved to an upstairs room, where it can remain intact.

The new stone wing consists of a large double lounge with the main bedrooms above. This runs at right angles to the farmhouse and joins the library wing which turns the whole house into a _⌐ shape. The library forms the complete first floor of the wing. From the far end of the oak panelled library, an oaken stairway leads to the courtyard which is a series of open archways. This forms a pleasant covered area. The library windows have Italian style wooden shutters. At the house end of the library wing, another staircase leads down into the hall. The bannisters are of oak, matching the panels. The stairway makes three right angled turns taking one completely round the focal point of the hall, the fireplace. The fireplaces throughout the house are of marble and the one in the hall has an oak surround. The staircase also leads up to the campanile, a roof supported by marble columns. Here J. H. James used to study astronomy. The courtyard is watched over by a large red clay eagle brought from Italy. While the Italian influence is strong, Mrs. Bowen has brought her own personal charm to bear on her home.

Mr. & Mrs. Bowen changed the name of the house to "Hy Brasail", the mythical "Isle of the Blessed" of the Gaelic legends.

The Council and Garden City

Though M.T.G.V.A. no longer existed, Garden City lived on. Dan Davies re-sold to the Council and the fourteen houses were completed. As a matter of interest, the roofs on the old fourteen are identical to some in Bedford Park. A. Hugh Mottram went on to great things. He was the architect selected to design the new town of Rossythe in Scotland and built the Clydesdale Bank in Edinburgh. Until his death he held many important architectural posts.

The Council bought the land around the fourteen houses with a view to future development which soon took place. The first tenants moved in on 6.12.1920 at a rent of 10/6-12/6 per week[9].

The second phase, fifty-four houses in all, took a long time. Several firms hit financial difficulties and the concrete boxlike houses were built by a Nottingham firm in 1923. The third phase was built by direct labour. The Borough Architect, Mr. Thackeray, submitted several designs and finally work was started. The plans were for eighteen parlour and eighteen non-parlour dwellings. These houses while not as different as the old fourteen were infinitely more attractive than the second phase. Thackeray used decorative tile work to good effect.

The last tenants took up residence in December 1924[10]. Thackeray went on to design houses in Aberfan, Heol y Bryniau, Heol y Castell and Rhodfa'r, Pant; Galon Uchaf and Brondeg in Heolgerrig. He lived with his family in Brondeg. It has been suggested that he had but little architectural training, but even if this is so, Merthyr should thank him for never did he revert to the old form of planning and he, as much as anyone is responsible for bringing working class housing in our town out of the shadows of the Industrial Revolution.

Government Legislation between the Wars

Sir Edwin Chadwick was perhaps one of the best known social reformers of the nineteenth century. His work as Secretary to the Poor Law Commissioners and his report "The Sanitary Conditions of the Labouring Population (1842)" helped to prepare the climate of public opinion which facilitated the passing of the Housing of the Working Classes Act of 1890. Later, King Edward VII then Prince of Wales added his voice to the growing chorus of those advocating decent housing for all. The slum clearance Act was eventually formulated, but had to be suspended for the duration of the Great War.

The current political slogan during the war was "Homes fit for Heroes" and when the war ended in 1918, the politicians found that the people expected them to provide the homes for heroes they had been promising for so long.

The Minister involved was Addison and the Housing Act of 1919 was named after him. Addison felt that the answer to the housing problem was to pay a fixed sum direct to each local authority. Unfortunately, he based his calculations on pre-war prices. The Act came to grief because houses in 1919 cost up to four times as much as those built in 1913, basic materials were difficult to obtain, and demand vastly exceeded supply.

By 1923, the policy had been rethought. This time, the Government felt, they had really done their homework, and they meant business. The first thing to do, they felt, was to set up an agreement with the unions to considerably increase the labour in the building trade. Prices were to be pegged at their existing levels, thereby avoiding Addison's greatest pitfall. A fixed subsidy of £75 per house for homes of a specified size to be built by private enterprise was made available. A grant for slum clearance schemes equivalent to one half of the loss incurred and a subsidy for building houses to let was to be given to local authorities. An increase in proposed rent subsidies from £6.0.0d. for twenty years to £29.0.0d. for forty years in theory doubled the value of the exchequer subsidy and would reduce the average rent from 15/- per week to 9/- per week.

This Act, called the "Chamberlain and Wheatley Act" compelled local

62

authorities to use all of the value of the Government and Municipal subsidy for the reduction of rents, until these reached in aggregate, a certain level, while leaving them free to adjust individual rents as they chose.

Family rent subsidies were worked out on an individual basis, by means of a "need" table brought out by the British Medical Association. One half of what was left after the amounts had been totalled and deducted from the income, was the amount considered available for rent. For example, a man, wife and four children aged 2, 6, 10 and 13 would need : Man and wife 19/-. Two children 10-13 years old 5/6 each = 11/-. Two children under 9 years old 4/- each = 8/-. Every person over 16 & working add 5/-. The total thus would be £2.3.0d.

On an income of £3.0.0d. per week, this left 17/-. One half of this, namely 8/6 was thus considered available for rent in this case. If the rental for a three bedroomed house was 13/2 per week, the subsidy would therefore be 4/8d.

The Government based these figures on the average wages for the period, which were £3.5.5d.-£3.15.0d. for skilled men and £2.10.0d.-£2.15.0d. for unskilled men. One drawback of this subsidy was that local authorities were sometimes loth to give a large subsidy, so men with large families were forced to live in houses that were less expensive to rent and therefore too small, leading to overcrowding.

On the whole, the Chamberlain and Wheatley Act worked well, giving, by 1927, employment to 200,000 men who otherwise would have remained unemployed.

By 1929, however, priorities had shifted. Not only was there a need for more housing, but slum clearance had to be accelerated . The advent of the "Greenwood Act" coined a new phrase—Improvement Areas. The terms stated simply that every individual removed under the Act meant a grant of £45 per annum to the local authority for forty years providing that for every five people removed, a three bedroomed house was built. Unfortunately, the Act did not specify that the house must be built for the same five people and that not all people in the improvement areas needed subsidies.

A circular was added to the Act pointing out the anomalies and including this statement : "It is the clear intention of Parliament that the benefits of the new grant shall not enure to persons for whom it is not intended."

The Hilton Young Act of 1931-1933, clarified the ideas of the Greenwood Act and reduced the interest rate on loans from 5% to 3½%. The Government were aiming to build a house able to be rented for 7/6 per week. The reduction of interest rate was to make it possible. "Slums will disappear by 1938" stated the Government firmly.

The 1933 Housing Act repealed all previous subsidies. A shift towards private ownership was encouraged. Building Societies were told to increase their mortgages to 90% of the value of the houses. Loans from banks, private investors and insurance companies were to be made easier.

People now had a choice; if they wished to own their own home, they would be able to find the means to do so; if they wished to rent, then local authorities would make houses available.

At last, housing was accepted as a national responsibility and a public service. No longer, it was hoped, would the working classes be forced to live in unsuitable, inferior accommodation. "Homes fit for Heroes" would soon be a reality at last.

Post War Housing

After the war, the Council decided to link Garden City and Galon Uchaf. Penybryn Estate was the result. This Estate is neither Garden Village type nor ribbon and as such is rather a negative place.

Haydn Terrace built below Garden City, was extended eastwards. The new houses were of metal and were supposed to be temporary. This estate still stands. Gellideg followed; I remember it seemed an enormous place when I was a child.

The largest estate in the area is, of course, the Gurnos Estate. It takes its name from the farm, over the land of which it sprawls. Said to be one of the largest housing estates in Europe, it is a town in its own right. It has its own shopping centre, health centre, public house, primary and secondary schools, and now the Prince Charles Hospital. Some of it, true, is badly planned, but even in these areas, there are many different styles. Contours of the land have been taken into account, the "groves" meander like tributaries of the main stream.

Houses are often set back from their neighbours, giving an interesting break up of surfaces. Where three storeys are used, an open staircase gives a welcome view of the sky, through the "block". The newer blocks of flats have plenty of green sward between them, showing that lessons had been learned after Dowlais flats had seen the light of day.

Heol Rhyd y Bedd means "the road to the grave" but the estate that bears this name is anything but a road to the end. This estate is very well designed, each "close" is separate, but an essential part of the whole. Colour is used to great effect and people seem to enjoy living there.

Private estates too, have blossomed. St. Mary's Close, Rectory Close and Lakeside Gardens include many styles and types of houses. They are colourful, happy places to be.

The estates get further away from the river. "Shirley Gardens" and "Castle Park Estate" are almost at the top of the mountain.

Town Planning began a long time ago. The Inaugural Dinner of the Town Planning Institute in this country took place in 1914. It has seen many changes[11].

Conclusion

1912 was an important year for Merthyr. Cyfarthfa Castle was converted into a Grammar School.

The Palace Cinema opened with a showing of "With Captain Scott

TINY HOUSE GEORGETOWN
(See Diane Green, Section 4)

STONE STAIRCASE AT GEORGETOWN
(See Diane Green, Section 4)

TRIANGLE, PENTREBACH
(See Diane Green, Section 4)

OUTSHOT DWELLING SWANSEA ROAD
(See Diane Green, Section 4)

OCCUPIED BACK TO BACK ABERDARE ROAD, MERTHYR
(See Diane Green, Section 4)

WEST GROVE MERTHYR
(See Diane Green, Section 4)

URBAN STREET, PENYDARREN
(See Diane Green, Section 4)

HIGH BRASAIL
(See Diane Green, Section 4)

ONE OF OLD FOURTEEN HOUSES IN GARDEN CITY
(See Diane Green, Section 4)

GARDEN CITY THIRD PHASE AROUND 1927
(See Diane Green, Section 4)

GALUN UCHAF
(See Diane Green, Section 4)

GURNOS ESTATE
(See Diane Green, Section 4)

CHARLOTTE STREET, OLD DOWLAIS
(See Diane Green, Section 4)

DOWLAIS FLATS
(See Diane Green, Section 4)

R.N. to the South Pole". He only went half way it seems for patrons had to return the following week to see the second half.

Merthyr's "Junior Member" Mr. James Keir Hardie caused a scene in the House when he asked Parliament a question on force feeding of suffragettes.

Dudley Stuart starred at the Theatre Royal as A. J. Raffles while at the Drill Hall you could watch "For the land we love or only a territorial"[12].

The King and Queen visited the town and toured Dowlais Works. Hy Brasail was built and the dream of Garden City began, the former would succeed, the latter doomed to failure. Further investigation has shown, that far from failing, Garden City was a turning point in the history of our town. With few exceptions, local building would never return to the miseries of overcrowding caused by strip or ribbon development.

Various groups tried to save the Triangle, built by industry, from industrial development. So much of old Merthyr has already been indiscriminately destroyed; streets torn down, communities displaced and Dowlais flats, like large barracks, rise from the ruins.

Many people stand and stare at Hy Brasail and well they might. An italian renaissance villa in a Welsh industrial valley town, it is like a pearl in a beautiful setting, located as it is in Vaynor. Few give Garden City a second glance. Despite trouble with modernisation problems, most residents do not wish to leave permanently. Here is a piece of history, a direct link with the International Garden City Movement. Here it was first realised in our town, that there was more to housing than a roof and four walls repeated as many times as possible in a given space. The ordinary working man too had a right to decent habitation. Housing was, is and should always be the creation of an environment, a place to live, a place to breathe, a place of which to be proud for rich and poor alike.

Acknowledgements

My grateful thanks to the following :

Mr. M. Harris and staff, Merthyr Public Library.

Mr. T. Witney and staff, Cyfarthfa Castle Museum.

Mr. & Mrs. W. Bowen of Hy Brasail.

Mr. I. Evans, Bragdy Cottage.

Mr. Mansel Richards.

Mr. K. Lloyd.

Mr. John Beynon, Tutor Librarian, Cardiff.

Mr. Frank Davies.

Mr. Arthur Davies.

The Residents of Garden City.

Research on Garden City was done on behalf of the Open University. Research into housing was done on behalf of the South Glam. Institute of Higher Education, Dept. of Art & Design, Howard Gardens, Cardiff. My thanks to Dr. Roy Crozier and staff for allowing me to print part of the results which formed the basis of my thesis.

References

1. The story of Merthyr Tydfil N.U.T. 1932 p. 50.
2. Verified by V. Harris, Merthyr Tydfil Historical Society. Sept. 77.
3. The Big Houses of Merthyr. M. S. Taylor. Merthyr Historian 1976.
4. Taff Street, Hovels or Houses. Thesis by K. Lloyd 1976 p. 28.
5. Garden Cities. Stephen Bayley. O.U. Press 1975 p. 4.
6. Edwardian Architecture and its Origins. Alistair Service 1975 p. 3.
7. Edwardian Architecture and its Origins. Alistair Service 1975 p. 3.
8. Garden City. Stephen Bayley O.U. Press 1975 p. 21.
9. Garden City. Thesis by D. Green 1975 p. 15.
10. Garden City. Thesis by D. Green 1975 p. 21.
11. The Evolution of British Town Planning. Gordon E. Cherry 1974.
12. Merthyr Express, various copies 1912.

5. JOSEPH GROSS

WATERSUPPLY AND SEWERAGE IN MERTHYR TYDFIL
1850-1974

(Illustrations 43 to 45 & 47)

Introduction

Few towns have better natural facilities for an ample supply of pure water and an adequate drainage of effluents than Merthyr Tydfil. The foothills of the Brecon Beacons, situated in easily reached proximity to the town, with their heavy rainfall and deep valleys, provide excellent facilities for the storage reservoirs required. The surface of the ground below Merthyr and its geological structure offer great scope for a proper drainage of the town. Yet in 1844, when the population had grown to 37,000 from a few hundred within a century, the sanitary conditions of the town were appalling. There was a complete absence of a supply of pure water, no system of sewers existed and the inhabitants lived in overcrowded houses in narrow streets and alleyways in which filth and excreta accumulated. These miserable living conditions led to frequent outbreaks of infectious diseases, which caused an appallingly high rate of deaths, particularly among young children.

Merthyr's poor health record was by no means unique among the rapidly expanding centres of population of the country during this phase of the industrial revolution. Slowly the public conscience was awakened, due mainly to the efforts of Edwin Chadwick, the great sanitary reformer. The Health of Towns Commission was set up and held a series of enquiries in the principal towns of England and Wales between 1843 and 1845. Sir Henry De la Beche conducted an enquiry in Merthyr in 1844 and found the conditions mentioned above. The reports of the various Commissioners led to the passing by Parliament of the famous Public Health Act of 1848.

The act set up a General Board of Health and provided for the establishment of Local Boards of Health in localities where no public health authorities existed. The introduction of such local boards depended on local demand and support, except in places with an exceptionally high mortality. The local boards were to be set up after a public enquiry, held by an inspector of the General Board of Health who had to ascertain the conditions of sanitation, water supply and related matters in the locality.

The passing of the act created great interest throughout the country. In Merthyr, T. J. Dyke, a well known medical practitioner, gave two public lectures concerned with the health of the town and the new act. As a result of these lectures a public meeting was held, at which it was decided to petition the General Board with the request to apply the act to Merthyr Tydfil. In consequence of this petition, a public enquiry took place in May 1849 and was conducted by T. W. Rammell.

Rammell's famous report shows that conditions in Merthyr had not improved since Sir Henry De la Beche conducted his enquiry five years earlier. Rammell's report describes the degrading circumstances in which so many inhabitants of our town lived. With regard to drainage and cleansing, he has this to say : "Although Merthyr has long been reported to be in an unsatisfactory condition as regards drainage, cleansing and water supply, I was certainly not prepared for so bad a case as my own senses and the testimony of numberless witnesses proved to be actually existing here. Merthyr having sprung up rapidly from a village to a town, without any precautions being taken for the removal of the increased masses of filth necessarily produced by an increased population, nor even for the escape of surface water . . . . ." "A rural spot of considerable beauty has been transformed into a crowded and filthy manufacturing town, with an amount of mortality higher than any other commercial or manufacturing town in the kingdom."

With regard to the want of privy accommodation he writes : "Badly formed as the streets, lanes and courts of Merthyr are in the first instance, ill tended and utterly neglected afterwards, their filthy and unwholesome condition is still further aggravated by the necessary consequence of an almost total absence of privy accommodation which prevails throughout the town . . . The majority of the inhabitants are making use of chamber utensils which they empty into the streets before the doors, sometimes into the river . . ."

As to the supply of water, the report has this to say : "The crowning evil under which the inhabitants of Merthyr Tydfil labour, as regards their social and sanitary conditions, is the utter want of provision for the supply of water; indeed not only are there no arrangements made in aid of the ordinary opportunities presented by nature for the procuring of this important article, but the demands made upon the natural supplies for the use of the iron works are so extensive and the waste by soiling that which runs off so considerable, that the poorer classes are put to great labour and loss of time in collecting very scanty quantities for domestic purposes."

He goes on to say that the inhabitants had to rely for their water-supply on private wells or a few natural springs. In a dry summer as few as three springs would be available and people had to wait their turn for six, eight and even ten hours. Eighty or even a hundred people could be seen waiting in this manner.

The lack of water supply and sanitation led to disease and premature death. The health statistics tell their melancholy story; they are based on a report by the first temporary Officer of Health, appointed for six months only in 1853, Dr. Kay. The average number of deaths in 1853 was 30.2 per 1,000 of the population (in 1971 it was 13.8 per 1,000). Of 1,000 children born in 1853, 199 died under one year of age (in 1971 the number was 17). The average age at death of the people of Merthyr in 1852 was $17\frac{1}{2}$ years (in 1976 it was 71 years). (The figures in brackets are based on information kindly supplied by the Mid Glamorgan Area Health Authority.)

Merthyr's Watersupply 1850-1865

As a result of Rammell's report, the Merthyr Board of Health was established in 1850, with Sir J. J. Guest as its first chairman. In September 1851 it was proposed to form a Joint Stock Company for the supply of water and by November applications for shares to the value of £20,000 were received, mainly from the ironmasters. However the Local Board of Health did not agree to the watercharges proposed by the promoters of the Water Company. As a result the promoters decided not to proceed with the Water Bill, which in the meantime had been submitted to Parliament. The Bill was taken over by the Local Board of Health. The Merthyr Water Works Act was passed in June 1852. It contained important clauses for the protection of the proprietors of the Cyfarthfa and Plymouth Works and of the Glamorganshire Canal Company. These clauses provided that in case the proprietors mentioned should raise objections to the plans of the waterworks, an umpire was to be appointed by the Board of Trade to decide upon them. Mr. Lynde was appointed as consulting engineer and drew up plans in August 1852. In July of the following year the ironmasters concerned and the Canal Company gave notice of objections. Mr. Brunel, the famous engineer, was appointed Umpire and made his award in 1854. On examining the plans attached to the award it was found that by "a most egregious oversight on the part of the engineer who had the fixing of the position of the reservoir, the site marked on the plan was about 200 ft. lower in the valley than it should have been". This would have meant that the reservoir would have been able to contain only nine million gallons of water instead of twenty million, and there would have been an additional cost of about £4,000.

Mr. Lynde had to prepare new plans which required an estimated expenditure of £75,000. Thus in May 1855 the local Board of Health decided to raise a loan for £80,000, but efforts to obtain it failed. By now the citizens of Merthyr began to complain about the long delay to obtain water and several letters were addressed to the General Board of Health in London with the request for intervention. However the General Board had no powers to compel the Local Board to take action.

In April 1856 Mr. Hill informed the Local Board that he had seen Mr. Hawkesley, an engineer who was well known for several large schemes of watersupply which he had designed in different parts of the country. Mr. Hawkesley had informed Mr. Hill that he Mr. Hawkesley could design a scheme that would cost considerably less than Mr. Lynde's. No action however was taken by the Board for another year.

The turning point came with the election of G. T. Clark as a member of the Local Board of Health in April 1857. Mr. Clark had worked as an engineer on the Great Western Railway under I. K. Brunel. He later became an Inspector of the General Board of Health and conducted several local enquiries under the 1848 Health Act. He was thus fully conversant with the details of this Act and the current techniques of watersupply and drainage. In 1854, as one of the trustees under the will of Sir John J. Guest, he took over the direction of the Dowlais Iron Company and greatly improved and expanded the works in the years to come. It was largely due to his drive and guidance that the Merthyr Board of Health first obtained an excellent supply of water and later constructed a comprehensive scheme of drainage.

Soon after Mr. Clark's election to the Board, a special meeting was called to put him in possession of the whole of the facts connected with the question of watersupply. At this meeting it was decided to ask Mr. Hawkesley to comment on two schemes for the waterworks then before the Board, or to report on any other, if a better scheme represented itself to him.

Mr. Hawkesley attended a board meeting in May 1857. He stated that he wished to take the water directly from the river rather than construct a large reservoir, as in his opinion and experience leaks often occurred in such reservoirs. As to the question of compensation to be given to the riparian owners for their loss of water caused by the new works, he preferred that compensation to be in money rather than in water, as this would be cheaper in the end.

At a meeting held in July it became clear that Mr. Crawshay would only agree to a scheme under the following conditions : That the riparian owners should be compensated for their loss of water in the form of water supplied, not in money. That the water supplied should be of the same quantity as the water abstracted. That the compensation water should be given from a reservoir, which was to be placed in the Taf Fechan valley, if the water was to be taken from that stream. The report of this meeting in the Merthyr Telegraph (4.7.1857) then states : "Mr. Clark at length succeeded in carrying his point that a letter be written to Mr. Hawkesley to prepare a scheme having regard to the limitations fixed by Mr. Crawshay."

Mr. Hawkesley submitted his proposals in October, 1857. This scheme, which was eventually carried out, provided for a storage reservoir to be built at Dolygaer with a capacity of 32,000,000 cubic feet; a pipe line from the reservoir and the Callan brook via the vicinity of Vaynor Church and a line nearly parallel to the tramroad alongside the Goitre pond, terminating in Penybryn in Penydarren. He proposed a pipe of 13 or 14 inch diameter. Filterbeds were to be constructed at Penybryn and a reservoir to store about one million gallons of water. From Penybryn a principal main would be taken for the supply of Penydarren and Merthyr proper. The supply of Dowlais would be effected by a small steam engine, which he proposed to erect near the filterbeds. This engine would elevate the required water to a covered tank holding 200,000 gallons to be placed near the top of Dowlais. He estimated the cost to be £45,000.

The Board accepted Mr. Hawkesley's scheme and proceeded to discuss the way in which it should be implemented. One alternative was to carry it out as a public works by the Board of Health. The other alternative was to form a private company. The chairman, Mr. Clark, said it was for the town at a Vestry Meeting to decide which way it should be. It was decided to advertise both schemes in the newspapers. The two advertisements appeared on 14.11.1857. Both stated the details of the proposed water works in the terms suggested by Mr. Hawkesley, but one called for subscriptions in a proposed private company, the other stated that the work would be undertaken by the Merthyr Board of Health. It was also stated that a Water Works Bill would be introduced in the next session of Parliament.

A Vestry Meeting held on 28.11.1857 voted in favour of a private company. Mr. Clark subscribed shares of £4,000, smaller subscribers called for another £4,000. Applications for the remaining shares of £36,000 were slow coming in and at a further Vestry Meeting of 5.12.1857 it was decided to abandon the plan for a private company and the scheme was carried out by the Merthyr Board of Health.

The new bill for the construction of the Merthyr Tydfil Waterworks was promoted in January 1858. The Crawshays insisted on the insertion of a clause which prevented the supply of water for the use of motive power and machinery. This had the effect of depriving the Board of a substantial source of income.

The Act was passed in May 1858. Mr. Hawkesley was appointed Consulting Engineer. The necessary land was acquired by June 1859. From then on the pipelaying and construction of the Penybryn filterbeds proceeded smoothly. The first water taken from the Callan brook and filtered at Penybryn reached Merthyr by the end of the year 1860. Twelve standpipes were erected in different parts of the town. The first water was served in the Board room on 19.1.1861. The Merthyr Telegraph describes the scene at the standpipes, when happy crowds of women clustered round them, filling all sorts of containers and cooking utensils and chattering till the early hours of the morning. The laying of the pipes and the construction of the filterbeds at Penybryn had taken 18 months, no mean engineering feat at that time, when all work had to be carried out by navvies, without modern mechanical aids.

One important result of an ample supply of water was the improvement it made possible in the fighting of fires. The fire service in those days and right up to the war 1939/45 was the responsibility of the Merthyr Police Force. Yet as late as 1859 they were without any equipment and had to borrow ladders and buckets at the scene of fires from inhabitants in the vicinity. Only in that year did the Merthyr Board of Health decide to provide two dozen leather buckets and ladders. In May 1861 hoses and jets were issued and the superintendent of police soon afterwards could report that they were used successfully.

The connection of the houses to the watermains proceeded quickly and by the end of 1862 5,000 houses had running water installed and the standpipes were withdrawn.

The construction of the reservoir however was delayed. The official opening took place on 6.10.1862 when the members of the Board of Health, after a lavish breakfast provided by Mr. Clark in Dowlais House, boarded a special train of the newly completed Brecon and Merthyr Railway and proceeded to Dolygaer. Mrs. Clark formally opened the reservoir by turning a valve. The reservoir however was not completed until February 1863 and from then on the watersupply of the town was derived from the head of the storage reservoir. Troedyrhiw was supplied in March 1863, Abercanaid in July 1864.

In June 1863 Mr. Clark brought up the question of the clause in the Water Works Act of 1858 which prevented the Board from supplying water for the use of machinery. Mr. Clark stated that he had obtained Counsel's opinion to the effect, that the clause had no legal validity. The motion was put to supply Dowlais works with water for use by machinery and carried by a narrow majority.

A year later the riparian owners, the Crawshays, Hill and the Canal Company, counter-attacked, when they obtained an injunction against the Board of Health and the Trustees of the Dowlais works, preventing them from supplying water for the use of machinery. Two months later the riparian owners offered to withdraw their objection if their supply of water was increased. Eventually a majority of the Board of Health agreed to an increase which Mr. Clark felt to be excessive and he resigned from the Board of Health.

In the election of 1865 he was re-elected a member of the Board and at the first Board meeting following the election he was again chosen as chairman with cheers and acclamation. In his speech accepting the chairmanship he referred to the great question of drainage on which they were of one opinion and that they were looking forward with hope to the completion of such a scheme. It is to the question of drainage that we must now turn.

Merthyr Sewerage 1850-1900

We have seen that Rammell's report of 1849 stated that Merthyr Tydfil was almost entirely destitute of drainage. Only two short sewers were referred to in this report, one in Victoria Street and one in George Town. A plan for a proposed system of tubular sewers for a part of Caedraw was attached to the report but was never carried out. Mr. Benest, surveyor to the Merthyr Board prepared a comprehensive scheme in August 1852, at an estimated cost of £33,000, but this too remained on paper. In 1853 the Workhouse was connected to the sewer in Victoria Street and in 1854 a drain was constructed in China at a cost of £51. In October 1853 we hear of four public privies at Ynysgau, possibly the first public lavatories. In 1855/56 a sewer was constructed from Plymouth Street to the Star Inn and thence to the lower part of High Street and Court Street.

Nothing further had been done by July 1863, when the Merthyr Telegraph published a leading article pleading earnestly with the Board of Health to supply the town with drainage, as the new water supply added to the nuisance of the open sewers in the streets. At last in September 1864 Mr. Harpur the Surveyor of the Board submitted a report for a comprehensive scheme of sewerage works to cover Merthyr, Dowlais, Abercanaid, Pentrebach and Troedyrhiw. He proposed to deliver the sewage to a point below Troedyrhiw, where it could either be applied to agricultural purposes or deodorized and passed into the

UPPER AND LOWER NEUADD RESERVOIRS
(See Joseph Gross, Section 5)

PONTSTICILL RESERVOIR
Valve Tower, Footbridge and Overflow Bellmouth   (See Joseph Gross, Section 5)

UPPER NEUADD RESERVOIR AND BRECON BEACONS
(See Joseph Gross, Section 5)

GARTH FILTER BEDS – Inlet Valve
(See Joseph Gross, Section 5)

river. The cost of the scheme he estimated at £27,000. It was decided to have 500 copies of the report printed. The plans for the sewerage works were forwarded to the Home Office and loan sanction for £27,000 was granted in April 1865. As a further safeguard it was also decided to ask Mr. William Lee, a well known expert in the field of sewerage, to examine Mr. Harpur's scheme and report on it. Mr. Lee eventually fully approved of the scheme.

We now come to the important meeting of July 1865. Mr. Harpur, the surveyor, submitted his detailed specifications for the drainage. These were approved. The Board had now to deal with the important question of the final disposal of the sewage. Should it be turned into the river Taff (at a point below Troedyrhiw as suggested by the surveyor), possibly after a process of so called deodorization, or should it be treated by applying it to a plot of land, a treatment which would require large additional expense. Several members expressed fear that legal action would be taken against them if they were to turn the sewage into the river, thus polluting it. Such actions had been taken in several places against Boards of Health. Mr. Clark however felt that there was no point in raising objections. There would be time enough to consider them if they were raised by other parties. The people were dying for want of sewerage. Imperious necessity behind them ought to compel the Board to carry out at once, and without delay, a scheme for getting rid of the sewage (Hear, hear and cheers). If the worst came to the worst, and there was an injunction to stop them, they must take the consequences. He for one was disposed to run any risk rather than go on as at present (hear, hear). The motion to advertise for tenders was agreed to.

I have described the scene at this dramatic Board meeting in some detail as it showed the force of character of Mr. Clark and his capacity to carry the Board with him in taking this calculated risk. An injunction for pollution was in fact, as we shall see, issued against the Board three years later when the sewage was eventually discharged into the river. The Board became involved in litigation and had to introduce a costly scheme of sewage disposal. The additional expense required was partly met from a sum of £10,000 which had previously been allotted to the erection of a new town hall. This town hall was not built until some thirty years later.

The first hole for the sewerage works was cut in November 1865. The sewer mouth then was situated at the southern boundary of the Taff Railway station. The sewage was treated with a sulphate of iron solution. By 1867 thirty-four miles of sewer had been constructed. The main sewer was completed in September 1868 comprising fifty-five miles. Two months earlier the sewage was temporarily turned into the river Taff below Troedyrhiw and soon afterwards the Nixon Coal Company of Merthyr Vale issued an injunction against the Board of Health because of the pollution of the river. This injunction prevented any further connection of house drains with the sewer. In 1869 the surveyor prepared a comprehensive scheme for the disposal of the sewage by irrigation of

73

farmland, and after a local enquiry by a Government Inspector a Provisional Order was obtained to purchase 90 acres of land in Troedyrhiw (1870). In the meantime the Court of Chancery suggested that some means should be adopted for straining the sewage and the surveyor therefore constructed two elongated straining tanks under the Parish Road in Troedyrhiw (early in 1869).

By November 1870 Lord Justice James placed Merthyr under the professional care of Mr. Bailey Denton, who recommended the adoption of Dr. Frankland's Intermittent Downward Filtration System of treatment of sewage. This method was based on research experiments only and Merthyr provided the first occasion to carry it out on a working scale. About 20 acres of the land situated in Troedyrhiw were divided into four plots of five acres each. They were provided with pipes placed six feet below ground. The sewage was directed to each plot for a period of six hours, then switched to the next plot and so on. It was left for 18 hours on the first plot so that it could filter through trenches to the pipes below and eventually left the plots as clear water. The plots were planted with vegetables and grass and gave high yields of excellent produce.

Once the sewage farm was completed, the injunction was lifted in 1872, and the remaining houses of Merthyr and Dowlais could be connected to the main sewers. Thus almost all properties were so connected by 1875. Another fifty acres of land adjoining the twenty acres mentioned above, used for filtration, were used for surface irrigation. These too were planted with crops with excellent results. The treatment of the sewage was completely successful. No offensive smells were given off and the water emerging from the filter and irrigation beds was pure and could be drank without ill effects by people and animals.

In 1878 an agreement was made between the Merthyr and Aberdare Local Boards of Health whereby the sewage of the Aberdare district was taken over and disposed of on the farm lands acquired by the Merthyr Board in Abercynon shortly before. The control of both sewage farms at Troedyrhiw and at Abercynon was placed under the control of a Joint Management Committee which consisted of seven members, of whom four were appointed by Merthyr and three by Aberdare. This Joint Farms Management Committee operated until 1972. The sewage farm at Abercynon consisted of 300 acres of land, of which 225 acres were under sewage treatment in 1908. The land was used mostly for grazing purposes and hay crops.

An interesting feature of Merthyr's sewage system are the ventilating shafts. These were erected at points where sewer gases accumulated, particularly at the highest point of each main sewer. In 1882 a number of four inch iron ventilating pipes were erected and in 1884 three thirty feet high brick stacks were erected in Dowlais. Of these one survives in Charlotte Street. By 1894 waterclosets were installed at 9,000 of about 12,000 houses in the area.

The Waterworks 1865-1974

Some years after the Pentwyn Reservoir, also called Dolygaer Lake had been completed it was discovered that a serious leakage occurred owing to the fact that the embankment had been constructed over a great geological fault crossing the valley. A limestone strata is embedded there in the Old Red Sandstone and the water seeps through it to an unknown depth. Repairs had to be undertaken from time to time in later years to try and stop the leakage.

In consequence of the expansion of the district and especially the deep coal sinkings in the southern portion, it was deemed advisable to construct an additional storage reservoir. The Lower Neuadd reservoir was completed in 1884. It is situated at a height of 1,412 ft. An independent 12 inch main was constructed taking the water to newly constructed filterbeds and service reservoir at Garth, Pant. From there Dowlais and Pant could now be supplied by gravitation and the steam driven pumps at Penybryn became superfluous. The capacity of the new reservoir was 75 million gallons. Further mains were constructed from the Garth reservoir to Treharris and Quakers Yard, the rapidly developing new mining villages.

In 1901 land was obtained for the Pengarnddu reservoir, which was constructed soon afterwards. The watersupply that year reached Bedlinog and Abercynon.

A further storage reservoir was built half a mile to the north of the Lower Neuadd reservoir. This was the Upper Neuadd reservoir, completed in 1902. It was built by the Merthyr Tydfil Urban District Council, the successor of the Merthyr Board of Health. The reservoir has a splendid masonry dam 75 feet high. It lies 1,500 feet above sea level and holds 340 million gallons. A temporary railway was built from Torpantau station of the Brecon and Merthyr railway to transport stone and other materials for the dam.

By 1910 demand for water increased still further. Other authorities wanted to be supplied from the Merthyr waterworks, Barry, the Rhymney Valley, Pontypridd among them. It was decided to build a reservoir at Pontsticill to be connected with the Dolygaer Lake. The Merthyr Tydfil Corporation Water Act was passed in 1911. The cost was then estimated at £400,000. However the war 1914/18 interrupted the work. After the war it was decided to form a joint water board with the other interested authorities. Thus the Taf Fechan Water Supply Board was formed in 1921, which took over the waterworks of the Merthyr Tydfil Corporation. This board was established by an Act of Parliament for the purpose of supplying water in bulk to the five constituent authorities, namely Merthyr Tydfil Corporation, the Rhymney Valley Waterboard, the Pontypridd and Rhondda Joint Waterboard, Llantrissant and Llantwit Fadre Rural District Council and Aberdare Urban District Council. The new reservoir is joined to the old Pentwyn Reservoir. The combined reservoir, situated at 1,082 feet above sea level, has a storage capacity of 3,400,000,000 gallons.

The dam is of earth, with a concrete tongue some 86 feet deep, resting on the Old Red Sandstone strata. Above this tongue a puddle clay wall some 100 feet high is flanked by an earthen embankment on either side and carries a macadamized road on its top. An interesting feature of the reservoir is that there is no spillway at the dam itself. The whole of the overflow is led away down a vertical overflow shaft inside the dam which leads to a horizontal outlet tunnel below the embankment. The overflow shaft terminates at its top in a bell mouth, faced with "Shap" granite slabs around the top edge. The valve tower, which adds a characteristic feature to the reservoir, is situated within the reservoir. It is octagonal in shape, built of dressed stone externally. Its upper part is machicolated and surmounted by a spire sheathed in copper. It is reached by a steel foot bridge.

New filterbeds were built below the dam. A new trunk pipe, the Low Level Trunk Main, conveys the water from the outlet of the reservoir to Merthyr Tydfil, Troedyrhiw, Treharris, Pontypridd and as far as Barry. This main consists of 37″ pipes, narrowing to 31″ near Pontsarn.

In 1955 the filtration plant in Pontsticill was extended and a pumping station installed, which can pump water from the Taf Fechan reservoir into the High Level trunk main from the Upper Neuadd reservoir. The use of the filterbeds at Garth had ceased some time before the war 1939/45.

In 1965 the Taf Fechan Water Supply Board was reconstituted as the Taf Fechan Water Board. The new board took over the distribution as well as the supply of water from 1.4.1966. Three local authorities in addition to those represented on the previous board joined the new one, Mountain Ash Urban District Council, Cardiff Rural District Council and Vaynor and Penderyn Rural District Council.

Sewerage 1900-1974

The original sewer between Troedyrhiw and Abercynon, laid down in 1880, was a simple brick barrelled sewer of 2 ft. diameter with wrought iron tubes. In the years following its construction it suffered severely from subsidence due to coalmining carried on in the area. It was replaced in the early 1920's by a concrete pipe 30 inches in diameter. Fifty unemployed persons worked on its construction. It was opened in 1924.

A new sewage disposal scheme was under consideration since 1935 but nothing was done when the war 1939/45 broke out. Similarly a new system of sewers for Merthyr was under consideration in 1939, when the District Commissioner for the Special Areas authorized expenditure for trial holes in the main thoroughfares. A major scheme of reconstruction was started in 1947 and the main sewers from the sewage farm at Troedyrhiw to Merthyr Tydfil and Dowlais were completed in 1952/53. The cost of £370,000 was mostly met from government grants. The main sewers were chiefly constructed of concrete pipes varying in size from 69 inches to 12 inches internal diameter. The drainage adopted, as the previous one, was of the "combined" system, where both sewage and surface water were carried in one pipe. Several storm overflow weirs were provided at points near the rivers, so that sewers could be relieved of excessive quantities of storm water. Thus the grosser impurities in the

76

sewers were retained at the weirs and the rest of the storm water discharged into the river consisted mainly of rain water.

By 1957 the problem of sewage treatment was again discussed by the Merthyr Tydfil Borough Council. By 1964 two possible schemes were under consideration, namely a separate scheme each for the Taf and Cynon Valley Authorities, or a joined scheme. Eventually it was decided to build two separate schemes. Merthyr's new treatment plant was to be built at Cilfynydd.

At this time too it was decided to reconstruct the trunk sewer from Troedyrhiw to Abercynon. An important point which came up for consideration was the problem of industrial waste. Many poisonous and otherwise harmful materials are produced by the diverse industrial firms now established in Merthyr. The disposal of these wastes could put a special burden on the sewage works, if they were channelled into the sewers untreated. It was eventually decided that the industrial firms would have to instal certain treatment plants at their own expense, but that no extra charge would be made for the rest of the effluvia running into the sewers.

The new trunk sewer from Troedyrhiw, now routed to the site of the new proposed treatment plant in Cilfynydd, was constructed between 1971 and 1975. It cost approximately £4.5 millions and consists of concrete pipes varying between 1,200 and 1,950 mm. All pipes are flexibly jointed to prevent damage by mining subsidence. Tunnelling of some $1\frac{1}{2}$ km. in length had to be constructed. One particularly difficult tunnel section was at Aberfan, where old mine workings and very mixed geological strata caused special problems. Four sewer pipe bridges were constructed over the River Taff.

A special problem was encountered in constructing a syphon under the River Taff as part of the Quakers Yard Branch Sewer. The bridge foundation of the old reinforced concrete viaduct carrying the main A470 trunk road from Cardiff to Merthyr Tydfil had to be specially underpinned, so that the syphon could be constructed 3 m. below it. The construction works caused dislocation of traffic and blocked roads and blasting in the vicinity of the houses caused the inhabitants much anxiety. The Council Minutes record several site meetings of the inhabitants, councillors and representatives of the contractors to iron out the difficulties and complaints.

The Consulting Engineers were Sir Herbert Humphries and McDonald of Birmingham, the main contractors Norwest Civil Engineering Ltd. of Bootle, Lancashire.

Reorganization 1974

In 1974 an Act for the Reorganization of Water Resources in England and Wales (The Water Act 1973) came into force. It created ten regional authorities which took over all water and sewerage services. The new authorities replaced the 29 river authorities, 160 water undertakings and 1,300 sewerage authorities which carried out these services at that time.

The whole of Wales came under the authority of the Welsh National

Water Development Authority, directly responsible to the Secretary of State for Wales. This authority thus took over the Taf Fechan reservoirs, filter beds and storage reservoirs, water pipe lines and all sewers and sewage treatment plants. They now became responsible for the scheme for a new sewage treatment plant at Cilfynnyd, originally commissioned by the Merthyr Tydfil Corporation. Work started in 1976 and is scheduled to be completed in 1978, at an estimated cost of £7,000,000.

References
1. Report on the Sanatary Conditions of Merthyr Tydfil by Sir H. T. De la Beche 1845 (Second Report of the Health of Towns Commission).
2. Report on the Sewerage, Drainage and Supply of Water and the Sanitary Conditions of the inhabitants of the town of Merthyr Tydfil by T. W. Rammell.
3. Merthyr Tydfil Board of Health Minutes 1850-1894 (incomplete).
4. Merthyr Tydfil Urban District Council Minutes 1895-1905.
5. Merthyr Tydfil Municipal Borough Council Minutes 1905-1908.
6. Merthyr Tydfil County Borough Minutes 1908-1974.
7. Reports of the Medical Officers of Health of Merthyr Tydfil 1854, 1865-1897, 1901-1970.
8. Public Records Office Box MH 13/125, 1847-1870.
   Extracts kindly supplied by Mr. Huw Williams.
9. Report to the Merthyr Tydfil Local Board of Health on the sewerage of the District and the disposal of the sewage by Samuel Harpur 1864.
10. The Sanitary History of Merthyr Tydfil by T. J. Dyke.
    British Medical Journal 1885 p. 192 ff.
11. The Merthyr Waterworks by T. F. Harvey. Proceedings of the Incorporated Association of Municipal and County Engineers 1899/100 pp. 45-69.
12. The Merthyr Sewage Farms by T. F. Harvey. Proceedings of the Royal Sanitary Institute 1908. pp. 648-655.
13. The Taf Fechan Water Supply Board by A. C. Quininborough, 1962.
14. Notes on Sewerage and Sewage Disposal of Merthyr Tydfil. R. G. D. Defriez, C Eng, MICE, The Consulting Engineer July 1950.
15. Trunk Sewer Troedyrhiw to Cilfynydd. Notes for the visit of the South Wales Association of the Inst. of Civil Engineers 5.6.1974 supplied by Sir Herbert Humphries & McDonald.
16. Area Health Profile published by the Mid Glamorgan Area Health Authority.
17. Merthyr Telegraph 1855-1881.
18. Edwin Chadwick and the Public Health Movement 1832-1854 by R. A. Lewis 1952.

6. JOSEPH GROSS

HOSPITALS IN MERTHYR TYDFIL 1850-1974

(*Illustrations 48 to 53*)

Introduction

Today, with our comprehensive health service, we tend to take our hospital facilities for granted. Intricate operations are performed daily, babies safely delivered, accidents treated quickly and efficiently. The skills of many specialists are available, trained nurses look after the patients, high standards of hygiene are achieved. It is difficult to realize, that in 1850 there was no hospital in Merthyr, although its population had grown to 46,000. Frequent accidents occurred in the ironworks, in the iron and coal mines, on the railway, the tramroads and on the canal. Epidemics such as scarlet fever, smallpox, typhoid and the dreaded cholera raged with fatal regularity. Tuberculosis was widespread. Yet treatment available for any of these could only be administered in the patient's home. We read about operations and amputations carried out on kitchen tables, of doctors' visits to bedrooms shared by six or seven people. Once a contagious disease appeared in one of the overcrowded houses, there was no means of isolating the patient and to prevent the illness from spreading (except the Houses of Refuge in the time of cholera).

Sir John Guest subscribed to the Infirmary in Swansea and could sponsor patients there. The Board of Guardians sent mentally ill, blind and dumb and deaf paupers to establishments catering for the so afflicted. These institutions were often run by private persons and were situated in different parts of the country, Devizes, Bath, Briton Ferry. These were also available for those who could pay for their services, but for the majority of the people no hospitals were provided.

Houses of Refuge

In 1849 occurred the second cholera epidemic. The Board of Guardians requested help from the General Board of Health. They sent Dr. Sutherland, the Medical Superintending Inspector, to Merthyr in June of that year. Dr. Sutherland recommended the erection of a temporary shed "for the purpose of a refuge for the healthy who shall be removed by the medical officer from such houses as are infected and overcrowded". The refuge was to be large enough to house 100 inmates. This was done and a wooden shed erected by Evan Rees, a carpenter. It was situated on ground "adjoining the new Burial Ground". Dr. Sutherland also recommended that the different ironworks be asked to provide Houses of Refuge for their workers.

The third cholera epidemic occurred in 1854. The Board of Guardians resolved on 23.9.1854 "that a House of Refuge be immediately erected in the Parish of Ffynnon Tydfil and that the same be immediately walled in". It was again to hold a hundred people. Two days later it was "ordered that the building be erected of brick, 48 ft. 4in. x 31 ft., with a kitchen 16 ft. x 12 ft. and that Mr. Evan Rees proceed at once with the work." This building, situated near the present Tydfil's Well Post Office in Brecon Road, survived until a few years ago.

The term House of Refuge appears for a third time during the fourth cholera epidemic in September 1866, when it was decided that the Workhouse be a Place of Refuge for the healthy of families attacked by cholera.

The Infirmary 1853-1929

The first hospital built in Merthyr was the Infirmary erected in 1853 as part of the Workhouse. This belonged to the Board of Guardians of the Merthyr Union, which comprised an area including the parishes of Merthyr, Aberdare and several others. The Infirmary provided hospital facilities for the destitute poor of the Union. It consisted of four men's rooms, four women's rooms, one fever ward, one lying-in (maternity) ward and two recovery rooms. There was accommodation for 65 patients. A House Surgeon was appointed in October 1853 with a salary of £25, the Guardians finding the drugs. A nurse and porter, man and wife, were also appointed. An assistant nurse was appointed in 1865. By 1863 two nurseries and an idiot ward were available. If infectious diseases broke out among the children, the only place to which they could be moved were the attics on the top of the workhouse. The bulk of the nursing was carried out by female inmates of the workhouse. Standards of nursing, in common with the rest of the country, were probably poor and only improved after the influence of Florence Nightingale made itself felt in the late 1860's.

One of the important aspects of the Infirmary was that no type of illness could be refused. Similarly the number of beds were not fixed and admission was not refused because there were no beds available. The procedure for admission however was clearly stipulated. A medical officer had to inform a Relieving Officer of any case to be removed to the Infirmary, who then accompanied the patient there. The numbers involved were large. In one year, 1863/64 the House Surgeon treated 557 patients, exclusive of those suffering from a slight illness. A dispensary was provided at the Infirmary in 1863. Water was supplied in 1861 and gas in 1865. The Workhouse had its own drainage connected to a public sewer in Victoria Street.

A new Infirmary building was erected in 1867. Ample accommodation was now available for the sick, with special fever wards. These consisted of two large and two small rooms. Two paid nurses were employed. A syphylitic ward was provided in 1882. A further new building was provided in 1897. It was designed in yellow facing bricks by E. A. Johnson of Abergavenny, at a cost of £10,000. In 1906 a new children's block was built, and additional wards erected in 1910. This was called "A" block and known as St. Paul's Ward. It originally housed male geriatric bedridden cases and also a small number of male patients certified for detention under the Mental Deficiency Acts. As vacancies arose, these latter cases were transferred to mental hospitals and "A" block became an entirely Male Geriatric Ward. A Maternity Ward was erected in 1911, at a cost of £3,014. A Lock Ward to house venereal diseases was also built at that time.

In 1920 a Ministry of Health Inspector visited the Infirmary. He recommended the appointment of a resident Assistant Medical Officer, the engagement of more and better trained nurses, and shorter hours of work for nurses. There should be a separate nursery for children under one year of age. In consequence of this visit, Dr. C. M. Probert was appointed Resident Assistant Medical Officer; two more sisters were appointed; evening meals were provided at 7.30 and tea at 4.30 p.m. replacing the last meal of the day served at 5.30 p.m. until then.

By this time the Infirmary held the largest number of beds among the hospitals in Merthyr. Conditions had vastly improved, so that private patients now sought admission in maternity cases and were admitted since 1922. It was not until 1924 that the authorization for admission by a Relieving Officer was replaced by a recommendation by medical officers of the Board of Guardians.

The Fever Hospitals 1866-1930

The Sanitary Act of 1866 authorized local authorities to provide hospitals for the sick. The only hospitals provided in Merthyr by the Local Board of Health were fever hospitals.

During the fourth cholera epidemic in 1866, the House of Refuge in Tydfil's Well was furnished as a Temporary Cholera Hospital. It seems that this was done by the Local Board of Health, as T. J. Dyke stated this in his report for 1866 to that Board. As we have seen, the building was originally erected by the Board of Guardians.

In 1869 a severe typhus epidemic occurred. Three measures were taken by the Local Board of Health :

1. They obtained the use of ten beds in the fever ward which had come into use in the new extension to the Infirmary built in 1867.
2. They fitted the House of Refuge in Tydfil's Well (used as a temporary Cholera Hospital in 1866) as a Fever Hospital for sixteen patients, with a sister in charge.
3. They built a new Fever Hospital in Queens Street, Pant. It was designed by the Surveyor of the Local Board of Health. A wooden structure, it had 32 beds and cost £1,000. The design of the hospital found the approval of the Medical Officer of the Privy Council, who reproduced the plans in his report for 1870 and recommended its principles of construction for general adoption.

The fever hospitals were only used intermittently, as outbreaks of infectious diseases occurred. In 1877 the Local Board of Health entered into an agreement with the Merthyr Board of Guardians to receive pauper patients in the infectious diseases hospitals for an annual sum of £225 and 1/4d. per day for each person accommodated.

The two fever hospitals became superfluous once the new Central Isolation Hospital in the Mardy was opened in 1907. The Pant Hospital, a wooden structure was destroyed by fire in August 1907 by order of the Council. The Brecon Road Hospital also ceased to be used for the treatment of patients. As it was a substantial brick building it remained in use for many years longer. Its kitchens were used to provide meals for needy children in 1908, 1909 and also during the General Strike in 1926. The building was used by the Corporation for stores and the Municipal Band also practised there.

Smallpox Hospital. During an outbreak of smallpox in 1902 the Council decided to erect a new isolation hospital. It was situated in Twynyrodyn. It was a corrugated iron building, had eighteen beds and cost £400. 93 cases were treated there in 1902, ten of whom died. When the new Mardy Isolation Hospital was built in 1907 it was too close to comply with the regulations of the Local Government Board. The smallpox hospital was therefore dismantled and re-erected in Mountain Hare. It was used intermittently as smallpox cases occurred until 1928, when it was partly blown down in a gale and the patients had to be removed to the Mardy.

In 1931 another site was chosen in Feddwhir near Aberdare. Four local authorities participated in the administration of this smallpox hospital until 1934. By then, due to progress in medicine, the incidence of smallpox had almost ceased. It was therefore decided to use the building as an Open Residential School for children suffering from rheumatism and certain other diseases. It remained however earmarked as a smallpox hospital, should an outbreak of the disease again occur.

The Mardy Central Isolation Hospital 1906-1948

The Mardy Hospital was built by the Merthyr Tydfil Municipal Borough in 1906 and opened by Keir Hardy on 23.3.1907. It stands in $4\frac{1}{2}$ acres of ground and cost £17,000. The hospital is built on the so-called pavilion plan, i.e. it consists of a number of separate blocks for isolation purposes. Originally there was a three storied building to house administration, kitchens etc., three pavilions and smaller buildings for laundry, mortuary, stables etc. Further pavilions were added from time to time. The hospital grounds originally contained a sizeable garden, the produce of which was used to provide vegetables and fruit for the patients. Livestock too was kept, namely chickens, ducks, geese and pigs.

The Medical Officer of Health for the Borough acted as Medical Superintendent until the retirement of Dr. T. H. Stephens in 1965. The contagious diseases treated consisted mainly of scarlet fever, typhoid, diphtheria and erysipelas. Scarlet fever was particularly prevalent until about 1920, affecting especially children under 10 years of age. Diphtheria was the next common disease. But whilst the numbers involved were less than those of scarlet fever, the number of deaths were almost three times as high. Fortunately modern methods of prevention and cure caused both illnesses to decline steadily and admissions in the last few years have been extremely rare.

The first patients suffering from tuberculosis were admitted in 1912. This followed a financial agreement with the Welsh National Memorial Association for Tuberculosis, to provide 16 beds in a Tuberculosis pavilion. Residents of Aberdare were also treated in the hospital following a financial agreement with the Aberdare Council. Towards the end of 1920 facilities for the treatment of venereal diseases were provided. The clinic continued until 1961, by which time treatment had become so effective that the service could be withdrawn.

In 1922 the hospital was approved as a Training School for Fever Nurses and continued until 1965, when the number of cases of infectious disease had declined so substantially that the nurses could no longer obtain the necessary experience.

Gwaunfarren House was acquired by the Merthyr Corporation and opened as a *Maternity Home* in September 1941 with 21 beds.

The Voluntary Hospitals 1860-1946

So far we have described two types of hospitals in Merthyr, those maintained by the Merthyr Board of Guardians and those kept by the Local Authority. We must now turn to a third type which appeared in the second half of the 19th century, namely the Voluntary Hospitals. These were of a kind which had long existed in London and other large cities and were maintained by gifts and bequests from individuals and groups. Patients treated paid no fees to the hospital or the doctors attending them. The reward of the doctors was deemed to be experience gained and prestige acquired. Three such hospitals were established in the Merthyr area : Mrs. Clark's Hospital in Dowlais, the Children's Hospital in Bridge Street, and the Merthyr General Hospital.

Mrs. Clark's Hospital in Dowlais 1860-1882

This was founded and maintained by the personal support of Mrs. Clark, the wife of G. T. Clark, one of the Trustees of the Dowlais Iron Works. It was closed in 1882.

The Children's Hospital in Bridge Street 1877-1888

The hospital was established through the efforts of the Rev. John Griffith, the dynamic Rector of Merthyr, Dr. T. J. Dyke and others. The premises in Bridge Street could accommodate 12 beds. Dr. Dyke was the honorary surgeon, Miss Adams the matron. Among the charitable efforts to maintain the hospital was a Calico Ball in 1880, which brought in £800.

After Mrs. Clark's Hospital in Dowlais had closed, there were no facilities to treat accidents. Operations, oftentimes of the most important kind, had to be performed in small rooms and under adverse conditions. More complicated cases had to be sent to Cardiff or Swansea Infirmaries. An attempt was made to create an accident ward in the Children's Hospital, but there were not sufficient funds. So it was decided to raise funds for a General Hospital.

Mr. W. T. Lewis obtained the support of the Marquess of Bute, who initially offered £1,000. The remainder of the required funds were quickly raised by public subscriptions. The architect of the building was T. Clarkson Wakeling. The original building consisted of two wards of ten beds each, namely St. Luke for men and Ann Lewis for women. There were also a children's ward of four beds. The foundation stone was laid by Sir W. T. Lewis in 1887. His statue was later erected in front of the hospital. The opening ceremony was performed on 1.10.1888 by the Marquess of Bute. The Merthyr Express published a special supplement for the occasion, which described the ceremony as a "brilliant demonstration and imposing pageant." The Marquess of Bute contributed £1,000 each for the Building Fund and Maintenance Fund. The owners of the local iron works and coal mines and their workmen subscribed the maintenance of the beds. Many smaller subscriptions were received. The children's hospital in Bridge Street was closed and the funds transferred to the new hospital.

It is interesting to read the rules governing the management of the hospital. Patients could only be admitted if recommended by their own surgeon and upon a note signed by a governor. The minimum subscription for governors was £2 a year. The following persons were not admissible as patients :

1. Those who were incurable or those whose complaints were deemed to be tedious of cure so as to preclude for a long time the admission of more urgent cases.

2. Patients suffering from insanity, epilepsy, tuberculosis or venereal diseases.

3. Persons whose admission might endanger the health of other patients, such as smallpox, itch and infectious diseases.

4. Persons suffering from asthma, as their condition may become worse through stay in the hospital.

5. Blind persons.

The treatment of the patients was in the hands of a group of Merthyr's medical practitioners, several of whom were highly qualified. They could usually obtain admission for their patients and attended them at the hospital. However by no means all practitioners residing in Merthyr belonged to the medical staff of the hospital.

The workmen of the iron and steel works, of the coal mines, railways, local government employees etc. paid weekly contributions to the funds of the hospital.

In 1897, as part of the Queen Victoria Jubilee celebrations, Sir W. T. Lewis endowed an accident ward. F. T. James, solicitor and Clerk to the Guardians, was High Constable of Merthyr in that year and commissioned a stained glass window in Sir W. T. Lewis' honour. It can be seen in the present nurses' dining room. All casualties and accidents were treated in the accident ward until 1953, when a new casualty department was opened in St. Tydfil's Hospital. All outpatients requiring orthopaedic, physiotherapeutical or massage treatment were also treated in the General Hospital until 1953 when specialist purpose built units were opened at St. Tydfil's Hospital.

The position of consultant surgeons was interesting. It came up for discussion in the Executive Board in 1915, when it was resolved that the consulting surgeons had a full right on the Board as Ex Officio members and that they could be summoned to meetings of the medical staff for any consultation that may be necessary, but that they were not to over-rule or interfere with the arrangements made by the working medical staff.

Another incident shows the growing influence of the workers in 1913. The workers contributed a large part of the revenue of the hospital. The Dowlais colliers and steelworkers requested that in addition to the present medical staff all Medical Men on the Panel of the new Health Medical Insurance Act be permitted to follow and attend on the Insured Persons in the hospital if they (the patients) so desired. This request was refused. However a year later the Executive Board agreed to admit three additional surgeons to the Medical Staff, namely one each from Merthyr, Dowlais and Merthyr Vale Districts of the workmen. These three sur-geons also became members of the Executive Board.

In 1922 two new wards were opened, the Berry and Sandbrook wards. They were wooden buildings and intended to last for 10 years only. They cost £12,000. Mr. Seymour Berry, later Lord Buckland, contributed £10,000. The wards were surgical wards and were named in memory of Mrs. M. A. Berry, Lord Buckland's mother, and of the mother of Lady Buckland (Mrs. R. Sandbrook). A full-time resident house surgeon was appointed about that time.

In 1930 the Lord Buckland Memorial Building was erected at a cost of £40,000. The bulk of this amount was borne by the executors of the will of the late Lord Buckland. The new block comprised accommoda-tion for outpatients, ophthalmic wards, operating theatre, X-ray equip-ment, equipment for therapeutic, diatermic and massage treatment and a Board Room and staff rooms. The number of beds increased to 118. About a year later a children's ward was opened.

A special feature of the hospital was the Annual Fete to raise funds. It was held every Whitsun in Cyfarthfa Park from 1927 till 1947. It was supported by many charitable activities in the various localities of the Borough, where whist drives, concerts and amateur dramatical per-formances were organised by local volunteers.

In 1933 the staff consisted of 12 hon. surgeons, one hon. dental sur-geon, eight consultant surgeons and physicians, and one house surgeon.

The Governors were the directing and policy making body. They met annually. However they were an unwieldy body. In 1938 there were 36 life governors and 85 governors. Anybody could become a governor for an annual subscription of no less than £2. In addition there were over 200 Workmen's Governors, representing various collieries, iron and steel works, the railways etc. In 1938 over half the revenue of some £11,000 came from the Workmen's Collection, paid by weekly deductions from wages. £9,000 came from the Annual Hospital Fete, the rest from donations, bequests and other sources. The annual cost per bed in 1938 was £124.8.10 for the year. There were 123 beds in that year.

The day to day running of the hospital was in the hands of the Executive Board, consisting of 34 members in 1938. Four of these were members of the medical staff, the majority representatives of the collieries, steelworks, and other employees' organizations.

During the war 1939/44 the Merthyr General Hospital was extensively used by the Emergency Medical Service. St. Luke's Ward and 46 extra emergency beds were used for soldiers' medical cases. The Government also took over St. Mary's Catholic Hall and the Kirkhouse Hall for hospital purposes. The Home Guard collected £2,000 after the war. This sum was used to furnish a Nurses' Home Annexe as a Home Guard Memorial.

The hospital had its own ambulance. Two other ambulances were kept in hospitals in Merthyr at that time, at the Mardy and St. Tydfil's Lodge.

Gwaelodygarth House was acquired for a Preliminary Training School for nurses in 1946 but not opened until after nationalization of the Hospital. A new X-ray installation was opened in 1946 by Arthur Horner, the General Secretary of the Miners' Union.

Pontsarn Sanatorium 1913-1948

Tuberculosis was one of the most dreaded diseases in the nineteenth and early twentieth centuries. There was hardly a family in Merthyr without one of its members suffering from consumption, which was only too often fatal. Many of the Paupers in the Institution suffered from it and in 1906 the Board of Guardians instructed their Medical Officer, Dr. Ward to look for a suitable site for a tuberculosis hospital. Dr. Ward was an authority on the treatment of tuberculosis and read a paper on "The treatment of consumptive patients by Union Authorities" at the South Wales and Monmouthshire Poor Law Conference held in Merthyr Town Hall in June 1907. Dr. Ward suggested two possible sites, one on Cilsanws Mountain, close to the Jewish Cemetery, the other in Pontsarn, just under Morlais Castle. The Pontsarn site was found to be more suitable because of its sunny position and protection from north and east winds. The Sanatorium was opened in 1913 by Dr. J. L. W. Ward. It was designed for 50 beds and cost £8,596. Non pauper patients were admitted for a charge of 15/- per week.

The Sanatorium was leased to the Welsh National Memorial Association for Tuberculosis on 1.12.1914. The lease continued until 1923 when the Association purchased the building for £10,537.

The Infirmary 1929-1948

The Local Government Act 1929, which came into force on 1.4.1930, abolished the Board of Guardians. However the Poor Law as such remained in force and the functions of the Guardians were transferred to the Merthyr Tydfil Borough Council. A special committee of the Local Authority was created by the Act, namely the Public Assistance Committee. All the assets of the Guardians were transferred to the Council, in particular the Workhouse with the Infirmary.

At this time, Dr. C. M. Probert was Medical Officer, Dr. E. L. Ward Medical Superintendent of the Infirmary. The nursing staff consisted of the Matron, six Sisters, five Staff Nurses and 28 Probationer Nurses. There were 337 beds in the Infirmary. The Public Assistance Committee decided in 1930 to employ Consultant staff. Dr. Parker was appointed consultant orthopaedic surgeon, Mr. Owen consulting surgeon and Professor Strachen consulting obstetrician and gynaecologist.

The Hospitals Under the National Health Service 1948-1974

The National Health Service Act of 1946 followed from the famous Beveridge Report of 1942. It came into operation on 5.7.1948. It consisted of three services :

1. The Hospital Services.
2. The services provided by the Local Health Authority.
3. The services provided by Family Practitioners : doctors, dentists, pharmacists, opticians.

All hospitals were transferred to the Minister of Health. This transfer concerned the voluntary hospitals, hospitals owned by local authorities and hospitals owned by other organisations. The Welsh Regional Hospital Board was set up to administer all hospitals in Wales, and under it local Hospital Management Committees. The Merthyr area came under the Merthyr and Aberdare Management Committee. Hospitals taken over in Merthyr comprised the Merthyr General Hospital, Tydfil's Lodge (the former Infirmary), now renamed St. Tydfil's Hospital, the Mardy Isolation Hospital, Pontsarn Chest Hospital, Fedwhir Hospital, Gwaunfarren Maternity Home and Sandbrook House. It also took over the Chest Clinic in Courtland Terrace.

The Merthyr Tydfil Borough Council became responsible for a number of health services dealing largely with preventive rather than curative medicine, such as care for mothers and young children, midwifery, health visiting, vaccination and immunisation and ambulance services. They were empowered to set up Health Centres, i.e. premises to be used by family practitioners consulting rooms as well as for clinics for specialists and consultants. Such Centres were not set up in Merthyr until 1972.

The merger of all hospitals under one authority had important consequences. It led to more uniform systems of administration. Particularly staffing, salary scales and appointment procedures were standardized and uniform systems of accounting and stores control introduced. The main change however was that in due course the hospitals became Consultant Hospitals, in which specialists played the dominant role and had all beds allocated to them. Thus the General Practitioners, who had played such a large role in the Merthyr General Hospital, lost their influential position. The change was a gradual one, it was completed in the General Hospital by 1956, in St. Tydfil's after the retirement of Dr. C. M. Probert in 1958, in the Mardy in 1965, when Dr. T. H. Stephens retired as Medical Officer of Health for the Merthyr Tydfil Corporation.

The following is a list of the hospitals taken over by the Merthyr and Aberdare Hospital Management Committee on 5.7.1948. The Senior Officers are those listed in the Report for 1951 :

Hospitals	*Beds*	*Senior Officers*
LOCAL AUTHORITY HOSPITALS		
Merthyr Corporation		
St. Tydfil's Hospital ...	607	Medical Superintendent : Dr. C. M. Probert Admin. Officer: Ivor Davies
Gwaunfarren Maternity Home	21	Medical Officer : Dr. Parry M. Morton Matron : Miss M. Walters
Sandbrook House Rheumatic Hospital ...	20	Med. Officer : Dr. Dilys Stephens Matron : Miss M. Jones
Mardy Isolation Hospital	120	Medical Superintendent : Dr. T. H. Stephens Matron : Miss M. I. Harries
Aberdare U.D.C.		
Fedwhir Smallpox Hosp.	72	
Mountain Ash U.D.C.		
Mountain Ash Isolation Hospital	24	
Lady Aberdare Maternity Hospital	15	Med. Officer : Dr. F. J. Doherty Admin. Officer : R. J. Phelps Matron : Miss E. Davies
Welsh Memorial Association		
Pontsarn Sanatorium ...	40	Med. Officer : Dr. E. A. Aslett Matron : Miss D. M. Owen
Voluntary Hospitals		
Merthyr General Hosp.	120	Admin. Officer : Mr. M. Williams Matron : Miss D. R. Grassick
Aberdare General Hosp.	102	Admin. Officer : Clifford Thomas Matron : Miss M. I. Wilson
Mountain Ash General Hospital	51	Admin. Officer : Mr. R. J. Phelps Matron : Mrs. C. Williams

Chest Clinics transferred from
Welsh Memorial Association

Merthyr Tydfil
Aberdare }   Med. Officer : Dr. E. A. Aslett
Penrhiwceiber

Details of staffing show that there were two House Surgeons in the Merthyr General Hospital and one in St. Tydfil's. There was one physiotherapist for the Merthyr General, and one pharmacist for all the Merthyr Hospitals. In 1951 the first full-time consultant was appointed for the group. He was Mr. R. D. Richards, F.R.C.S.

Radio installations with earphones to each bed were provided before the war (in the Mardy in 1936). Television sets were first obtained in 1952.

Gwaelodygarth House, which had been acquired in 1946 by the Merthyr General Hospital, was opened by Dr. S. Creswell on 14.9.1950 as a Preliminary School for Nurses. It was used as a residential unit until 1975.

Fedwhir was used for a recovery hospital since 1959, but remained designated as a smallpox hospital. When a smallpox outbreak occurred in Wales in 1962, all patients were transferred to the Mardy and the hospital made ready for smallpox cases. Fortunately the outbreak subsided before any such cases were received at Fedwhir and the previous patients returned.

In 1953 important improvements took place at St. Tydfil's Hospital. A Group Pathological Laboratory was opened as well as an Orthopaedic Department and Outpatients Department, including a Physiotherapy Department and Hydrotherapy section. 41 consultants attended at the hospitals in the group. The report for that year gives details of the facilities available for the training of nurses. There were two separate complete Nurses' Training Schools for State Registered Nurses (SRN) at the Merthyr General Hospital and at the Aberdare and Mountain Ash General Hospitals respectively. Training for Fever Nurses (R.F.N.) was available at the Mardy Hospital. An Assistant Nurses' Training School (S.E.A.N.) operated at St. Tydfil's Hospital, Merthyr. A Preliminary Training School for entrants to S.R.N. and R.F.N. courses was held at Gwaelodygarth, Merthyr.

From 1957 onwards the number of tuberculosis patients declined both in Pontsarn and at the Mardy. 17 beds in Pontsarn could be set aside for chest diseases other than tuberculosis, such as asthma, bronchitis and pneumoconiosis. Pontsarn Sanatorium was closed as a hospital in 1960 and later converted into flats.

Another disease which showed a steady decline in that period was diphtheria. Dr. T. H. Stephens in his report of 1959 attributed this improvement largely to the work done by the local Health Authority, who had carried out a comprehensive immunization programme for the children of the Borough. This was also done for poliomyelitis. The treatment of these diseases had become much easier with the introduction of the new antibiotics, and the stay in hospitals shorter.

A survey in the 1964 report shows that in that year the number of beds were only three quarter of those in 1949, yet almost 70% more patients were admitted and discharged. In the Outpatient Clinics, four times as many new patients were seen and over five times as many attendances occurred. The number of clinics had increased three and a half times. By 1968 the number of consultants and senior hospital staff who were employed full-time or made regular visits had reached 35, representing 16 specialities.

Area Profile 1972. The position of the hospitals in 1972 is shown in a document called Area Profile published by the Mid-Glamorgan Health Authority in 1974. The hospitals in the Merthyr area are described as follows :

St. Tydfil's Hospital provided 281 acute beds covering most of the major specialities and was the largest unit in Merthyr Tydfil. Specialities provided included geriatrics, trauma and orthopaedics, general surgery, general medicine, paediatrics and gynaecology. As the base hospital, it provided certain departments operating on a group basis, namely pharmacy, pathology, central sterilizing, group administration and stores. Outpatients facilities together with Accident and Emergency departments were also provided.

Gwaunfarren Hospital numbered 30 beds, half of which were used for post natal cases and half as pre-convalescent beds. A day hospital was opened in 1968.

Mardy Hospital provided 120 beds used for general medicine, infectious diseases, diseases of the chest and for preconvalescent purposes.

The Merthyr Chest Clinic, used since 1944, was no longer required and other uses of the building were under consideration.

The Merthyr General Hospital provided 126 acute beds complementary to those in St. Tydfil's Hospital. They were used for general medicine, paediatrics, general surgery, ear, nose and throat cases and ophthalmology.

The training of nurses provided at this time took place in the Merthyr Tydfil School of Nursing and consisted of courses for the training of State Registered Nurses (S.R.N.) and of State Enrolled Nurses (S.E.N.)

Health Centres for which provision had been made in the National Health Service Act of 1946, were eventually introduced in the Merthyr area in the early 1970's. They were built by the Merthyr Tydfil Corporation in Merthyr (The Hollies) and Dowlais, both opened in 1972, and in Treharris. The Treharris Centre was originally a clinic, but was converted into a Health Centre in 1974. The Hollies was the largest Health Centre in Wales in 1972. It provided

a. a day centre for handicapped elderly persons.
b. Surgeries for five practices staffed by 14 general practitioners.
c. Local Authority clinics and dental facilities.
d. Administrative premises for the present Health Services including the School Health Service.

Four clinics were in use in 1974, all provided by the Merthyr Corporation. Two of these were purpose built, the ones situated in Gurnos and Gellideg, whilst the ones in Troedyrhiw and Aberfan were housed in older premises.

Merthyr Council also provided a new ambulance station in 1966.

A new District Hospital, the Prince Charles Hospital was started by the Health Authority in 1972 in the Gurnos in Merthyr, and is due to be opened in 1978. It will have 362 beds, ten operating theatres and all departments of a modern hospital, providing a wide range of specialities. It will become the major hospital of the Merthyr and Cynon Valley Health District.

Reorganization of 1974

The National Health Service was reorganized by an act of 1973, which came into force on 1.4.1974.

The main principles laid down in 1948 remained unaltered. The Welsh Office became responsible for the overall control of the health services of the whole of Wales. Eight new Health Areas were created, corresponding to the new Welsh Counties. The Health Areas were further divided into Health Districts. Merthyr comes within the Merthyr and Cynon Valley District, with offices in St. Tydfil's Hospital. This District forms part of the Mid-Glamorgan Health Area.

The Area Health Authorities are responsible for the overall control of the hospitals, the Family Doctor Services, Community Health Services and Ambulance Services. The Health Districts are responsible for the day to day management of the hospitals in their district, the Health Centres and Clinics.

Community Health Councils have been set up in each district to allow the inhabitants access to and information concerning the health services in their district.

References

Board of Guardians, Merthyr Union. Minutes 1836-1930.

Merthyr Tydfil Board of Health. Minutes 1850-1894.

Merthyr Tydfil Urban District Council Minutes. 1895-1905.

Merthyr Tydfil Borough Council Minutes 1905-1974.

Reports of the Medical Officer of Health of Merthyr. 1854, 1865-1897, 1901-1970.

Report on the Sanatary Conditions of Merthyr Tydfil by Sir H. T. De la Beche 1845.

Report into the sewerage, drainage and supply of water and the sanitary conditions of the inhabitants of the town of Merthyr Tydfil by T. W. Rammell 1850.

Annual Reports and Minutes of the Executive Board of the Merthyr General Hospital. Incomplete.

Notes on the Merthyr General Hospital, kindly supplied by Miss D. R. Grassick.

Annual Reports of the Merthyr and Aberdare Hospital Management Committee 1948-1971.

Notes on the history of the hospitals in Merthyr Tydfil, kindly supplied by the Merthyr and Cynon Valley Health District.

Description of the opening ceremony of the Merthyr General Hospital. Merthyr Express 6.10.1888.

Obituary of T. J. Dyke. Merthyr Express 27.1.1900 and South Wales Daily News 22.1.1900.

The role of Dr. Dyke in the Public Health Administration of Merthyr Tydfil 1865-1892. (Unpublished Swansea University MA Thesis) by B. A. Frampton.

Poor Law Administration in the Merthyr Tydfil Union 1834-1894 by Tydfil Davies Jones. Morgannwg Vol. VIII. 1964.

Area Profile. Mid Glamorgan Health Authority. Kindly supplied by the Area Administrator.

The Hospitals 1800-1948 by Brian Abel Smith. Heinemann 1964.

English Public Health 1834-1939 by W. M. Frazer. Bailliere, Tyndall & Cox 1950.

ST. TYDFIL'S HOSPITAL
"The Workhouse" built 1853.   (See Joseph Gross, Section 6)

ST. TYDFIL'S HOSPITAL
Infirmary built 1897.   (See Joseph Gross, Section 6)

MERTHYR GENERAL HOSPITAL
(See Joseph Gross, Section 6)

GENERAL HOSPITAL ACCIDENT WARD 1895
(photo taken March, 1976).   (See Joseph Gross, Section 6)

SITE OF SMALL POX HOSPITAL IN MOUNTAIN HARE 1906-1928
(photo taken in 1976).   (See Joseph Gross, Section 6)

PONTSARN SANATORIUM
(See Joseph Gross, Section 6)

THE OLD IRON BRIDGE
(See Leo Davies, Section 7)

7. LEO DAVIES

THE OLD IRON BRIDGE—MERTHYR

(*Illustration 54*)

The 'Old Iron Bridge'—known as the Merthyr Bridge until 1809—was commissioned and paid for by William Crawshay. It was designed and built by Mr. Watkyn George the Principal Engineer of the Cyfarthfa Iron Works.

Work on the bridge started in the middle of 1799 and it was completed in April/May 1800. The Iron Bridge of Shropshire—1779, the bridges at Sunderland over the River Wear—1796 and Buildwas at Coalbrookdale and, no doubt, a few other iron bridge experiments, in other iron making areas, had already been completed and put to use. The 'Merthyr Bridge' joined this very early and illustrious group of pioneering designs.

T. E. Clarke recorded in 1849 "the Iron Bridge was built about fifty years since by Mr. Watkyn George. The stone bridge that had been erected previously fell owing to a very heavy flood after a long frost of about fourteen weeks which brought down great quantities of ice and woodwork from the river above the bridge".

F. Pedler refers, in his 'History of the Hamlet of Gellideg', to a plan of 1790 which shows a bridge near Parliament Lock—two hundred and seventy yards below Morlais Brook. It is most likely that the fallen bridge to which Mr. Clarke referred and the bridge site indicated on the plan, are one and the same. To date this plan has not been located and no further details obtained.

These circumstances substantially underwrite the motive for building the 'Merthyr Bridge'—indeed it was essential. With no river crossing at this point the inconvenience to Merthyr people, and particularly to those living in the Hamlet of Gellideg, most of whom worked at the Cyfarthfa undertakings, must have been considerable. In the presence of keen competition between the Iron Masters—in all things (it couldn't have pleased William Crawshay overmuch that the Dowlais Iron Company's Jackson's Bridge—1793—was the only means of crossing the Taff in the village of Merthyr), Mr. Crawshay's gesture might not have been entirely altruistic.

Mr. Watkyn George, with the facilities of the Cyfarthfa Iron Works behind him, conceived a structure fabricated with cast iron frames or sections. Until this point what iron bridges had been built in the locality were simply one piece castings which acted as carrying beams and parapets simultaneously. They were limited to twenty to twenty-five feet in length, about four feet wide and in one and a half inch section thickness. These frames were suitable for relatively short spans across canals, brooks and feeders. The lower boom of the cast frame carried the transverse members on which the roadway was placed—either by being placed

93

to rest directly on the boom or engaged with underslung bosses which were integral with the main casting.

The existing bridge over the Glamorganshire Canal at Rhydicar—1794—is an instance of this design. Contained in a print in 'Wood's Rivers of Wales' which illustrates the Penydarren Iron Works there is a works bridge which crossed the Morlais Brook as it passed through the Iron Works. The detail of the form and scale of the main castings could only mean that our oldest iron bridge relic of Rhydicar—which fortunately is still with us—and the long gone Penydarren Iron Works Bridge were cast in moulds made from the same patterns.

Spanning the River Taff presented Mr. George with the problem of spanning sixty-five to seventy feet—from bank to bank. He realised that single cast iron beams were impractical. Their projected size would be excessive, both in the creation of the castings themselves and their susceptibility to failure, bearing in mind the shock loading of continuous pounding of the iron rimmed wheels of the wagons which would require to use the bridge. An idea of the volume of this traffic is shown later in Superintendent Wren's census.

He therefore elected to fabricate a structure using numbers of cast iron beams and frames. He decided on using three main sections generally equal in length—twenty-two to twenty-four feet long—the section thickness was one and a quarter inches—the upper members or booms were four inches wide and the side and bottom ones were six inches wide. The width of the frame itself, which would eventually form the parapet, was five feet.

With the flexibility he was now afforded, he adopted a cantilever on the two sections mounted on the buttresses. He included, on these sections, additional cantilevered supports within the casting frames themselves—coming up from the lower point of the buttress mounting at a more acute angle. These measures gave considerable advantage to the final strength of the assembled structure. The centre portion would be slightly convex—four inches over twenty-two feet six inches.

The profile of the bridge was therefore a minor approach to the well established and more conventional radial arch form found in stone bridges, the strength of which has been proven by service over thousands of years.

When one is considering the life expectancy of a bridge the advantage that stone has, as a base material, over iron is considerable. Iron, at the time, was in good supply in the area and it had merits of ease of manufacture and would entail less construction costs. However performance history using iron in bridge construction was very limited, perhaps thirty years on simple erections.

The Merthyr Bridge then, with its three segments forming the approximate of a shallow arch, automatically caused it to be a structure of a lower order of strength when compared to a stone arch with its multiples of segments in the voussoir.

The angled stone buttresses, erected on each bank, carried the cantilevered sections and when they were in position the slightly convexed centre portion was dropped into position in the 'gap'. The abutting edges of the beams, before being secured, were spaced by oaken packing pieces about two and a half inches thick and equal in width to the beam edges. Once beams and the wooden packing were in position the nuts were tightened down on the holding bolts. The introduction of the packing pieces was, I am convinced, Mr. George's method of ensuring flexure in the completed assembly which would have been completely rigid without them—a circumstance on this scale in cast iron would have tempted failure.

Criticism of the design, and this feature in particular, is referred to later.

Resting upon the bottom and slightly heavier sections of the beams were a set of cast iron cross members with strengthening centre 'ribs' along their lengths. They were placed side by side over the whole length of the bridge. They were twelve feet long, twelve inches wide and had a section thickness of three-quarters of an inch. The centre rib averaged six inches high and had the same section thickness. "In situ" they provided a road width of ten feet and six inches. Stone sets were inserted between the stiffener ribs forming the road surface.

The finished length of the bridge was sixty-six to sixty-eight feet. No dimension of height above water level has been located. We know that it stood on its own account through the floods of a hundred and sixty-three years.

Watkyn George and his team must have been very busy throughout 1799 because on January the 23rd 1800 "Notice was given for filling up both ends of the 'Merthyr Bridge' and making a road over it. It was settled to make a road twenty yards on the west side and sixty yards to the east side and to cover the bridge with iron slag from Cyfarthfa. David Edmunds, having delivered a proposal for doing the said work for the sum of seventeen guineas, which said proposal is accepted—he, the said David Edmunds engages to complete the work by the first of April next—to the satisfaction of Mr. Watkyn George, Henry Jones and James Rees the General Surveyor".

The minute was signed by Henry Jones, Watkyn George, John Lewis and Francis Rees.

In April 1800 traffic moved over it for the first time and it was kept in full use, excepting short intervals for repair, until 1880 when the new Ynysgau 'skew' bridge or the 'New Iron Bridge' was completed and put into service.

Over those eighty years incidents and comments were numerous.

On April the 17th 1800 Mr. Edward James received payment for building a wall by the Merthyr Bridge.

The residents of the Parish of Hoelwermod (Town District) could not have been too pleased at being 'summoned' on March the 9th 1801, for no payment toward repairing the road from Merthyr Bridge (by the Mill) to Morlais Brook.

On July 6th 1801 Mr. Henry Jones was "authorised to agree with a person for the building up of the abutments of the Merthyr Bridge and keep same in repair for three years and is not to give more than twenty pounds for doing the same".

September the 22nd 1801 saw "The common bridge over the Taff called Merthyr Bridge has been indented for defect of repair and leveries have been raised upon the indictment. (Merthyr Bridge by Merthyr Mill)".

The various retaining walls connected with the Bridge could not have been well constructed—repairs to them were listed through 1803, 1805, 1807 and 1809. On this last report the first reference was made to the 'Iron Bridge' and it read "It is ordered to appoint a committee to super-intend the repair of the wall from Mr. Evan Lewis's House to the Iron Bridge and the abutments above the bridge".

Further mention, although not directly connected with the Iron Bridge was made on October the 10th 1809 when, due to frequent flooding "It was authorised to build a wall from the upper end of Caedraw to the Plymouth Weir to keep the river from the Turnpike Road leading from the village of Merthyr to the Iron Bridge—to be built to Mr. Richard Hill's direction".

Mr. Wm. Williams of Cyfarthfa, on August 5th 1817, recommended that the Iron Bridge be repaired. He proposed that iron plates, with ribs, should be laid over the old bridge and screwed to the present bearers so as to form a platform and that the surface be pitched with stones or iron as may be deemed proper.

Considerable repairs were effected judging from the size of the total bill submitted—£354-1-10$\frac{1}{2}$. The nature of the repair did not seem to follow what Mr. Williams' suggested. A bill submitted in November 1817 for £196-11-6 was attributed to the supply of castings (this charge was part of the £354-1-10 overall account) therefore there must have been considerable replacement of cast items on the structure. Credit was claimed on two of them which were unsuitable. Further charges by Mr. Thos. Jones (Smith) and Mr. Edward Powell totalling £147-0-2$\frac{1}{2}$ must have been mainly connected with labour charges. One could presume therefore that the castings were transverse bearers, if, as Mr. Williams stated, the roadway itself required attention. It appears that Mr. Wm. Williams supervised the work himself and was paid ten guineas for his pains.

For the next thirty-five years little record of repair or maintenance costs were to be found and no doubt the apparent absence of such activity lead to the outspoken and critical comments to the Local Board of Health by Superintendent Henry Wren in March 1852. He referred to the dangerous and dilapidated condition of the Iron Bridge. He was asked to make a report.

He wrote as follows : "I have made an inspection of the Iron Bridge and have no hesitation in pronouncing it unsafe for traffic in its present state nor would I advise the expenditure, which would be required, to put it in thorough repair for the following reasons :—

(1) It would be necessary to take down and re-erect the structure which would be as costly as putting together a new bridge.

(2) The principles of erection are radically bad. The Bridge con-

sists of iron girders in three segments bolted together and abutting, at the junctions, against pieces of timber. The roadway is bolted on the girder and braced underneath with timber. The abutting pieces and bolts are quite decayed and two of the transverse braces underneath are so strained as to be nearly broken through. The result will be that if a heavier load than usual should be on the Bridge the bolts will give way and the Bridge collapse in the middle.

If the Board, at any time, should decide on erecting a new bridge then it should be constructed below the present one and in the line of Victoria Street and Swansea Road."

As a result of this report a committee was set up to inspect the Bridge —it consisted of Messrs. John Evans, B. Martin and S. Francis.

It appears that they completed their task of inspection fairly quickly and they stipulated that the Bridge should be repaired.

On the 7th of June 1852 the following expenditures were authorised for payment by the Board.

"Total expenditure of repairing Bridge of £66-12-6½.

Itemised as follows :—

Mr. Evan Rees	Carpenter's Labour ...	£11- 1- 1
Mr. Mathew John	Iron Work	£10- 3- 0
Mr. Wm. Marshall	Mason & Labourer ...	£ 3- 2- 1½
Mr. Thos. Jones	Stone	£ 6- 0- 0
Messrs. Watson and Richards	Timber supplied and used	£35-14- 5
Mr. David Evans	Sundry Blacksmith Work	£ 0-11-11"

George Borrow in his 'Wild Wales' came to Merthyr Tydfil from Hirwaun in 1854 and before reaching his destination in Merthyr for his overnight stay he crossed the Iron Bridge—he wrote "I went through a filthy slough, over a bridge and up a street from which dirty lanes branched off on either side, passed throngs of savage looking people talking clamourously, shrank from addressing any of them, and finally undirected, found myself before the Castle Inn at Merthyr Tydfil."

The repairs carried out in 1852 show that Superintendent Wren's report had roused the conscience and concern of the Local Board of Health to some extent. Little heed was however paid to his plea that early consideration should be given for a replacement bridge. Eight years had to pass before a further mention of the matter was made by the Board. As a preliminary move and again at the instigation of the Superintendent who, with the ever increasing volume of traffic now using the bridge, had visions of a calamity, the Board decided to take a census of the traffic now using the Bridge.

On the 5th of July 1860 the Superintendent submitted his report. It was a comprehensive analysis and reflected the very considerable movement of the population over the river Taff.

It read : "In compliance with a request from your Board I caused the traffic over the 'Iron Bridge' Merthyr to be taken from 8.0 a.m. to 8.0 p.m. for seven days : viz. from the 25th of June until the 1st of July and beg to give you, on the side, a tabular statement of the same.

I may add there is a very great traffic over the Bridge both before and after these hours particularly on Mondays, Wednesdays, Saturdays and Sundays."

"Henry Wren—Superintendent"

TABULATION

Traffic over the 'Iron Bridge' Merthyr Tydfil from the 25th of June to 1st of July 1860 both days inclusive—from 8.0 a.m. to 8.0 p.m.

Day	Foot Passengers	Horses	Car-riages, Gigs etc.	Carts, Wagons, Drays etc.	Cattle	State of Weather
Monday	9,218	129	5	267	17	showery all day
Tuesday	8,080	141	7	347	113	fine all day
Wednesday	4,837	68	3	188	185	wet all day
Thursday	6,687	111	3	302	137	wet all day
Friday	7,597	120	7	381	15	wet morning fine afternoon
Saturday	11,119	131	12	350	31	fine all day
Sunday	9,938	73	9	—	9	fine all day
Totals	57,716	773	46	1835	507	

Merthyr, at this time, was still growing rapidly and had still some twenty-five to thirty years before reaching its peak. It is no wonder Mr. Wren had misgivings about the future safety of the Bridge. His tabulation amply justified his proposals for the construction of a replacement bridge based on his earlier recommendations.

He submitted a comprehensive description of the new bridge supported by three plans which provided details of the line it was to take, the view of the elevated sections of the bridge and the third plan provided working drawings of the iron work.

He suggested a new line for the bridge should form a "direct communication between Victoria Street and Penry Street which will effect greater facility for the traffic than the inconsistent turns at the present site".

He continues : "The heavy traffic which will pass over the new bridge, if created, renders it necessary to make it considerably stronger than is usual for a road bridge and an increased disposal of metal and materials and consequently of an expense which I estimate at £1,700 to erect the bridge in all respects and if the work is executed in the summer it could be finished in three to four months."

The board examined Mr. Wren's proposals and they issued an order that they were to stand over for one month. That stay or standover lasted over twenty years. It was not until the 15th of March 1880 that the replacement bridge—called 'Ynysgau Bridge' with its 65 degrees skew was completed.

In the meantime, during these twenty years, the old 'Iron Bridge' took the battering that an ever increasing traffic load inflicted.

Conditions and circumstances of pedestrian and wheeled traffic using the Bridge during this period are reflected in two items which were reported by the Press.

On April the 12th 1872 a little girl, whilst crossing the Bridge was knocked down by a laden cart and her legs were severed when the wheels passed over them.

In 1913, a reader of the 'Merthyr Express', seeing an old photograph of the 'Iron Bridge' from the Ynysfach Cinder Tip (before erection of the new Ynysgau Bridge) was moved to reminisce when he was a ten year old boy in the year 1878. He claimed how he marvelled at the skill of the waggoners bringing the hay from the Vale of Neath Station to the Cyfarthfa Stables in Nantygwenith Street. Each waggon had four wheels and required a four horse team to pull it, all of which made the negotiating of the sharp bend of the boundary wall of Ynysgau Graveyard very difficult. The waggoners had to obtain a good line to the 'Iron Bridge' to ensure they could cross in safety.

So it was not until March 1880 that the grossly excessive burden for which the old 'Iron Bridge' was never designed and built to accommodate was now directed over the 'Ynysgau Bridge'.

Until the end of the Second World War it was used sparingly as a footbridge (the stone setts made it uncomfortable to walk on). At this time it was fenced, at each end, and remained so until its inglorious and somewhat brutal dismantling in November 1963.

Its introduction, at this time of the explosion of industrial activity in, the then, Village of Merthyr Tydfil, in the first years of the Nineteenth Century was timely. Its construction and subsequent existence had a positive purpose and throughout its eighty years, of hard—indeed excessive use, it served that purpose well.

Its design in that very early year of 1799 was adventurous and inspiring.

It was worthy and well qualified to be preserved, as it stood, as a relic of Merthyr Tydfil's contribution to progress—in the widest sense—but we had to destroy it.

A fragment of the original casting was analysed—the hope being that, some, as yet, unknown secret of alchemy would be detected. The limited penetration of corrosion, over 178 years, would indicate that the iron might have contained some recognisable feature or element. As in earlier trials—it was not to be. The Chemical analysis was :—

Carbon	3.86%
Manganese	.67%
Silicon	.95%
Sulphur	.053%
Phosphorous	.87%

Apart from being a little low on Manganese and a little high on Phosphorous—to the general average of normal grey cast iron—there was nothing in the analysis or the micrographic study to indicate anything unusual.

References

Vestry Books of the Parish of Merthyr Tydfil.

Minutes of the Merthyr Tydfil Board of Health.

Minutes of the Merthyr Tydfil Borough Council.

Reports—the "Merthyr Express" and "Merthyr Guardian" covering the period.

8. JEREMY K. KNIGHT

EARLY CHRISTIAN ORIGINS AND SOCIETY
IN SOUTH WALES
(Illustrations 55 & 56)

During the summer of A.D. 177, in the reign of the Roman Emperor Marcus Aurelius, a group of people, many of them immigrants from Asia Minor, were arrested in the French city of Lyons. The precise charges against them under Roman law are not certain, but were perhaps broadly those of fomenting public disorder and of criminal conspiracy. Popular rumour charged them with immorality and atheism, but their real crime was that they belonged to a novel religious sect of which most people knew little, but about which sensational rumours tended to circulate. They were Christians and the letter which the survivors of the subsequent persecution sent to the Churches of Asia and Phrygia, from whence many of the victims had come, describing their sufferings and deaths, is the earliest surviving document of the Christian faith from the western parts of the Empire, outside Italy.[1]

We cannot trace the spread of Christianity in Britain and Gaul in any detail, but it would seem that during the third century at least three inhabitants of Roman Britain died as Christian martyrs. Usually, the body of such a martyr would be recovered by his (or her) fellow Christians and buried in the normal cemetery of the town, outside the walls. It was usual at this period for both pagans and Christians to commemorate the anniversary of the deaths of relatives and friends with ceremonies at their tombs, often accompanied by ceremonial meals, at which it was believed the spirit of the person remembered was present. In the case of a Christian martyr, such a ceremony was the affair not only of his earthly relatives, but of the whole Christian family within that city and it commemorated not only the day of his death (his "heavenly birthday" as Christians sometimes put it), but also the anniversary of his heroic witness to his faith. In time, the place of his tomb would be marked by a walled enclosure, or by a small Christian chapel, known as a *Memoria* or *Martyrium* which would become a focus of Christian devotion and many Christians would seek to lie in death close to the body of the venerated martyr, who was now often seen as an intercessor with God, both in earthly problems and on the last day.

The *martyrium* of St Albanus or Alban outside the walls of the Roman town of Verulamium was visited by the Gaulish bishop Germanus of Auxerre in A.D. 429. Germanus is known to have carried dust and perhaps relics from the tomb of the martyr back to Auxerre.[2] About a hundred years later someone in central France, perhaps near Auxerre, wrote an account of the martyrdom of Alban. This *Passio*

Albani was used by the sixth century British writer Gildas and later by Bede and the fame of the martyr led to the development of the medieval abbey of St Albans over his tomb, whilst the site of the town itself shifted from the Roman Verulamium to that of the medieval abbey and the tomb of St Alban.[3]

Gildas is also our primary source for the martyrdom of Julius and Aaron "citizens of the City of the Legions",[4] but neither Gildas nor anyone else gives us any account of their deaths and we do not know the source of his information, or whether by "City of the Legions" he meant the fortress of *Legio II Augusta* at *Isca* (Caerleon), or, if he did, whether he had correctly understood his source. It was not unknown for similar sounding placenames to lead to confusion in such matters and it is just possible that Gildas could have been misled by a martyrology or other written source which referred to martyrs of, say, *Legio* (Leon) in Spain. There is however circumstantial evidence to support the traditional siting of the martyrdoms at Caerleon.

Literary material dealing with Christian martyrs tended to proliferate in the middle ages rather than diminish, but no source can be found which might have misled Gildas in the way suggested above and unless one invents the hypothesis of a lost British source of the fifth or early sixth century which vanished without leaving any other trace of its presence, one has to conclude that Gildas's source was not a written one. Christianity may have had a rather similar appeal for sections of the Roman army to that of certain other "mystery" religions which promised redemption through a saviour God, for example the cult of Mithras, and there are a number of Legionary martyrs associated with Legionary fortresses in various parts of the Empire. Their *passios* make it clear that situations could easily arise where duty as a soldier clashed with duty as a Christian, particularly where the Christian N.C.O. was called upon to take part in official worship of the Regimental colours, or the image of the Emperor. Gildas's statement is thus historically credible. It also finds support in the topography of the area around the Legionary fortress. One of the principal cemeteries of Roman *Isca* lay across the river from the fortress, along a ridge up which climbed the Roman road to Caerwent. On this ridge there stood in the middle ages a chapel of St Alban, near the house now called Mount St Alban. Levison has explained how the name of St Alban came to supplant those of Julius and Aaron,[5] but there is no doubt that the chapel is that described in a charter in the 12th century Book of Llandaff as *Merthir* (Julius) *et Aaron* (the *martyrium* of Julius and Aaron).[6] Its siting corresponds to the classic pattern of the grave of a Christian martyr in the cemetery outside the city walls and on the Rhineland excavation has revealed in several such cases a sequence of martyrs' grave, Roman *martyrium*, early chapel, later church and medieval abbey following each other.[7] It is very possible that at Caerleon a Roman *martyrium* could have become by the sixth century a *Merthyr Julii et Aaron* known to Gildas and which served as the basis of his brief statement about the two martyrs.

A considerable number of Romano-British towns have produced archaeological evidence for the presence of Christian believers, usually in the form of objects bearing the Christian chi-rho monogram. In the case of Caerwent, such evidence appeared in 1961, when Mr George Boon of the National Museum of Wales was re-examining a late fourth century group of pottery and metal vessels found in 1906 in a Roman house at Caerwent and now preserved in Newport Museum. He noticed a lightly incised *graffito* on the underside of the base of a pewter bowl from this group, partly concealed by a thin layer of powdery oxide from the corrosion of the metal. When this was removed, the *graffito* proved to be a chi-rho monogram.[8] The group of vessels had been found concealed in a pit in a courtyard of the Roman house. A large pottery jar had been buried in the pit and inside it were two pewter vessels (including the one with the chi-rho monogram), five pottery vessels, a knife and an iron hook, which may be a meat-hook or possibly a suspension hook for a lamp. An inverted mixing bowl had been placed over the mouth of the large jar and, according to the original account, sealed down with mortar. It was difficult to avoid the conclusion that the whole group had been deliberately concealed, possibly to prevent the vessels from being put to base uses after having been used in a religious ceremony. Possibly the group relates to the early Christian *agape* or church supper, an evening service held in a private house, whose order of service opens with the lighting and blessing of the lamps.[9] Even without this hypothesis, the find perhaps provides evidence of a Christian community in Caerwent in the late fourth century, no doubt presided over, like similar urban Churches throughout the Roman world, by a priest bearing the title of bishop.

How far this late Roman Church survived to form the foundation of the post-Roman Church of western Britain is uncertain and it has been suggested that the Welsh Church of the sixth century onwards was a new post-Roman foundation which owed nothing to the Romano-British Church of the fourth century, and was perhaps introduced by Gallic missionaries, much as Ireland was evangelised by the Gaulish trained Briton St Patrick.[10] The problem is too complex to discuss adequately here, but one or two points may be made. Firstly, whilst there is a large and growing body of archaeological evidence for fourth century Christianity in what was to become England, all but the fringes of Wales were devoid of the Roman towns and villas at which Christianity might have established itself. On the other hand, there are one or two faint hints that something of the Roman Christianity for which we have found some evidence at Caerleon and Caerwent may have survived. If we are right that the source of Gildas's information about Julius and Aaron was a *martyrium* outside Caerleon, which was still the subject of popular veneration in his day, this implies the survival of a Christian community, probably centred on Caerwent, for the *Merthyr Julii et Aaron* lies on the line of the Roman road from Caerwent to Caerleon. Similarly, the life of St Sampson, a south Welsh contemporary of Gildas, who died as Abbot of Dol in northern Brittany, depicts St Dubricius visiting a monastery which is probably Llantwit Major, about A.D. 500, to conduct ordinations as diocesan bishop.[11] The extent of a see at this date normally coincided with that of the territory administered from a Roman tribal *Civitas* capital or other town and Llantwit almost certainly lay within the *Civitas* of the Silures, administered from *Venta Silurum* (Caerwent). The core of the Life, to which this tradition belongs, probably dates to about A.D. 610 and if the writer was not merely reflecting current Merovingian practice of his own time it could suggest the survival of an organised sub-Roman church in south-east Wales.

Any such survival would have been confined to a limited area in the Romanised coastal plain of Gwent and South Glamorgan and for the remainder of Wales we have to turn to the series of about 140 latin inscribed memorial stones (ie tombstones) of the fifth to seventh centuries which form our main source of material evidence for the Christianisation of Wales.[12] Their distribution is weighted towards the west of Wales, with, (including stones carrying inscriptions in the Irish ogams script), 36 stones in Pembrokeshire, 22 in Carmarthenshire, 19 in Brecknockshire, 9 in Glamorgan and 1 in western Herefordshire. Their absence in the most Romanised areas of Gwent and lowland Glamorgan is striking. The forms of the inscriptions vary. In the south-west, particularly in Pembrokeshire, they normally take the form of A filius B (A son of B) e.g. MACCATRENI FILI CATOMAGLI (Maccatrenus son of Catomaglus—E.C.M.W. 297 from Brawdy, Pembs.). A third of the Pembrokeshire stones are bilingual with parallel Irish (ogam) and latin texts, as are a quarter of the Carmarthenshire stones, whilst a number of the personal names on the stones are Irish, e.g. Maccatrenus. In North Wales, ogam inscriptions are rare (2 on a total of 45 stones) and the most common form of inscription reads e.g. CVNOGVSI HIC IACIT—(the stone) of Cunogusus, Here he lies— E.C.M.W. 9 from Llanfaelog in Anglesey. In South East Wales, with which we shall be mainly concerned, the prevalent formula combines the Filius of Dyfed with the Hic Iacet of Gwynedd—e.g. CATACVS HIC IACIT FILIVS TEGERNACVS—E.C.M.W. 54 from Llanvihangel Cwmdu in Brecknockshire. The formula HIC IACIT (a late Roman vulgar Latin form of the more correct HIC IACET) links our memorial inscriptions with those of post-Roman Gaul, where the same formula was in use in the Rhône Valley for the brief period c. A.D. 420-50, after which it was replaced by other and longer formulae. There are a few Hic Iacet inscriptions in western Gaul, in the area between Bordeaux and Nantes. These are not closely dated like some of the Rhône Valley stones, but probably provide the link between the latter area and Britain.[13] Links between western Gaul and western Britain in the sixth and seventh centuries are independently shown by finds of western French pottery on sites like Dinas Powys near Cardiff.[14]

Four of these Early Christian memorial stones once stood in the upper Taff valley above Merthyr, close to the line of the present

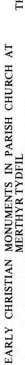

EARLY CHRISTIAN MONUMENTS IN PARISH CHURCH AT
MERTHYR TYDFIL
Artbeu stone on left—Annicius stone on right
(See Jeremy K. Knight, Section 8)

THE MEMORIAL STONES IN THE ADJACENT ILLUSTRATION
WITH THE CROSS AND LETTERS TRACED IN CHALK
(See Jeremy K. Knight, Section 8)

BUST OF THOMAS STEPHENS BY JOSEPH EDWARDS
(See Margaret Taylor, Section 11)

MERTHYR TYDFIL, SATURDAY.

A NATIONAL APPEAL.

ISSUED UNDER THE AUTHORITY OF HIS MAJESTY'S GOVERNMENT.

VOLUNTEERS

URGENTLY REQUIRED.

MEN, WOMEN AND CHILDREN MUST BE FED.

ESSENTIAL SERVICE MUST BE MAINTAINED.

For these PURPOSES VOLUNTEERS are NEEDED.

ARE YOU PREPARED TO SERVE? IF SO, GIVE IN YOUR NAME TO-DAY.

You will be called upon in your turn. Arrangements for Pay will be made according to duties Performed.

REGISTER YOUR NAME TO-DAY AT—

Milbourne Chambers, (First Floor)

(The Local Volunteer Recruiting Office)

Glebeland Street, Merthyr Tydfil.

FRANK T. JAMES,

Chairman of Volunteer Service Committee.

VOLUNTEER SERVICE COMMITTEE.

Vice-chairman for Recruiting.

ABERDARE: Major R. D. Williams, 3, High-street, Aberdare,
LLWYN VALE: Mr. Bert Thomas, Magistrate, Llwyn Vale,

APPLICATION FORM.

Name (Surname first) _____
Address _____
_____
Present Employment _____
Work volunteered for (in order of choice) _____
(1) _____
(2) _____
(3) _____

With acknowledgements to the Merthyr Express – 8 May, 1925
Appeal for volunteers during the General Strike.
(See Huw Williams, Section 10)

Merthyr to Brecon road. As they, and a few others like them, are virtually our only source of information on the people of the Merthyr region in the early Christian period, it is worth looking at them more closely. To understand their setting, we must first look at the topography of the valley.

On its eastern side, a series of streams run down from the high moorland ridge along narrow valleys. From north to south, the most significant of these valleys are the Nant Crew, the Nant Ddu, the Nant Wern-Ddu or Cwm Llysiog, the Nant Gwineu and the Nant Car. The topography of the valley bottom has been much altered by the series of reservoirs which now dominate it, together with their attendant works and belts of conifers, but earlier editions of the 6 inch Ordnance Survey map show that there was once a quite extensive area of enclosed agricultural land along the valley bottom. Some of this still survives above the road, which runs a little below the boundary between the enclosed land and the barren moorland slopes. A series of farms once stood alongside this road, near the points where it crosses the stream valleys. These were mostly demolished when the reservoirs were built, but are shown on the earlier O.S. maps. They enjoyed the shelter of the stream valleys and could use the streams for watering their stock, whilst they were also well placed to exploit both the enclosed farmlands in the valley and the seasonal grazing on the open moorland. The sixth century memorial stones were all found in or near one of these farm buildings, normally re-used as gateposts or lintels.

The farm of Aber-Car stood (until the building of the Llwyn-on reservoir) at the point where the road crossed the Nant Car brook (Grid Ref. SO 00851259—Westwood's statement in *Lapidarium Walliae* p.64 that it stood 100 yds north of the 13th milestone from Brecon is a slip—this should read 300 yds north of the 14th milestone). The 1905 6 inch O.S. map shows its buildings clearly, including the barn and cow house north of the stream on one of whose lintels Iolo Morgannwg first noticed the Anniccius inscription (E.C.M.W. 41), which reads ANNICCI FILIVS . . . HIC IACIT TECVRI IN HOC TVMVLO. *The (monument of) the son of Anniccius. Here lies Tecurus in this tomb.* The site of the Farm now lies under the belt of conifers flanking the road. The stone was removed to Merthyr by Charles Wilkins and set up on his lawn at Springfield, together with a fragment of a second inscription which he had found built into the farm buildings reading . . ETA FILI(A) . . . *eta the daughter of . . .* (E.C.M.W. 41). Sometime after 1885, the Anniccius stone was moved to St Tydfil's church, where it is now fixed to the interior wall near the pulpit, but it is not known whether the . . . eta stone was ever moved, for nothing has been heard of it since 1885.[15]

The Nant-Ddu stone (E.C.M.W. 66) has a somewhat similar history to the Aber Car fragment. It was first seen by Theophilus Jones, the historian of Brecknockshire, in use as a gate-post "within a 100 yards of the twelfth milestone on the turnpike road from Brecknock to Merthyr" (i.e. near SO 00231503, close to the point where the Nant

Ddu brook crosses the road). It was later moved to Merthyr with (apparently) the intention of placing it in the Museum of the Royal Institution at Swansea, but it seems to have been hidden (or according to one account broken up) to prevent its removal to Swansea and though Charles Wilkins claimed to have traced it to a brewery, it has vanished as completely as the other. It read . . . TIRI (FILI)VS CATIRI. (The monument of) . . . tirus, the son of Catirus.[16]

In 1957, during an archaeological survey of the valley, Mr Derek Webley discovered a fourth inscribed stone, re-used as a gatepost in the farmyard of the demolished Nant-Crew farm. It reads (C?) AMAGLI HIC IACIT NI . . . II *Camalgus lies here* . . . and has now been moved into a place of safety in the porch of Cefn Coed church.[17] The previous year, Mr Webley had rediscovered another stone, last seen in 1695, in the Cwm Criban valley, a tributary of the Taff Fechan.[18] This stone is not inscribed in latin, but in an Irish script known as ogams, consisting of a series of notches cut on the angle of a stone, rather on the same lines as the Morse code. This script, possibly developed from a system of sheep tallies, where notches were used for counting flocks of sheep, was invented in the Cork-Waterford area of south-east Ireland, or possibly among Irish colonists in Dyfed in the fourth or early fifth century. Its appearance in Brecknockshire and upland Glamorgan must be due to Irish immigrants, travelling eastwards from Dyfed much as their descendants and fellow country-men of the nineteenth century travelled eastwards from the north Pembrokeshire ports to the South Wales coalfield and its ironworks. The south Welsh uplands are not unlike areas of Southern Ireland and small bodies of Irish immigrants may have been able to settle in unoccupied spots on these uplands and resume a largely pastoral life not unlike that which they had left behind them.

Though the use of the formula *Hic Iacet* suggests that these folk were Christian there is no indication on any of the find spots of the stones that a church at any time stood there. Recent research on the development of churches in western Britain and Ireland has emphasised the way in which many of them grew out of small enclosed cemeteries, perhaps the property of extended family groups, to which a church, often initially of wood, was later added.[19] We have seen how the siting of the recent farm sites in the Taff valley was largely conditioned by the topography of the valley, and though there is no evidence for the original siting of the memorial stones, they were probably not carried a great distance for re-use. We shall probably not be greatly wrong if we visualise the Taff valley in the sixth century with a series of small family farms scattered down it in rather similar sitings to the later farms, each having near it a small burial plot, probably enclosed in some way. Christian Churches and churchyards were still few and widely scattered in this upland country. The medieval parish of Merthyr was of vast size and on Dartmoor, where a similar situation prevailed, great hardship was caused by the necessity of conveying bodies many miles across the moor for burial in the existing churchyards—as a fifteenth century petition for the establishment of a parish church at Widdecombe in the Moor makes clear. The church was not yet powerful or organised enough to insist on this in such remote areas, but the apparent absence of churchyard burial does not mean that the sixth century folk of the Taff valley were not Christians.

There is not room to describe the other fifth to seventh century memorial stones of these uplands in detail. A stone from Hirwaun Common, recorded in a Welsh publication of 1827, has long since disappeared.[20] The memorial of Macaritinus son of Bericius from Seven Sisters is now in Swansea Museum,[21] and the tombstone of an Irish man named *Gluvoca*, inscribed in ogams and with a later cross cut on it is now in Cyfarthfa Castle museum.[22] This originally stood on open moorland at Pen-y-Mynydd near Ystradfellte. Three other stones however can still be seen in their original contexts. Beside the Roman road known as Sarn Helen, running between the forts of Neath and Coelbren, is an impressive standing stone eleven feet high with an inscription commemorating Dervacus, the son of Justus.[23] Dervacus was buried on bare moorland, his stone looking down on a sheltered valley in which his farmstead may have lain, but two stones from Ystradgynlais are in a very different setting. These are built into the fabric of St Cynog's church, having been moved to their present positions when the church was restored sometime after 1876.[24] These two memorials and the large circular churchyard suggest that here we are dealing with one of the early churches served by small groups of monks or canons which served as mission stations in the early period of the Welsh church.

During the seventh century, these latin inscribed memorial stones die out and are replaced by stones usually bearing no more than a simple pecked or incised cross. St Tydfil's Church at Merthyr has one of the rare inscribed examples, bearing the name of one Artbeu, together with a ringed cross. Its date probably lies somewhere between the seventh and ninth centuries.[25] It is now inside the Church, next to the surviving Aber Car stone. There are two similar cross-slabs from Llanwonno Church, on the block of upland between the Aberdare and Rhondda valleys,[26] whilst at Eglwysilan Church above Caerphilly is a slab carrying a figure of a warrior with sword and shield, recalling similar warrior figures of this period from Ireland and Gaul.[27] These stones show how new churches were coming into being in the seventh and eighth centuries, each serving a block of upland between two valleys and usually sited beside the ridgeway running along its crest. From one of these Churches—that which was to become known as the *Martyrium* (or Merthyr) of Tydful, the town of Merthyr Tydfil takes its name.

We have already seen how the graves of the Christian martyrs became centres of devotion for local Christian communities and how the martyrs were regarded as intercessors between God and man. Gradually, this devotion spread from the graves or *martyria* of those who had died during the persecutions to the graves of certain revered bishops (Martin of Tours is an important example), who were regarded as the equals of the martyrs in holiness and as intercessors. From these bishops, the practice spread to the graves of monks, priests, hermits, holy men (and women), as localities from one end of the Christian world to the other sought divine protectors for their own local community. We know nothing of Tudfil, save much later legends of no historical worth, but the devotion which grew up around her (or indeed his) martyrium was only one local manifestation of a process familiar throughout the Early Christian world.

1. The full text of the original letter is now lost. An abridged version survives in Eusebius *Historia Ecclesiastica* Book V, 1-3. A translation is available in the Penguin Classics series.

2. Bede *Historia Ecclesiastica* I, 18.

3. W. Levison "St Alban and St Albans" *Antiquity* 15 (1941), 337-50. For the date and origin of the *Passio Albini* see Levison 344-50.

4. Gildas *De Excidio Britanniae* 10.

5. Levison, op. cit 340-42.

6. J. G. Evans and J. Rhys (edd) *The Text of the Book of Llan Dâv* (Oxford 1893), p225 (partial translation on p377).

7. For a summary of this evidence, with references, see C. A. Raleigh Radford in *Christianity in Britain 300-700* ed. M. W. Barley and R. P. C. Ranson, (Leicester 1968), 31-5.

8. G. C. Boon "A Christian monogram at Caerwent" *Bulletin of the Board of Celtic Studies* 19 part 4 (May 1972), 338-44.

9. On the *agape* see J. A. Jungmann *The Early Liturgy to the Time of Gregory the Great* (trans. F. A. Brunner, London 1960), 107.

10. For some recent expressions of such views see e.g. Kenneth Painter "Villas and Christianity in Roman Britain" in *Prehistoric and Roman Studies Commemorating the Opening of the Department of Prehistoric and Romano-British Antiquities* (of the British Museum) (ed G. de Sieveking, London 1971), p167, where the faith of the post-Roman folk of the Celtic speaking West is described as "an entirely new affair, unconnected with . . . fourth century Christianity" or Professor Emrys Bowen *Saints, Seaways and Settlements in the Celtic Lands* (Cardiff 1969) where the introduction of Christianity to post-Roman Wales is attributed to Gaulish missionaries.

11. The text of the Life of St Sampson was published by R. Fawtier *La Vie de S. Sampson* (Paris 1912). There is an English translation by T. Taylor *The Life of St Sampson of Dol* (London 1925).

12. V. E. Nash-Williams *The Early Christian Monuments of Wales* (Cardiff 1950—hereafter abbreviated E.C.M.W.). This is the standard and authoritative work. A full bibliography of individual

stones, also by Nash-Williams, appeared in the *Bulletin of the Board of Celtic Studies* 8 part 1 (Nov. 1935) 62-84 (counties alphabetically from Anglesey to Flintshire) and 8 part 2 (May 1936), 161-88 (Glamorgan to Radnor).

13. The French stones were published by Edmond Le Blant in *Inscriptions Chrétiennes de la Gaule Antérieures au VIIIe Siecle* (Paris, 2 vols, 1856 and 1865) and *Nouveau Receuil des Inscriptions Chretiennes de la Gaule* (Paris 1892). These are difficult books to obtain and most of the Rhône Valley stones will also be found in F. Cabrol and H. Leclerq *Dictionnaire d'Archaeologie Chrétienne et de Liturgie* Vol 10, 1-81 (article "Lyon") and Vol 15, 37-9 (article "Vienne").

14. L. Alcock *Dinas Powis, An Iron Age, Dark Age and Early Medieval Settlement in Glamorgan* (Cardiff 1963); C. Thomas "Imported Pottery in Dark Age Western Britain" *Medieval Archaeology* 3 (1959), 89-111.

15. The story of the Aber-Car stones can be followed in *Archaeologia Cambrensis* 1853, p. 332; 1858 p. 162; 1886 p. 93; 1901 p. 61. See also J. A. Westwood *Lapidarium Walliae* (Oxford 1876-9), p. 64.

16. Theophilus Jones *History of Brecknockshire* (Brecon 1805-9), ii, p. 624; J. A. Westwood *Arch. Camb.* 1853, 332 and *Lapidarium Walliae* 54-5; Charles Wilkins *Arch. Camb.* 1886, 94.

17. D. Webley "The Nant Crew Stone: A New Discovery" *Arch. Camb.* 1958, 123-4.

18. D. Webley "The Ystrad Ogam Stone, A Rediscovery" *Arch. Camb.* 1957, 118-120.

19. Charles Thomas *The Early Christian Archaeology of North Britain* (Oxford 1971), 68-90. For two important excavations of early church sites see M. J. O'Kelly "Church Island near Valencia, Co. Kerry" *Proceedings of the Royal Irish Academy* 59C. (1958), 57-136 and Charles Thomas "An Early Christian Cemetery and Chapel of Ardwall Isle, Kirkcudbright" Medieval Archaeology II (1967), 127-88.

20. Royal Commission on Ancient Monuments (Wales) *Inventory of the Monuments of Glamorganshire, III, The Early Christian Period* p. 39. The inscription appears to have read ERECOR(I) (?Fili) MAGLORICVNI HIC IACIT.

21. E.C.M.W. 268. See also Aileen Fox "The Siting of some Inscribed Stones of the Dark Ages in Glamorgan and Breconshire" *Arch. Camb.* 1939, 30-41, particularly pp. 32-3.

22. E.C.M.W. 74, first recorded in *Archaeologia* 1777, p. 24.

23. E.C.M.W. 73. See also *Arch. Camb.* 1939, 31-2 and 1940, 210-16.

24. E.C.M.W. 75-6, *Arch. Camb.* 1855 p. 6, 1886 p. 341. *Lapidarium Walliae* p. 63. The letters of No. 75 were worked over and deepened sometime between its discovery and the taking of the photograph in E.C.M.W. The person responsible for this missed the last two letters, which have therefore been overlooked by later writers. The inscription reads ADIVNETI (the stone of Adiunetus) not ADIVNE as in E.C.M.W. No. 75 was originally built in the steps of an external staircase on the south side of the church, No. 76 into the exterior of the east wall of the church.

25. E.C.M.W. 248. The stone was first noted when built into the east gable wall of the church, prior to its restoration.

26. E.C.M.W. 227 and R.C.A.M. op. cit. in note 20, pp. 43-4, Nos. 889 and 890.

27. E.C.M.W. 195—dug up in Eglwysilan churchyard in the summer of 1904.

9. ALUN MORGAN

EARNING A LIVING.

INDUSTRIAL DEVELOPMENT 1918 TO 1939

The years between the two world wars witnessed economic depression in many corners of the world. The severity of this varied in both length of time and depth of distress. As far as Britain was concerned few, if any, areas suffered as prolonged or severe depression as did Merthyr Tydfil. Even basic statistics convey this distress in powerful fashion. Between 1921 and 1939 almost 20,000 people left the Merthyr Borough and yet unemployment *within* the area trebled between 1921 and 1935.

For the majority of its population life in Merthyr had never been easy as far as making economic ends meet was concerned. From its sprawling, tumultuous birth in the early industrial revolution local people had struggled with often appalling social conditions and the vicissitudes of economic 'boom' and 'slump' which so characterised nineteenth and twentieth century capitalism.

However no slump ever hit Merthyr with such severity as that which began in earnest in the mid nineteen twenties but whose roots were a lot further back. A slump which by 1935 created an unemployment rate among adult males of 60% and in one part of the Borough, Dowlais, 80%.

The causes of this misery were a combination of world wide economic factors, inherent weaknesses in the British economy and chronic weaknesses in Merthyr's own industrial structure.

These local weaknesses were in many ways an exaggerated form of Britain's economic weaknesses—a dependance on a few labour intensive industries whose outdated and uncompetitive organisation made them easy prey to any economic reverse let alone the catastrophes which were to punctuate the inter-war years.

In 'Merthyr Politics' (ed. Glanmor Williams) Joe England writes of Merthyr's economic base "Merthyr at the beginning of the century was living on borrowed time". Thus by 1900 the twin pillars of steel and coal, on which the town's economic wellbeing totally depended were in decline at a local level. The local ore deposits were proving inadequate in both quality and quantity. For every ton of local ore used in the industry of the area two tons were being imported from Spain. The coal industry was also in difficulties especially in the northern half of the Borough around Dowlais and Penydarren. In these parts many of the pits were small, old-fashioned and unproductive by the standards set through the newer, larger pits elsewhere in South Wales. Besides this the problems of attracting newer forms of industry to the area were considerable largely due to a communications network which was reasonable in relation to Cardiff but terribly inadequate to other areas of England and Wales.

Symptoms of economic decline had been appearing since the turn of the century. In 1891 part of the huge Dowlais steel works was moved to Cardiff and 1910 the once mighty Cyfarthfa iron and steel works was closed altogether. Several small levels around Dowlais also closed down. Suddenly the outbreak of war in 1914, and its consequent demands for massive quantities of steel and coal, breathed new life into the area's failing economy. Production was stepped up dramatically at Dowlais steel works and Cyfarthfa re-opened.

In November, 1918, the armistice at last ended the carnage of war and Europe considered its far from settled future. One of the most immediate consequences was a sudden drop in demand for the raw materials of war and subsequent slump in steel and coal producing areas. By 1921 Merthyr was back in the throes of economic distress; although later withdrawn 3,000 steelworkers at Dowlais were given a month's notice. But once again international events drew a veil over the reality of Merthyr's decrepid economic system and its grim future. These events were a long strike in the major American coalfields in 1922 which, following on the heels of coal shortages caused by the 1921 Lock-Out in the British coalfields, created a large but temporary demand for Welsh coal and, following on, the occupation of the rich German Ruhr coalfield by French forces over Germany defaulting on payment of war reparations in 1924—once again this boosted demand for Welsh coal. Thus in that year 2,500,000 tons of coal were mined in the local mines which provided employment for 14,000 men—over 6,000 of these would be out of a job by 1931. By this time also over 4,000 steelworkers had lost their living.

The cause of this was a series of staggering economic blows which delivered a critical impact on Merthyr. The first came in 1925 when the Chancellor of the Exchequer, Winston Churchill, decided to place Britain back onto the system which valued currency in relation to gold, the Gold Standard. The result was a quick rise in the cost of British raw materials and manufacturing goods thus causing an equally sudden drop in demand.

The second blow came with the 1926 Miners' Lock-Out which lasted six months and began with that enigmatic nine days, the General Strike. A principal feature of the Coalowners case *before* the lock-out was that wage cuts were necessary to save many pits. After six months without profit the owners acted ruthlessly by deciding to keep many small pits closed permanently—in this aspect Dowlais and Penydarren suffered badly. In the south of the Borough at Merthyr Vale and Treharris there was no real danger of the big, productive collieries closing down but in these the increased mechanisation, coupled with fairly low demand, meant a reduction in the number of men they employed.

A further setback came with the final closure of the Cyfarthfa works in 1928 and in this localised gloom the collapse of the American Stockmarket in 1929 must have seemed the final blow. The worldwide effects of this collapse were quickly manifest and they brought depression to hitherto relatively prosperous areas—what it would bring to already depressed areas such as Merthyr is not hard to imagine. In October, 1930, the main section of the Dowlais works were closed with the loss of 3,000 jobs. This event almost shattered Dowlais, a town which largely owed its very development to the steel works. A person with a job became a rarity in the village.

To those who lost jobs prospects of finding another in this area made up solely of depressed industries were extremely remote. With unemployment in the main industries rising steeply a chain reaction now set in which resulted in the many service industries suffering due to the decline in spending power by the town's work force and their families. Thus once flourishing shops, cafes, pubs and other places of service or entertainment sacked workers to cut losses while some closed down completely. The famed entertainment centres of the Temperance Hall and Theatre Royal played to dwindling audiences whilst the football team lost its place in the Third Division (South). Beset by rising costs and small crowds it conceded a still-intact record 135 goals in its Final League season—somehow symbolic of the town's fortunes.

Merthyr, then, was a victim of unplanned, unregulated, rapacious economic growth (which had brought problems enough in itself) which had now quickly turned in to catastrophic decline.

A particularly critical factor in this economic slump was female unemployment. Although the historical impression of the period persists with notions of "a woman's place being at home" around 3,500 women were employed in Merthyr according to figures compiled in 1931. Their occupations were mainly as maids, cooks and general cleaners in domestic service or as assistants in shops, cafes and public houses. As economic hardship grew many "service" shops were lost and for considerable numbers of households females joined males in the out-of-work queues. For increasing numbers of Merthyr people the choice they faced was becoming ever more stark—accept long-term unemployment or move away. With the great worldwide depression, triggered off by the Wall Street Crash of 1929, still intense neither migration nor emigration offered any real hope of relief.

To the growing army of unemployed relief was small. The 1928 rate of payment for an unemployed man was £1-3-0 (£1.15) plus 2/- (10p) for each of his children not in work. From 1931 the rate of benefit was calculated by examining all possible sources of revenue available to the claimant—this was the so-called Means Test, it was hated by nearly all subjected to it, many finding the whole process humiliating and distressing. Ironically since the end of World War I South Wales had increasingly become an area of declining wage levels. For those in employment, a reflection of the sharp drop in the area's economic fortunes. Thus in 1930 a miner in the Merthyr area averaged around £2.00 per week in wages and some miners from the area who found work in pits some distance away discovered that after travelling expenses had been accounted for they were actually *worse off* than if they were receiving unemployment benefit.

Unquestionably a weekly income of £2.00 was, by 1931, totally inadequate to meet the basic needs of a family unit in the way of sufficient nutrition, warmth, shelter and clothing. Giving evidence to the 1935 Royal Commission, set up to examine the town's plight, the Mayor of Merthyr stressed that the condition of many employed was little better than the unemployed. Nevertheless jobs were often coveted and employers always had the massive bargaining weapon of a half-dozen men outside the works ready for any job inside.

The consequences of such poverty as existed in inter-war Merthyr were grimly predictable. In 1928 a correspondent of 'The Times' wrote on the plight of the unemployed in South Wales : "As the months go by first boots and clothing wear out and then bedclothes and utensils ... men and women are starving; not starving outright, but gradually wasting away through lack of nourishment." Social deprivation was rife. The number of women in the 15-35 age groups suffering from tuberculosis was more than double the rate in the rest of England and Wales (apart from a couple of equally unfortunate and deprived communities in the north-east of England). One in five infants died before the age of five, the young aged before their time and the old suffered chronically. In 1935 a report by Merthyr Borough Health Officer, Dr. Stephens, vividly portrayed the condition of Merthyr's school-children; it stated firmly that the disease caused by lack of proper nourishment, malnutrition, was alarmingly prevalent. A bone disease caused by lack of nourishment, rickets, was rampant and diseases such as tuberculosis, diphtheria and pneumonia claimed many lives. Significantly the report stated that these diseases were in marked decline in most areas of Britain but in Merthyr they were, in some cases, on the increase.

The effect of the economic depression upon the physical appearance of the town was also alarming. The intense hardship forced many shops to close, buildings became even shabbier and dilapidated. In addition government regulations stipulated that money paid to the unemployed had to be found by the local authority. This proved an impossible burden for Merthyr's Council—in 1932-33 the amount paid in unemployment benefit was more than *the whole* of the Council's services had cost in 1919. To raise the vast amounts of money the Council needed the rates on property had to be constantly raised. By 1937 these were the highest in Britain. However because of the depression the value of property *dropped* sharply throughout the 1930's thus creating a vicious circle. Thus by 1938 the value placed on all property in the Borough amounted to just £200,000—unemployment benefit alone cost *twice* that amount. There was no alternative but to appeal to central government for financial help. Some grants were given but these were not very large. The Council was spending virtually all its resources on meeting the cost of unemployment relief with the result that the rest of the Authority's services were bound to suffer; rubbish gathered, buildings became shoddy, grass grew in the streets, street lighting became almost non-existent.

The town was therefore on its knees. After 1935 the general economic condition of Britain began to improve considerably, however, the shattered, economic communities such as Merthyr and Jarrow* saw no benefit from this—if anything their plight became worse. In this desperate situation the political reactions and activities of the area are worth examining. Up until the 1922 election a Liberal candidate had always topped the poll (with the exception of the 1915 bye-election when the 'Britisher' candidate, C. P. Stanton had won). From 1900 to 1915 James Keir Hardie, the Labour candidate, also represented the boroughs of Merthyr and Aberdare as the second of its two M.P.'s.

From 1918 Merthyr became a single-member constituency separated from Aberdare and in 1922 the Independent Labour Party (I.L.P.) had won it in the shape of Richard Wallhead—a position he held in the 1924, 1925, 1929 and 1931 elections. Low wages, terrible social conditions, growing unemployment and the promise of a better alternative for society were strong reasons for the growth of socialist support in the Merthyr area.

In 1934, just about at the peak of Merthyr's misfortunes, Wallhead's death necessitated a bye-election. At this there were four candidates; J. Victor Evans (Liberal), S. O. Davies (Labour), J. Campbell-Stephens (I.L.P.) and Wal Hannington (Communist). It was a fiercely contested campaign with each candidate forcefully putting forward alternatives to solve the local and national economic crisis. The result was victory for the Dowlais Miners' Agent, S. O. Davies, standing on a platform of "Constructive Socialism versus Reaction", he polled over 18,000 votes. The Liberal candidate finished some 8,000 behind this total while the I.L.P. and Communist candidates polled just over 3,000 apiece and each lost their deposit. The political indicators of this result were clear. The Liberal Party, once a most formidable political power in the area, was in decline. Its local organisation was a shadow of its recent past and its policies seemed to no longer offer either appeal or relevance for the depressed working class. Another powerful political force, the I.L.P., was also in considerable trouble—sandwiched between the trades union backed Labour Party and the new, militant socialism of the Com-munist Party. This movement had fielded a very strong candidate, Wal Hannington. He had shown a keen sympathy and understanding of the economic plight of places such as Merthyr in his book 'The Problem of the Distressed Areas' and was also national organiser of the National Union of Unemployed Workers. Despite this Mr. Hannington lost his deposit and illustrated that despite their deprived condition many Merthyr people were unwilling to support ideas of revolutionary social-ism and shied away from it as too much of a "shot in the dark". More than anything the result was a triumph for the left-wing parliamentary socialism identified with people such as Aneurin Bevan, M.P. for Ebbw Vale, and S. O. Davies himself.

Politics, of course, is not simply about elections but involves many

---

*The North-East town where the closure of the shipyards had caused unemploy-ment and distress comparable only to Dowlais.

other areas of activity also. The Communist Party was most active in organising and representing the grievances of the unemployed, there was a broad left-wing opposition to the Means Test and other policies felt to be detrimental to the area's already awful condition. The Conservative Party was by far the most powerful in Parliament but did not contest an election in Merthyr in the nineteen thirties. Far more to the extreme right the Blackshirts formed a local group led by ex-Communist, ex-wrestler, Arthur Eyles. This small group made their presence felt in demonstrations, marches and fights with left-wing groups but their appeal to Merthyr people was never more than extremely limited and their presence was short-lived. In the political agitation of the nineteen thirties Merthyr was a discernible part. Although the length and depth of economic depression was such that many must have become imbued with a sense of fatalistic apathy there is enough evidence to suggest that significant numbers of Merthyr people questioned and protested against their condition. There were, for instance, sizeable Merthyr contingents on the Hunger Marches from South Wales to London; blacklegging in nearby collieries was strongly resisted by groups of local trades unionists and activists of the N.U.U.W. Some men, mainly from the Communist Party, took their beliefs and struggle from Merthyr to Spain. There they formed part of the International Brigade fighting the rebellion led by Franco. The townspeople served notice that they were not about to tolerate an erosion of their already appalling living standards when massive demonstrations were staged against new Social Security regulations, introduced in 1935 — one large rally erupted into angry disorder and windows of the Unemployment Assistance Board (U.A.B.) at Isgoed House, Pontmorlais, were stoned. These rallies were part of a nationwide campaign against the new regulations which were withdrawn hastily after a few weeks.

The monarchy, however, still seemed to command the loyalty and respect of most. The Silver Jubilee of 1935 was celebrated with enthusiasm locally as Merthyr festooned its dilapidated shell with flags and bunting. Possibly Merthyr people were simply grateful to have any opportunity to briefly forget their troubles and celebrate. In 1936 Edward, Prince of Wales, visited Merthyr and Dowlais. Large crowds saw him gaze almost in disbelief at the closed shops, the derelict appearance of the area and the idle expanse of the huge Dowlais works through which his parents had entered triumphantly via the mighty Coal Arch some twenty-five years previously. His utterance "Something must be done" has lived on as possibly the understatement of the thirties—albeit a sincere one.

It would be misleading to state that nothing was done to attempt to alleviate the misery of communities like Merthyr. New industrial development was dreadfully hampered because of the extremely high rates, the run-down appearance of the area and a suspicion (unfounded as it turned out) that long years of unemployment would create a lazy, inefficient labour force.

Some initiatives came from central government, at this time in the

116

hands of a Conservative dominated coalition, the National Government. It had never seemed able to understand the causes and the nature of the economic crisis and offered little other than advocacy of patience to solve it. However the government could hardly fail to appreciate that certain areas of Britain were heavily over-dependant on the old, staple industries of coal, steel textiles and heavy engineering—South Wales was one of these areas.

Slowly but surely areas of Britain such as the West Midlands and the South-East began to climb out of economic depression, basing this recovery on newer forms of industry such as electronics, domestic appliance manufacture, vehicle construction, chemicals and light engineering. However in the areas of traditional heavy industry such as Merthyr no industrial growth took place whatsoever. Merthyr's link with these areas of economic growth was simply one of exporting, unloading its population into them. Thousands left for London, Birmingham, Coventry, Leamington, Slough and other corners of England. While the economic plight of these areas improved that of Merthyr remained desperate—its whole economic foundation had collapsed in ruins.

To such areas governments, between 1934 and 1939, attempted to provide some forms of economic relief. None were to prove very successful. At first they merely relied on persuasion. A circular was issued by the Board of Trade in 1934 asking firms if they would contemplate establishing branches in areas worst hit by depression—5,829 circulars were sent out and 1,313 firms replied. Of these 12 firms said they would establish branches. The next step was the creation by government of 'Distressed Area' status for certain regions of which Merthyr was one. This provided for various forms of government assistance but these were on a relatively small scale and the very title 'Distressed Area' seemed to create a deterrent effect on prospective industrial development.

A third, more positive development was the creation of trading estates by government. Treforest was the largest one near to Merthyr and although it did provide some new employment the scale of local unemployment in Merthyr and regional unemployment in South Wales meant that this was a drop in the ocean.

Merthyr's problems were so acute that in 1935 a Royal Commission was set up to investigate the area's problems and attempt to advocate some solutions for them. The Mayor of Merthyr Tydfil gave lengthly evidence to it in which he pointed a vivid, accurate portrait of gloom and despair. In addition he outlined plans drawn up by the local authority to bring new work to the area; these included moving a section of the Woolwich Arsenal to Merthyr. However the Commission rejected these plans and its Report recommended that Merthyr lose its County Borough status so that the burden of finding money to supply unemployment benefit would be lifted from its present local base to the wider one of the County of Glamorgan. Implicit in this thinking is the assumption that any short-term improvement in Merthyr's economic position was out of the question. The Report was, in short, little help to a town facing catastrophe.

Those who stayed in the area wanted more drastic action than this. The constituency M.P. delivered an angry attack on the Prime Minister during a debate in the House of Commons soon after the Report was published. He asked "Does the Right Honourable Gentleman know that the conviction is spreading in South Wales today that Government has deliberately abandoned it to its poverty and destruction? ... We are not accepting quietly the destruction of the coalfield and the crucifixion of a little nation." All the Government could point to was its *Special Areas* scheme offering incentives to firms wishing to establish plants in the depressed regions. Between 1932 and 1938 this resulted in 235 factories being set up in the depressed areas—in the same period over 2,000 were set up in the Midlands and Greater London—none were set up in the Borough of Merthyr Tydfil.

The increasingly menacing sound of Fascist jackboots on the European continent led to a slow rearmament programme getting under way in Britain from 1935 onwards. This brought some relief to South Wales, the main example being the re-opening of the strip-mill at Ebbw Vale in 1938 and increased production of coal and steel elsewhere. But for Merthyr's small coal levels and derelict steel works there was simply no chance of a new lease of life. Their closure was permanent and new jobs in the surrounding valleys were quickly snapped up by people from them for they too had known long years of unemployment. *The fact was that even in a depressed region Merthyr's situation was critical even in comparison with its far from fortunate neighbours*—throughout the depression its unemployment levels were around 15% higher than the rest of the Glamorgan valleys and were only matched by the stricken communities of Jarrow and the Gwent towns of Blaina, Brynmawr and Nantyglo. In these places only the pawn-shops prospered.

By the beginning of 1939 there was no sign of any real improvement in Merthyr's sorry plight. Because of this the Parliamentary Economic and Political Planning Unit issued a report in March, 1939, in which they virtually advocated killing the town off quietly. This document, Report on the Location of Industry, looked at the town's 7,000 plus unemployed male labour force and its migration figure of hundreds *per month* and concluded : "The sole justification for a large town on this site has been the abundance of profitable coal and iron deposits, and no detached person would be likely to favour going to live at such a spot after the minerals have ceased to make it worthwhile." The Unit advocated *that the town be completely abandoned and that its population be moved in full to the coast or to the Usk valley.*

Thus one reputable body was already counting Merthyr out after its fight with economic misfortune. But ironically the supreme element of destruction, war brought fresh life to this economic corpse. With the commencement of war in September, 1939, Merthyr re-emerged as an industrial centre because its remote, hilly geographic situation may have been a serious handicap to new industrial peace-time development it was extremely useful as protection for industry against air-raids. In addition the locality had large areas of vacant industrial sites on which construction and operation of munition factories could take place immediately. On top of this there was a large pool of readily available male and female labour while the vastly increased demands of war for both coal and steel would bring new employment opportunities in nearby pits and the steel works at Ebbw Vale and Cardiff.

The consequence of this was that by 1941 male unemployment in the Merthyr Borough had fallen to just over 1,000 and many women found work in the newly opened factories (it must be remembered that one factor in the dramatic fall in male unemployment, 1939-41, was that many young men had been called up to the forces). After fifteen years of unemployment many people were at work again, days spent aimlessly on street corners or in pool halls, days at attempting to live off a pittance and fighting off hunger—these days were now a thing of the past. However it was clear that only freak conditions resulting from war had brought this improvement. Merthyr still had no economic diversity and no economic base for long term development. Once war and its freak conditions were over it was quite possible that economic dereliction would quickly re-descend upon the town.

The immediate impressions, once war had ended, seemed to confirm these grim predictions. Demand for steel and coal dropped suddenly, munitions factories closed and large numbers of servicemen were demobbed home to seek work. By mid 1946 Merthyr was once again a place of very high unemployment; over 7,000 were out of work and once more hundreds began to leave the area in search of better opportunities.

Crucially, however, there had been a change in political and economic strategy from those of the 1930's. The ideas of parliamentary socialists such as Aneurin Bevan and S. O. Davies that the State should own certain vital industries and services had become far more widely accepted. Along with this the theories of economist, J. M. Keynes, were now seen as prophetic. These revolved around the notion that governments should not be obsessed with balancing budgets but instead spend to deliberately boost the economy and create employment. The general election of 1945 had brought a surprising but sweeping victory. In the ranks of the new government there were few who did not subscribe to at least one of these viewpoints. The result of this was that swift action was taken to aid troubled areas such as Merthyr. Measures such as The Distribution of Industry Act (1945) and the Town and Country Act (1947) brought new economic hope to the area. Hoovers began an expansion which, with a few stutters, has gone on ever since. New factories were set up by Teddington, O.P. Chocolates, Ceramics, Thorn and Lines Brothers. There was, at least, more economic diversity than ever before and a real prospect of long-term economic growth. By 1951 unemployment was at its lowest level for thirty years.

Economic depression was lifted but such a shattering twenty years leaves more permanent problems and consequences. Merthyr began to recover its confidence—the soccer team revived and became a mighty force in non-league football; the rugby team reformed; shops re-opened alongside new businesses setting up in town. Snooker, boxing, greyhounds and pigeons now became leisure time pastimes instead of the centres of workless, aimless lives. But the depression left a bitter, haunting legacy. The virtual bankruptcy of the borough over such a long period had meant that virtually no scheme of house building, school or hospital development had taken place on any large scale. This left postwar Merthyr with huge problems of re-development. In the extensive schemes that were launched another legacy of the depression is clear—those who put the redevelopment into practice seemed to be full of resentment and hostility toward Merthyr's past. The result has been some extremely necessary social improvement but also a large scale destruction of interesting buildings which formed part of Merthyr's historic heritage.

Since 1951 Merthyr and district has undergone some great physical and social change along with mixed fortunes. Some of the firms who came to the area after the war have since closed, depopulation continues but these problems are on a scale much less serious than in pre-war years. The town has a stability and confidence which certainly suggests that the plans to abandon the town were rather premature and that the economic future of the area is now more certain than at any time this century.

The industrial birth of this community in the late eighteenth century had been a turbulent, tough, sometimes violent one. Gradually factors such as the growth of radical ideas, the rise of non-conformist religion, the growth of State and self-education and the evolvement of working class organisations produced a more stable community base within which the worst degradation, crime and vice of the middle of the nineteenth century had all but disappeared. Merthyr was still a very boisterous community (e.g. in 1975 it was reported that there were 188 convictions for drunkenness while in 1910 there were 1,070 for the same offence). But all the time a more responsible sense of community was developing as virtually a challenge to the dehumanising conditions of industrial society in late Victorian and Edwardian Britain. Despite the extreme severity at the inter-war depression Merthyr and its people did not return to its former violent, racy past but instead displaced a strength at spirit, a strength of community and a belief in humanity which provided a resistance and resilience to the worst indignities of stark economic deprivation. It was this spirit which is Merthyr's greatest triumph from a desperate period in her history—how she emerged battered but fairly intact from a decade which her population came to know simply and expressively as 'The Hungry Thirties'.

Notes

For this article I am particularly grateful to three articles as sources of expert analysis and detailed information. These articles are :—

B. M. Brunt—*The Contemporary Economic Problems of Merthyr Tydfil.* (Merthyr, 1972).

J. W. England—'Merthyr since 1918' in *Merthyr Politics* (ed. Glanmor Williams, Cardiff, 1965).

E. Willis—*Economic Changes in the Borough of Merthyr Tydfil since 1939*. (Merthyr, 1971).

I should also like to express my sincere thanks to Mr. David Bevan, Archivist at University College, Swansea and Mr. Hywel Francis, Tutor-Librarian at the South Wales Miners' Library, U.C. Swansea, for their co-operation in allowing me to study source material of a primary nature.

10. HUW WILLIAMS

MERTHYR TYDFIL AND THE GENERAL STRIKE OF 1926

(Illustration 57)

The first weeks of May 1976 last were remembered and celebrated
as the 50th anniversary of the calling of the General Strike of May,
1926, the single most important event in the industrial history of Great
Britain this century. It lasted for nine days, May 3-12 until the strike
action was called off on unconditional terms by the General Council
of the Trades Union Congress. The miners, the main participants in
the strike were not consulted at the TUC's surrender to the Government, and were to continue their stoppage and remain out of work for
a further seven months until they were almost literally starved back in
the November on the coal owners' terms of lower wages and an
additional working hour from seven to eight per day. It was the biggest
industrial struggle that had ever taken place to that time, the only
general strike to have taken place in this country, and the last official
national miners' strike until those of 1972 and 1974. It was also a
glorious failure, almost inevitable in its results, and, by its end finally
in November, very much an anti-climax for the hopes of so many
people. Within the borough of Merthyr Tydfil, the whole incident was
something of a non-event, a very tame affair which the townfolk took
in their daily stride of life. Perfect peace and order was maintained
throughout the strike period, and there was no violence whatsoever.
Yet every mode of life was affected to some extent by the stoppage,
and Merthyr society was to be profoundly changed by the events and
consequences of that year, 1926.

It was neither a *general* strike—the miners were the majority involved
aided briefly by their fellow unionists—nor was it actually a *strike*, but
rather a lock-out of the men by the coalowners in the face of the
threat of strike action from the miners. Its impact was felt almost
immediately. The town came to an abrupt standstill; buses and railways
stopped running from the morning of the first day, May 4, factories
closed and all the Borough's pits stopped production. The miners
brought their tools up from the pits to be handed in, and were paid
off from their work, and the pit ponies were soon brought to the
surface as well. It was the first sunlight many of them had ever seen
in their lives, and a sure sign that it was going to be a long struggle.
Work though continued on the Taff Fechan reservoir dam at Pontsticill
on the northern outpost of the town, probably forgotten in the heady
days of May, and some large shops did manage to remain open. The
Maypole Dairy Co. Ltd. boasted in the local press after the strike
ended that it had continued trading owing to the loyalty of its staff
throughout the strike. Any transport that there was in the town for
the time of the strike was provided by private vehicles, although there

122

could have been very few cars in the Merthyr of 1926. The owners of cars were asked in an appeal in the *Merthyr Express*, May 8 to get in touch with the Road Transport Officer at Bank Chambers, Merthyr to provide their vehicles for public service in the town. Public transport resumed on the 12th of May when the bus and railway services recommenced.

The national press had been unable to publish during the strike owing to the action of the printers, and, in turn, the usually beefy 24 pages of the *Merthyr Express* were curtailed to a 12 page issue for a fortnight, "produced under the greatest difficulties". The local press was soon under attack from the pro-miners' group, and the Libraries Committee of May 10 requested that certain local papers including the *Express*, the *Western Mail*, which had managed somehow to print throughout the strike, and the *South Wales Echo* be removed from the Borough's libraries, as they were representative of the "black-leg" press. It was decided finally to include all newspapers on the libraries' tables, including the Government's *British Gazette*, then edited by Winston Churchill, and the unions' *British Worker*—to give as full a coverage as possible from all points of view of further developments.

After the strike had been called off life slowly returned to normal from mid May. Those involuntarily laid off work through the strike action of others soon returned, and production resumed slowly again in the Borough. Thus ended the month of May, "a month pregnant with gloom and shameful memories". The strike actual had ended after nine days, but the miners were to stay out for another six months; and it was this prolonged lock-out rather than the nine days which was to be the real test for the people of Merthyr Tydfil.

The issue was about coal: the coalowners had been trying since 1921 to reduce wages as a means of alleviating their losses from the pits. The miners had resisted so far these threats to their livelihood, and by May 1926 were standing firmly behind their slogan, "Not a penny off the pay, not a second on the day". Merthyr's historical legacy producing an insecure economic base after the First World War, almost totally dependent on coal and iron and steel, assured the town of future industrial problems. The post-war dislocation on the national and international economies severely affected Merthyr more so than many other areas. In 1913 over 3 million tons of coal were mined by 13,500 miners within the Borough, a record. By early 1926 local coal-owners were complaining that "there was not one colliery that could possibly make a shilling profit for the next year or two". The year 1925 had proved disappointing, and Merthyr was "one of the grievously striken districts" in Wales. Only 1500 miners were left in employment in the Borough; 8500 were unemployed by the end of 1925. The sheer impact of the strike was therefore greatly lessened in one sense by this fact—that some 12% of the Borough were unemployed even *before* the strike had begun.

Both sides, the Government and the unions, had been preparing for a showdown before May 1926. The Government had held in reserve since 1921 certain provisions under its emergency powers which it now evoked in May 1926. Warships were sent to the major ports about the South Wales coalfield. Under the Organisation for the Maintenance of Supplies (OMS) the Government issued directives throughout the country to ensure the adequate supply of essential services such as food, light, heat, transport, and to recruit a force of volunteer labour to provide these services.

At the beginning of December 1925 Merthyr Council had received from the Ministry of Health contingency plans for maintaining local services in the event of an emergency. A "decentralised organisation" was thus in preparation before 1926, and when the strike became a fact in the May, the Merthyr and District Volunteer Service Committee was set up to administer local arrangements to cope with the stoppage. The Committee was divided into separate offices each with its own duties under a head officer: Frank T. James, Clerk to the Merthyr Poor Law Union was the Chairman; the Food Officer was W. H. P. Shoot; the Road Officer was Isaac Edwards, also President of the Merthyr Tydfil Chamber of Commerce and Trade; and Postal services were under the charge of the town's Postmaster, J. Jones. The *Merthyr Express* May 8 printed a front page "National Appeal issued under the authority of His Majesty's Government" for volunteers to maintain essential services. "Men, women and children must be fed", and local volunteers were asked to apply to the Local Volunteer Recruiting Office, Milbourne Chambers, Glebeland Street, Merthyr. By Thursday, May 6 over 300 local recruits had been enrolled and the numbers, it said, were being augmented hourly. A State of Emergency had been proclaimed, and on May 7 the Government had enacted its Coal Emergency Regulations, whereby the Council was to safeguard coal stocks and provide facilities for their distribution now that the pits were at a standstill. A twelve man committee was thus set up to deal with this issue, and Merthyr's coal merchants were instructed to supply persons with not more than 28 lbs of coal per week. Any infringement of the regulations rendered one liable to prosecution.

Under the Emergency arrangements of the Government in operation from the end of April, the Home Office was also directing local councils to strengthen their existing police forces and make provisions to meet any such demands as may be made upon them. Merthyr Council was urged to establish a first Police Reserve which would complement the regular force if needed. There is no evidence however that such a reserve force was in fact created or that it was ever used to help the regular police in Merthyr. Good order prevailed within the Borough during the strike, and the regular police force coped adequately with the local demands upon it. (Merthyr Watch Committee was even reporting six vacancies in the police force throughout May.) Certainly the Council, and with the advice of the Chief Constable, resisted the pressures of Central directives to recruit more men than was necessary, arguing that they were the better judges of local mood. It was certainly one of the main reasons for the peaceful conduct of the strike.

The nub of strike activity in Merthyr was centred on the Merthyr Trades and District Council, founded in 1900. Together with the Merthyr Council, these two virtually ran affairs in Merthyr during May 1926, and for the several months afterwards into the Summer and Autumn. A Trades Council was the local branch of the Trades Union Congress (TUC) to which it sent representatives. In turn, the local branches of unions were affiliated to the local Trades Council. Fifty-two lodges, three unemployed organisations and 85 delegated and a total of 142 affiliated members belonged at Merthyr. The Merthyr Trades Council had been in readiness for a strike from the April, and had co-opted the Dowlais Co-operative Society, the Troedyrhiw and Merthyr Co-operatives and several union branches in preparation for a struggle.

Recently, a unique historical item of the time has come to light. A *Souvenir* Brochure of the Central Strike Committee of the Merthyr Tydfil Trades Council was found at the TUC Library in London, and has been reprinted in facsimile. This Brochure reveals a sophisticated four-tier strike organisation active in Merthyr in 1926 organised by 56 members on the Central and District Committees. Mr. D. Shankland was the President, there were six central sub-committees dealing with food, finance, communications, intelligence, permits, and sports and entertainments. There were in turn four district strike committees at Treharris, Merthyr Vale and Aberfan, Troedyrhiw and Dowlais, each with its own district strike sub-committees for food, finance, permits and sports and entertainments. So efficiently was the district network operating that the Central Strike Committee, after initially setting up the district system, could afford to meet only in the evenings to receive reports from the district sub-committees.

The Strike consolidated around the local Trades Council and its several strike committees organised food distribution in the town. Transport movements into and out of the town were vetted and only essential supplies to hospitals were allowed through the valleys on issue of permits. Sports and entertainments took over more time as the strike proceeded into the Summer months. A detailed picture of the work of one district strike committee can be gained from the work of the Treharris Strike Committee which was composed of miners, railwaymen and other workmen with the help from colliery officials as well. Employers and employed worked side by side in this respect for the common good of Merthyr's people. In common with the other wards in the Borough, The Treharris Committee issued relief notes for 6/- to "financial members" of the South Wales Miners Federation (SWMF), and issued relief in kind to those who were not entitled to receive assistance from either the Board of Guardians or the Miners' Federation. Treharris Silver Band played concerts in aid of the district relief fund and £310 was collected by various means by early July.

The several miners' meetings held throughout the strike give a fair reflection of the changing mood of the men, from one of solidarity and defiance against the Government and the owners at the beginning of

125

the strike to the realisation of inevitable defeat and awful submission to the owners' and the Government's terms at the end of the long struggle by early November. The local miners' leaders prominent in the dispute were the two agents in the Borough, Noah Ablett, agent for Merthyr district, and S. O. Davies, agent for the separate miners' lodge at Dowlais, "the David and Johnathan of the South Wales coal-field" as the *Merthyr Express* (never very sympathetic towards Ablett and Davies) referred to them. Both men were "hardliners". Ablett was one of the foremost Marxists in the South Wales coalfield; educated at Ruskin College, Oxford, he was part author of the famous radical pamphlet *The Miners' Next Step* (1912). The younger S. O. Davies had also been making a name for himself throughout the coalfield, and by 1926 was Vice-President of the South Wales Miners Federation. He later became Labour MP for the Merthyr Tydfil constituency from 1934 until his death in 1972. Both men in their several speeches urged the miners to stand firm and resist a return to work on the owners' terms, but Ablett eventually realised painfully the inevitability of defeat, before the younger Davies, and was prominent in negotiations with Lord Buckland for the reopening of the Plymouth pits in Merthyr in the November of 1926. For his troubles in thus securing the jobs of some 1600 men which were threatened by the miners' stoppage, Ablett was forced to resign his position on the Executive Council of the Miners' Federation. The Merthyr miners were still in militant mood in October when they passed a resolution to be forwarded to the SWMF meeting asking that all maintenance men be removed from the pits, a drastic step which would render the pits unsafe on any eventual return to work. However S. O. Davies did not waver in his resolve. At the end of the strike he refused to accept the Conciliation agreement for the return to work on the owners' terms.

It has already been emphasised that peace and good order were observed throughout the strike in the town; no troops or extra police were needed at any time within the Borough. This calm owed much to the work of the local union leaders, to the Merthyr Trades Council, the sympathetic Merthyr Labour Council and the lenient attitude of the Merthyr police—some would say too lenient by far in 1926. For a town steeped in an industrial history of conflict within the coal and iron industries, firmly conscious and rooted in its substantial radical heritage, this passiveness might come as a surprise to many. When the strike ended both the Mayor and the Chief Constable thanked all labour leaders and trade unionists for the splendid way they had insisted on maintaining law and order during the crisis. The Chief Constable, D. Mansel Davies, in his annual report for 1926 stated that not one person had had to be brought before the magistrates for any offence directly connected with the strike. Merthyr escaped some of the more ugly incidents of the neighbouring Aberdare and Rhondda valleys, where buses were stoned and workers molested on returning to work. Significantly, the proper tone had been set in Merthyr at the annual Miners' May Day rally at the Miners' Hall, where R. C. Wallhead, the Labour MP for Merthyr addressing the meeting urged the men not to get involved in disputes with the authorities and thus give people a chance to involve them in physical conflict, but "to conduct yourselves quietly". This was to remain the keynote throughout the struggle in Merthyr: "conduct yourselves quietly".

With the drift back to work in the Autumn there was the threat of potential trouble, and even violence at Dowlais, though none actually occurred openly, when it became known that a number of Dowlais miners were preparing to return to the Nantwen and Bedlinog collieries at the beginning of November before official approval had been given for a return to work by the miners' union. Local miners' leaders were urged to advise their workmen to keep the peace and so prevent extra police from being drafted into the district from outside. It was being alleged that police protection for those workmen wishing to return to work at Dowlais and Treharris was insufficient, a charge which was immediately rejected by several Merthyr Labour councillors. Nevertheless, local police leave was cancelled, and 33 constables were sent to Caeharris railway station, Dowlais, from Merthyr, to escort 17 miners off the returning train to their homes amidst crowded streets of interested onlookers gathered to express their disapproval of these "black-legs". Suffice to say that the same 17 did not venture to return to work for more than three successive days after that; the social leprosy which they had incurred by returning to work prematurely was instantly effective in the clannish, tightly-knit community which was then Dowlais Top in 1926. The drift to work rose to "stampede" proportions by early December after the miners' union had officially called off the stoppage, and men were signing on in their hundreds daily at the large Merthyr Vale, Treharris and Abercynon pits. Most pits were reported to be back to near full strength by the end of the year. That may be for the first few post-strike weeks, but Lord Buckland who had taken over the Plymouth colliery echoed the owners' feelings, "the mineowners will once more be masters in their own homes". For irrespective of the reports of the initial "stampede to sign on", known agitators and active local unionists were deliberately recruited last if at all after the strike. Numerous miners never worked again after 1926 in Merthyr and thousands were forced by unemployment to leave the South Wales valleys for possible jobs in London and South-East England. It was not the coalowners' province to be generous in their hour of victory; the victimisation of proven "troublemakers", although never openly conceded by the management, was certainly the order of the day after 1926.

How did the town fare through the strike months of 1926?

No unemployment pay was made to those who were taking deliberate strike action. Merthyr Poor Law Union was obliged by law to refuse payments to those not involuntarily unemployed, and very little strike pay was available for the miners from their union. The SWMF was still paying off the costs of the last strike of 1921. Up to the end of May Merthyr miners had received no strike pay whereas it was being alleged that other unions had been managing to pay their members; for instance, it was said the railwaymen were receiving £1/15/0. Otherwise, it was to the Parish as the traditional resort that the miner and his family turned for relief. Merthyr Union had paid out in relief by way of loans over £340,000 during the 7 months from May 1926. The Merthyr Board of Guardians tried manfully to cope with the utterly hopeless colossal problems of relieving those affected by the strike. By the second week of May Merthyr was bankrupt, "overwhelmed and overdrawn" by £58,000. Thereon, relief continued only by the device of massive loans from the central Ministry of Health, and further overdrafts. One in three persons was in receipt of Parish relief from the Poor Union by the beginning of June in Merthyr, that is 17,500 families representing over 66,000 individuals. A sum of £15,000 was being paid out regularly each week to over 66,000 people by the Autumn; over £130,000 were left unpaid on the Rates; arrears on the Council's housing amounted to over £4,000 by September. The relief problem only got worse as the stoppage lasted into the Winter. Extra staff were employed to administer relief payments, and extra relief stations were opened in the local chapel vestries in the Borough. The scale of relief offered was, 18/- for a male, 23/- for a man and wife, and 2/- for each child over 14 years. The price of massive loans from central Government however was the gradual reduction in this scale after the Summer. Several cases of destitution amongst single men on strike were received at the Union House in town. Their plight was much the worst in Merthyr, and several deputations from the miners' leaders and the Trades Council attended the Council to try and alleviate the condition of these men. By the Autumn every family in Merthyr must have been sorely feeling the pinch of the miners' stoppage.

Other than the statutory method of help, the main form of voluntary relief was the soup-kitchen, or "canteens" as they were poshly called. This was the main work of the district strike committees, to set up as soon as possible these soup-kitchens to feed the strikers and their families now that no more wages were entering the households of the miners. The response from the townsfolk was magnificent, as kitchens appeared from almost nowhere within a short space of time. Strikers and soup-kitchens after all went hand in hand throughout all the major coal strikes in South Wales. This was a tightly-knit community in the early Summer of 1926 in Merthyr, in full-bodied communal action, when called upon to help in this way, and this action kept alive through the long strike months the miners' spirits and morale. It was also, of course a means of self-preservation for the mass of people in the town with little or no savings to fall back on after the first few days of the strike. It also gave those who chose to help the feeling of being involved in something worthwhile. The Mayor's Central Fund was soon set up to relieve local distress, and over £1,000 had been subscribed by early June from churches and chapels, district unions and individuals. One of the most generous contributors throughout the strike year was the Merthyr teachers' union. The kitchens commenced from early June throughout the Borough, from Troedyrhiw to Dowlais. All garden and allotment produce that could be obtained were used as well as some more dubiously acquired contributions from surrounding farmers who were occasionally relieved of some of their livestock, usually at night, for the larger appetites of the many in the town. A hard-worked committee organised the district kitchens from headquarters at Hope Chapel, Merthyr, which was open from 8 am until 6 pm engaged in distributing roast and boiled beef to 4-6,000 workmen. The central staff rationed the food to the 25 or so canteens about the town. There were seven at Dowlais, where the fare provided by the kitchens was described as excellent, three at Penydarren and four in town itself. The Merthyr Miners' Central Food Council provided some 450 adults with a hot meal each Thursday as well.

School children were fed at the schools canteens which were being run under the voluntary supervision of the Borough's teachers. (The unstinting work of the Merthyr schools teaching staff has never been fully recognised, for the way they helped to alleviate the real threat of widespread distress in the town throughout the 1920s. For their gallant work in 1926 they were then obliged to take a pay-cut themselves in 1927). Some 250 children were fed each morning and afternoon at St. John's Hall, Troedyrhiw by the local headmaster there. As much as three meals a day were given to over 6,000 children by mid-May. The numbers thence declined for the rest of the year, a sign it was said that families, now receiving relief, were making an effort to feed their own children at home. It was the unanimous opinion of Merthyr's teachers that the children in receipt of regular school meals were in fact better off than they had ever been before, and the same was true of several families now forced to turn to the authorities for help. There were few barefoot children, if any at all, to enhance this popular image of coal-strikers in the South Wales valleys, but boot repairing was a popular pastime for the unemployed miner, and from November, the Chamber of Trade and Merthyr and District Miners Boot Fund was set up to provide adequate footwear for the miners about to return to the pits.

Merthyr's churches and chapels played their part too in providing relief, both spiritual and temporal. Local chapel vestries were used as meeting places. Though the clergy could not take it upon themselves to become involved in the local politics of the strike, they worked hard nonetheless to help those in distress. Merthyr's miners provided a large part of the local church and chapel congregations. Before the strike had begun, the influential Rector of Merthyr, the Rev. J. Richards Pugh, in his annual review of the past year, 1925, had condemned strike action in no uncertain terms. "Strikes and lock-outs, I have no hesitation in saying do not belong to the kingdom of God; they are the product of the jungle and of the animal in man". That said however, several Dowlais Free Church ministers had forwarded a resolution to the Mayor by early May expressing their desire to co-operate in alleviating the local distress with the Council. An interesting sidelight here is the career of one local churchman; the Rev. William Evans, a former curate of Dowlais was the Mayor of Hackney in London Eastend in 1926 where the Government deployed armoured vehicles to ensure food supplies reached the City of London and suburbs from the docks, and troops guarded the streets. Hackney was to become a known refuge for the Hunger marchers from South Wales who were to walk to London in the 1930s. Through this admirable local effort on the part of councillors, teachers, clergy—in short everyone, the worst potential effects of the distress caused by the lock-out were hardly realised in 1926.

Relief from the boredom of unemployment was the other major task of the district strike committees, in order to keep spirits buoyant and morale intact during the Summer and Autumn of 1926. An incredible programme of sports and entertainments was organised for the town that year. For the miner, the Summer of 1926 was proper "strike weather"; the weather was gloriously fine, not unlike the Summer months 50 years later! A full calendar of rugby, football and cricket matches was organised, and held in a noticeably holiday carnival atmosphere. Merthyr Town FC then played Third Division League football, but the match to remember was one held by the Aberfan and Merthyr Vale Strike Committee at the end of May, when a comic match under the auspices of the Rechabite Hall comedy party took place between single and married teams for a prize of a faggots and peas supper. There was a surplus left and so a challenge was issued to any other team to play for this dubious prize. A lock-out cricket tournament was organised on the "Dowlais Oval"—the Bont, in aid of the communal kitchens. The price of admission to the municipal bowling greens and baths was reduced because of the strike, and the popular pastimes of pigeon breeding and racing, quoits, coursing could be indulged in to the full. Time there was now in May to give the house its annual coat of whitewash. Reg Lee in his reminiscences of Dowlais remembers going to the Dowlais "Cwm" to cut bucketfuls of lime for this purpose. Men could tend to their garden, catch up on reading from the town libraries, and just relax, albeit for a very brief moment.

Numerous concerts were given throughout the Borough in true musical Merthyr style. The Dowlais Choir would travel to Abercynon and give a concert there, and Abercynon would return the compliment to the north of the Borough later. A Dowlais Drama Week was held at the Oddfellows Hall in the October; a Dowlais Eisteddfod in November at the Dowlais Schools, under the auspices of the local entertainments committee, where there were 133 entries. The highlight of the Summer in Merthyr however was a splendid carnival procession held at Cyfarthfa Park at the beginning of August in perfect weather, "the best show of its kind ever seen in the town". The local report is worth quoting in some detail to give an idea of the sheer involvement of people with nothing much better to do at that time, in these wholly

130

self-inspired events. The line-up was, the Zulu warriors, the Japs and Pengarn Negro bandsmen "dressed as if to the manner born" with not a detail in their clothing overlooked. A mile length procession was headed by the Merthyr Vale Silver Band, and the Town Ward Band followed, then children in fancy costumes, a slave driver with negroes, gypsies, "Black and White", "Little Tich", "Simple Simon", and other characters from the music halls of the day, and more jazz bands, all marching with soldier-like precision. Georgetown canteen jazz band brought up the rear. All proceeds were in aid of the communal kitchen fund.

Jazz band fever had gripped Merthyr and Aberdare soon into the strike. Indeed 1926 was known locally as the "jazz band strike". The gazooka, a kind of trumpet was the main home-made instrument employed as numerous bands were formed in the town to provide entertainment for all and sundry. Fifty such bands attended the Quakers Yard jazzband festival, again held in aid of local distress funds, at the end of September. These bands were certainly an important form of working-class culture in the coalfields of England and Wales. Music and sport helped defeat idleness and boredom and took the mind off the wordly needs, if only for a brief respite as the stoppage dragged on through 1926. What the people of Merthyr could turn their hands to with the least resources merely illustrates the cultural depths and richness of such a community even in the severely straitened times of the 1920s and 30s.

All the pits in Merthyr remained shut for the best part of seven months, and it became common practice in this as in other strikes previously in the valleys for the miners and their families to scavenge for coal on the "patches" found on the coal tips above the town where the skilled miner would have little problem in opening up his own private coal level to supply himself and his friends with coal. So long as the coal thus obtained was used purely for domestic consumption, for the miners' own purposes in his home, the police virtually turned a proverbial blind eye to this coal getting from the hills above Merthyr town. A bag of coal fetched about 1/- to 2/6d in the town, and it became common for some people to work the coal patches and sell their coal. This was soon frowned on by the miners' union who formed a vigilance committee to try and prevent this large scale sale of coal. There was a well-used trade route for this coal from Dowlais eastwards through Tredegar and then to Newport. It is not surprising to learn of several persons seeking to earn a little extra to make ends meet by indulging in this relatively small scale coal trade. The Thomas-Merthyr Coal Co. had adopted a policy of allowing anyone, not just its own employees to take coal from its lands on issue of a voucher from the Company. This lenient attitude on the part of the authorities however began to change towards the end of the strike and certainly in the following years after 1926 when conditions forced many families to pick for coal regularly. The taking of Company coal of course had always been illegal, and fines of 10/- and 15/- for a second offence were often meted out in the Merthyr magistrates court. The duel between coal picker and the local police became keener from 1927, when the halcyon days of the strike Summer turned to the harsher long term depression of the late 1920s and 1930s.

There was very little organised theft in the strike, although the temptation must have presented itself to many people as a way of helping to make ends meet. Everyone had to pull together, and there was little room for individual greed which could go undetected by neighbours in such closely-knit communities which formed Merthyr town in the 1920s. "Legal thefts" (for want of a better term) were in order for the "happiness of the greater number" to supply the communal kitchens. There were some substantial mysterious moonlight losses from the GWR goods yards at Merthyr railway station towards the end of 1926, when a cask of butter and 56 lbs of cheese "disappeared". Otherwise, the unblemished conduct of everyone in the town throughout the strike reflected a communal harmony above political issues which no one openly transgressed.

The General Strike of 1926 was a political failure for the miners and for the British working class. By virtue of Merthyr's dependence on the occupations of iron and steel, and coal, the town felt the effects of the long coal lock-out more so than many other towns. The strike heralded the final defeat of the local coal and steel industries on their former substantial scale. Merthyr's pits never recovered from the 1926 stoppage; the Dowlais Works closed in 1930. The strike was for Merthyr a story of jazz bands, summer sports, concerts and soup kitchens. The bitterness followed in the years immediately after 1926, with the advent of Company Unionism challenging the position of the SWMF and the jobs of its members, and this cut far deeper into the Borough's fabric, into people's loyalties and characters far more than any previous strike had done. After 1926 the basic industries of the town irreversibly collapsed and mass unemployment ensued for much of the inter-war years in Merthyr. Thirteen thousand people had left the town by 1935 never to return.

There were the casualties of the strike to consider as well, not least the miners and their families. The local branches of the Co-operatives were stretched to the hilt having given so much credit to the strikers and their families. Several local bankruptcies were notified in the press; for example, the Greyhound's Head Inn at Cefn Coed was forced to close as a consequence of the strike. The Treharris Workmen's Fund of £268 towards the establishment of a Merthyr Technical College had been used to relieve local distress instead. Merthyr within a decade after the Strike had been transformed from a buoyant prosperous industrial town to a withering shell; there were serious plans to move the whole town to a coastal site in the 1930s. That was the enormity of the change, as much the consequence of impersonal forces, "the system". The human side of the coin, often forgotten in the grim inter-war years in Merthyr is strikingly evident in the town in 1926, where the General Strike brought out the best in its people, a solid working class community at its corporate and effective best. For Merthyr, and the valleys, the General Strike was a lesson in self preservation, and more, an essay in human dignity against over-whelming odds.

Notes & Bibliography

* I should like to thank Mr. W. M. Richards formerly of Cyfarthfa Castle School who first suggested this study to me several years ago and for helping me in its early preparation; and to several of my neighbours of Morlais Street, Dowlais for their interest shown and assistance given towards this paper: the late Mr Sam Jennings and Miss Eunice Jennings; and Mr Dan Lewis and Miss May Lewis.

This article was first presented as a lecture to the Merthyr Historical Society, 5 April 1976 to celebrate the 50th anniversary of the General Strike of 1926. It was slightly revised for publication in the *Merthyr Express* in six weekly parts, May 13 to June 17 1976. An earlier uncorrected typescript of mine is in Merthyr Public Library.

There is no single book or chapter on Merthyr and 1926. The files of the *Merthyr Express* at Cardiff Central Library and the Office of the Glamorgan Archive Service, Cardiff were consulted as the principal source of information. (The *Merthyr Express* 17 July 1926 commented: "The historian of the future need have no difficulty in finding an abundance of reliable data in the pages of the *Merthyr Express* when he comes to deal with the period of the General Strike of 1926.")

Also consulted were the Merthyr Tydfil Council Minute Books, No. 21, 1925-1926; the County Borough's Education Committee Minute Book, No. 26, 1925-1926; and the Merthyr Board of Guardians Union Minute Book, No. 55 at the Glam. Archives Office, Cardiff. (Ref. GRO U/M)

The most interesting item is the *Merthyr Tydfil County Borough Souvenir of the General Strike* (nd). This has been reprinted and is available from the Librarian, the South Wales Miners' Library, 50 Sketty Road, Swansea, SA2 0LG (price 30p & 7½p postage). This pamphlet contains several illustrations including one of the Merthyr Tydfil Central Strike Committee and Officers of the District Strike Committees, with an identifying key to each member; a Report from the General Secretary; and a detailed "Diagram Illustrating Organisation Of Central Strike Committee' and an Explanatory Note.

Several useful books were consulted. The general background to the period can be obtained from:

†*C. L. Mowat, *Britain Between The Wars 1918-1940* (1955).

On the Merthyr background to 1926 see:

*D. G. R. Belshaw, *The Changing Economic Geography of the Merthyr Valley* (Merthyr, 1955); *Margaret S. Taylor, *Fifty Years A Borough* (Merthyr, 1956); and chap. 4 in *Merthyr Politics: The Making Of A Working-Class Tradition*, ed. Glanmor Williams (Cardiff, 1966).

On the Strike itself detailed accounts are found in:

† Christopher Farman, *The General Strike May 1926* (1972).

*Patrick Renshaw, *The General Strike* (1975).

*G. A. Philips, *The General Strike: A Study in the Politics of Industrial Conflict* (1976); a contemporary account is in *R. Page Arnot, *The General Strike, May 1926: Its Origin and History* (1926, repr. 1975).

On the miners themselves see:

*R. Page Arnot, *South Wales Miners* Vol. 11 (1975) esp. chap. X. Within this chapter, pp. 301-316, "The Minutes Of A Council Of Action" are that of the Bedlinog Council. For the background story see also his *South Wales Miners* Vol. 1 (1967).

Local studies useful for comparison with the Merthyr story, as well as more general accounts are found in:

† Jeffrey Skelley ed. *The General Strike, 1926* (1976) and see esp. ch. 7 Sect. 2 on South Wales; and Margaret Morris, ed. *The General Strike* (Penguin, 1976)† esp. ch. (c) Sect. 5 on "The Pontypridd Area".

† The special 1926 issue of *Llafur* (The Journal of the Society for the Study of Welsh Labour History) Vol. 2, No. 2, (Spring, 1977) is devoted entirely to articles on the 1926 Strike following the Llafur-NUM Weekend School at Treforest, April 1976, including reminiscences of the Strike in Aberdare.

†* R. L. Lee covers the period in his account of Dowlais, *The Town That Died* (1975).

Full references of the above can be obtained from the author.

(†—paperback   *—available at Merthyr Public Library)

11. MARGARET S. TAYLOR

THOMAS STEPHENS OF MERTHYR (1821-1875)

(Illustration 58)

Until 1915 there was a chemists's shop at No. 113 Merthyr High Street that bore the name of Thomas Stephens. It stood opposite St. David's Church. The famous owner was Thomas Stephens, and he died in 1875, forty years before his name was removed from the shop front.

There is nothing remarkable in running an efficient pharmacy, or druggist shop as it used to be called, but Thomas Stephens has acquired lasting fame through the service he rendered to Welsh literature and history. In making English and continental scholars aware of the great literary heritage of Wales, he ranks even higher than Lady Charlotte Guest who spent eight years translating into English, with valuable erudite notes, the *Mabinogion*. Her completed work appeared in 1846. Three years later came Thomas Stephens' masterpiece, *The Literature of the Kymry,* deliberately written in English although he was a Welsh scholar, but with the intention of making Welsh literature more widely known.

In the preface he says of his countrymen, "Their history, clear, concise, and authentic, ascends to a high antiquity; their language was embodied in verse . . . and their literature, cultivated and abundant, lays claim to being the most ancient in modern Europe." *Literature of the Kymry* was immediately translated into German after publication, then later into some European languages.

This great scholar was not born in Merthyr, but in Pontneddfechan, Vale of Neath, on April 21st 1821. His father was a bootmaker in the village and his mother the daughter of a Unitarian minister. They were ordinary folk, but well read, and in their little house Tŷ-to-cam (House with the crooked roof) there were friends calling to hold argumentative learned discourses with the couple, and as the boy listened he too developed critical faculties and became steeped in Welsh culture.

As he grew older he was sent to a boarding school in Neath where he received the usual classical education then given in grammar schools, but with important additions. The headmaster, the Reverend John Davies, was also a Unitarian like Stephens' parents. The name of the sect expresses belief in one Divinity, not Three-in-One, and because of its denial of the Trinity it was abhorred by other Nonconformist, or Dissenting, sects at that time. During the early nineteenth century in Wales it was characterized by the spirit of unfettered enquiry pursued by its adherents. In fact, it came to attract many intelligent young men who were disinclined to accept conventional dictates. One of these was William Crawshay the Second, builder of Cyfarthfa Castle, who, for a short time, attended services in the Unitarian chapel at Merthyr, but the Riots of 1831 made him fearful of liberalism in practice and his interest ceased.

Thomas Stephens was taken away from school in 1835 when he was fourteen, and apprenticed for five years to a Merthyr druggist named David Morgan. This was the shop of which Stephens became owner when Morgan retired. The change of environment must have been terrifying for a teenage boy. He left a secluded rural village for a town containing four great ironworks from which issued the constant roar of machinery, while at night, when the furnaces were opened, the sky looked as if a blazing volcano were erupting. Merthyr was then approaching the height of prosperity. The custom of whitewashing exteriors applied even to workmen's dwellings, while there were less huddled-together houses for agents and engineers, and for the ironmasters such splendid residences as Dowlais House, Penydarren House, and Cyfarthfa Castle. It was a place very much alive—alive with industry and alive with a growing awareness of culture.

During the years of his apprenticeship, Thomas Stephens worked hard to become skilled in pharmacy, also studying wider subjects like chemistry that would help him. This was in the cause of duty. In leisure hours he indulged his passion for reading, a passion that almost amounted to a compulsion with him, but he often found it difficult to obtain books he wanted and this difficulty caused him to be such an advocate of public libraries later. Mr. Morgan, his employer helped him, though not always approving of the place chosen by Stephens for reading, sometimes a bath tub. But read he must, even missing sleep to do so. His was a mind that continually sought knowledge, especially the truth about any matter—a result of his Unitarian upbringing.

He started competing at eisteddfodau at an early age, but it was at Liverpool he had his first real triumph. In 1840 he gained a prize for "History of the Life and Times of Iestyn ap Gwrgant, the last native Lord of Glamorgan." A year later he won £10 at the Abergavenny Eisteddfod for "History of Remarkable Places in the County of Cardigan." So he continued. In 1848 the Prince of Wales (later Edward VII) offered a prize for an essay on "The Literature of Wales during the twelfth and succeeding centuries." According to the historian Charles Wilkins, who was very friendly with Thomas Stephens, when the bardic name of the winner was proclaimed the successful bard was asked to rise and identify himself. Although twenty-seven he looked much younger than his real age, and all were astonished when this slight, pale young man stood up.

This literary piece formed the basis of *Literature of the Kymry*, published a year later. The sub-title states it to be "a critical essay on the history of the language and literature of Wales during the twelfth and two succeeding centuries : containing numerous specimens of ancient Welsh poetry in the original and accompanied with English translations." There was a second edition in 1876. By permission of Queen Victoria, the book was dedicated to the Prince of Wales, and Lady Charlotte Guest approached Her Majesty's secretary to ascertain correct procedure for asking royal sanction for this. The Guests were great friends of Stephens. Sir John paid for the cost of the book's publication by Longmans, something that was permissible then, but is not today, save with rare exceptions. Nowadays, the publisher produces a book at his own expense, then pays the author royalties on the sales.

Literature of the Kymry, brought immediate fame to Thomas Stephens in Wales and in the rest of Britain, then abroad when it was translated. The first translation was into German, a language Stephens had mastered well enough to be able to read reviews published in that country. But he did not rest on his laurels. Throughout his life he continued reading and studying and writing. A full list of his works is given at the beginning of *Literature of the Kymry*, second edition. Later I will speak about the controversial *Madoc*, but first I want to show how he took to heart his adopted town and strove for its welfare. He lived in Merthyr for forty years, became a well-known figure, and was honoured by being given the office of High Constable (equivalent of Mayor) from 1858 to 1859.

One of his earliest and dearest projects was the formation of a library, since he as a student experienced difficulties in obtaining books and did not wish others to suffer in that way. Stephens and a few others started a discussion class or "conversational club" in the winter of 1846. One historian says the book collection resulting from this began in the Temperance Room behind the Market; another that it was near the Plymouth Arms. Wilkins describes the beginning. "The first selection of books was Knight's Shilling Library, which I, the first librarian, carried in a box once devoted to Warren's [boots'] blacking! Our next step was to the Temperance Hotel in the Glebeland, where, by dint of subscriptions, about fifty volumes were put on the shelves. The Rev. J. C. Campbell . . . was on the committee, and I well recollect his anxiety on the first evening of our migration lest all the books should be taken out on the first night." According to T. E. Clarke, writing in 1848, over thirty pounds was spent on flooring and papering walls before the library was ready. Sir John Guest gave one hundred and eighty volumes, and the Marquis of Bute gave ninety, once the institution was established. For many years Charles Wilkins continued as librarian, presumably honorary. Thomas Stephens was honorary secretary from 1846 until near the end of his life.

Besides circulation of books, the institution was a cultural centre, and lectures were a regular feature. Stephens would give at least one during the season, and he did not confine himself to literary topics. For example, on December 1st, 1849, he spoke on Electricity. The lectures were long. The *Cardiff and Merthyr Guardian* in 1850 reports him as speaking for one and a half hours on "The migration of the Kymry from the eastern cradle of the human race to their final settlement in the British Isles."

In 1856, larger premises were purchased and these were in Thomastown. According to Wilkins, the library stock was now "nearly three thousand volumes of the gems of English literature." However the Thomastown room was not large enough to hold all who came to attend the winter lectures. The *Cardiff and Merthyr Guardian* of February

19th, 1864, states, "The attendance at the 'readings' on Thursday was so numerous that the members and friends were compelled to adjourn from the Library to St. David's Infant schoolroom...The exertions of Mr. Stephens...[4 others] with selections from music and literature were applauded."

Under the bardic name of CASNODYN, Thomas Stephens was President of the Cymreigyddion Society. He supported the Temperance Society, fought for badly needed improved sanitary conditions in Merthyr, and, in 1850 he was elected to serve on the Public Health Board. Anything he could do to help Merthyr, he was ready to undertake. In 1850 it was proposed to build a town hall. The present building was erected more than forty years after this, but on the site originally chosen. This site, opposite the Castle Hotel, was not fixed upon for sixteen years—1866, because a strong body of opinion favoured Market Square. Thomas Stephens was on the initial committee when it was decided the cost, estimated at a thousand pounds, should be borne by shareholders financing the venture with twenty-five pound shares. At a meeting held on April 27th, 1850, Stephens is reported as being present and asking if the enterprise were to be a public or a private undertaking. He wanted it to be "a private undertaking for the public good."

He was responsible for the purchase of land at Cefn for a cemetery. As a Unitarian, he could not be buried at any of the church or chapel graveyards because he was not a Christian, but in Cefn there was an unconsecrated section where the bodies of non-Christians could be interned. Stephens remained faithful to the religion in which he had been brought up. He regularly attended the Unitarian Chapel in Twynyrodyn, called in T. E. Clarke's list "The Old Meeting-house", built in 1747, and whose minister was the Reverend O. Evans. I have not been able to discover if this occupied the site of a later Unitarian Chapel that still stands in Lower Thomas Street, although it has been closed for many years. In *Chapel Architecture in Merthyr Tydfil*, by Anthony Jones and published in 1962, this is designated as imitation gothic. It has a most elaborate frontage, and belongs to some time after 1870 when pseudo-gothic characteristics were frequently occurring, so this cannot be the building where Thomas Stephens was a faithful attender for so many years. But he was not married in a Unitarian Chapel. His marriage to a Miss Margaret Davies, an old friend, took place at the Parish Church Llangollen on September 11th, 1866. He was then forty-five years of age.

A few other dates in his life are noteworthy. From 1851 to 1868, he concerned himself deeply with local politics. This was the time when H. A. Bruce, later Lord Aberdare, represented Merthyr in Parliament. In 1862, came the colliery disaster at Gethin Pit No. 2, and Thomas Stephens was honorary secretary of the relief fund. In 1864 he took over the management of the Merthyr Express. In 1875, at the age of fifty-four, he died.

One photograph of him remains, but taken in maturity. It shows a keen sensitive face with long nose, dark curling hair and beard. He was

138

said to have had a very pale complexion. He had a pleasant, cheerful manner, but was not a witty, joking person, and he was remarkably industrious. When writing *Literature of the Kymry*, Wilkins says, "he would often be closely occupied up to the small hours of the morning from the time he had closed his shop, and it was frequently the case that, wearied out, he would go to sleep on the sofa, waking up when the servant came to light his fire."

Wilkins pays tribute to his strict honesty. "It stamped his social career, and was illustrated by everything he wrote. He never formed an opinion or a belief, and then ransacked the literary world to support it; but studiously searched, diligently read, and the result was his estimate to which he tenaciously clung. Note his essay on Madoc. "Stephens was a Welshman. His country bore the Madocian wreath of honour. Not Spain, but Wales claimed the praise for first discovering America. The essayist, the historian, and the bard had supported these claims, and Wales would hear of nothing in opposition. But Stephens, after diligent examination of authorities, careful sifting of evidence, came to a contrary conclusion, and though his fame as a rising author was in jeopardy, he openly avowed his opinion, and alone defied the world."

How did the controversy over Madoc arise, and who was Madoc? At the National Eisteddfod of 1858, held in Llangollen, the subject for the essay competition was "The discovery of America in the twelfth century by Prince Madoc." The winner was to receive a silver medal and twenty pounds. Six entered, of whom one was Thomas Stephens.

Owain, king of Gwynedd, had several sons, and when he died in 1170 they all began to quarrel amongst themselves. One, Madoc, grew tired of this strife, took a large boat, and with his retainers sailed away westwards. The legend continues that he returned after many years, stated he had discovered a fine new land—America—and persuaded a number of Welsh folk to go back with him and found a settlement there.

This was the story, handed down from generation to generation, and gaining immense popularity in Queen Elizabeth the First's reign because it claimed the American continent for Britain, not for her enemy Spain. Later, a certain Morgan Jones, a Puritan who emigrated to escape persecution, was captured by a tribe of Red Indians in Virginia, and was about to be executed when he prayed aloud in Welsh. Among the spectators was an Indian of another tribe, who recognised the meaning of Morgan Jones' utterances, intervened, and secured his release. The story was widely circulated in 1740 by an historian, Theophilus Jones, so that the truth of the legend became even more firmly established in the minds of Welshmen—namely that Madoc and his company had founded a settlement, whose descendants, though classed with Indians, had pale skins and spoke Welsh, or a language akin to Welsh.

In 1791, a scholarly dissenting minister, Dr. John Williams, included this in a book that had great influence. Then the romantic-minded Edward Williams, better known as Iolo Morganwg, began to talk of going to America to seek for the mysterious tribe. He did not do so, but a certain John Evans of Caernarvonshire undertook the investigation.

Evans found a fair-skinned group called the Mandans, spent six months with them, but as he never heard a word of Welsh spoken by them, he came to the conclusion that they were not of Welsh descent, and decided Madoc's descendants did not exist.

Yet the Madoc legend persisted in Wales, and in England. In 1893 a long narrative poem called *Madoc* was written by the English poet Southey. So there was nothing extraordinary for this subject to be set in a national eisteddfod competition, but it was naturally assumed all competitors would accept the story to be historical fact. In this spectacular 1858 eisteddfod at Llangollen, five did, but the sixth, Thomas Stephens, did not. He argued that another record concerning Prince Madoc's life stated he never left Wales and that he met with a violent death at home; also that there was no allusion to Madoc's supposed discovery of America until after Spain laid claim to the New World; finally, there was the fruitless quest by John Evans.

Thomas Stephens held this point of view after detailed research, and his belief that truth must prevail. Truth must be adhered to however unpopular this might be. And to proclaim the Madoc story a mere fanciful tale was unpopular. It lost him the eisteddfod prize. By common consent the judges agreed his entry was the best, but they took refuge in arguing over terms of reference. Some declared that the essay set was "The discovery of America in the twelfth century by Prince Madoc," and was intended that this be taken for granted, not for it to be disproved, so it would be wrong for Stephens to be awarded the prize. Obviously this was a mere quibble, made to provide an excuse for withholding proper unbiased judgement. At least two of the judges resigned because they believed Stephens' essay was the best so he should be proclaimed winner, whatever the antagonism against his conclusion. In the end, no award was made. The essay, with additions, was published in book form by Longmans eighteen years after Stephens' death.

Possibly some of you saw the television programme given on St. David's Day 1977 by Professor Gwyn Williams. It dealt with Madoc and the fair-skinned Indians. From what Professor Williams said, and also from a speech he made at the 1975 Soroptimist dinner, he is convinced of the authenticity of the Madoc story. It was certainly not impossible for a Welsh prince to cross the Atlantic Ocean in a small boat in the twelfth century. There were others, who did so.

Some years ago I visited Iceland, and in the capital city of Reyjavik was a statue commemorating an Icelander, Leif Erikson, whom it was claimed, reached North America about the year 1000. This statue had been presented in 1930 by the United States. It dealt a blow to me who had always believed what I was taught in school, namely that Christopher Columbus was the discoverer of America.

Forgive the digression, but I have recently been on a tour of the cities of Leon and Castille in northern Spain, and in churches and monasteries and palaces one saw the wealth of treasure—especially gold—brought from the New World by Columbus and explorers who followed him. As you know, he was a poor Genoese navigator who believed that the world being round (this was now an acknowledged belief) a ship sailing far enough westward would reach the East Indies and India. In the city of Burgos, we visited the home of the Constables of Castille, where, after the second voyage in 1498, the joint sovereigns, Ferdinard and Isabella who had financed Columbus received him on his triumphal return. Then at Salamanca, there was a Dominican monastery where he had argued with clerical and university savants to convince them of the feasibility of his plans.

Of course Columbus never realised he had discovered a New World. He thought he had landed in India, and I heard a delightfully pithy summary of his mistake. "Christopher Columbus set out on a voyage but did not know where he was going. When he arrived he did not know where he was. When he returned he did not know where he had been."

To return to Thomas Stephens and the Madoc story. Whichever side one takes, one must feel intense admiration for his intellectual honesty, his search after truth, and his determination to keep to what he believed to be the truth. Although he was such an ardent lover of Wales, and anxious to increase her prestige, yet principles came first. To quote from the *N.U.T. Story of Merthyr Tydfil,* "he refused to glorify his country by supporting any claims that were based on tradition only, or on the inventions of over-imaginative poets." In more flowery language, a German critic says, "He has sealed the Celtic mythological heaven, and through rifts made by his lance has scattered the false gods and goddesses who disported there."

The Madoc controversy has always impressed me because I do admire the courage and honesty of this man of great scholarship, and I have never cared greatly whether Stephens' conclusions were right or wrong. He stuck to what he believed, even though it meant unpopularity with many people, and certainly the loss of a coveted prize. *The Literature of the Kymry* is justly his preeminent claim to immortal fame, but locally his work here promoting libraries and other social amenities deserves our respect and gratitude.

The sculptor, Joseph Edwards, made a bust of him, and this, I believe, still stands in the University College of Wales at Aberystwyth. There ought to be a prominent memorial in this town, a memorial to an adopted son of whom Merthyr people can justly be proud.

12. HUW WILLIAMS

SOME SOURCES TOWARDS
A HISTORY OF MODERN MERTHYR TYDFIL:
A BIBLIOGRAPHICAL NOTE

Merthyr Tydfil as the leading industrial town in Wales from the Industrial Revolution of the late 18th century until the last quarter of the 19th century has probably acquired as much literature about itself as any other town in Wales. As one of the foremost printing and publishing centres in Wales until 1930, the book trade in the town was a flourishing concern. Newspapers, numerous periodicals, journals and magazines, novels, ecclesiastical letters and sermons abounded, as well as books covering all subjects in both Welsh, which was the first spoken language for the majority of Merthyr people in the 19th century although it is probable that only a handful could have had the ability to read, and in the English language.

This article is in the form of a brief bibliographical note, with some accompanying comments, which hopes to draw the attention of the reader to some of the major texts written on the subject of the history of Merthyr Tydfil, and some of the not-so-well-known sources which may be consulted locally. It is *not* an exhaustive or complete list by any means, and does not pretend to be so. Most of the works cited here, unless specifically otherwise stated, are available for loan from the public libraries of Merthyr Borough Council, or may be consulted for reference purposes in the library.

The majority of books, pamphlets and articles referring to Merthyr town and Borough have been recently gathered together in the Library's *Local History: A Guide To The Local History Collection At The Central Library, Merthyr Tydfil* (1976) available from Merthyr's libraries at 20p. All the titles here are arranged by author under several subject heads: Industrial; Social; Education; &c. Two other bibliographies of a more general nature have emanated from The Call To The Valleys '74 Conference held at Aberfan; Alan Morgan's *The South Wales Valleys in History: A Guide To Literature* (Tŷ Toronto, Aberfan, 1974) is an admirably comprehensive guide to over 500 items, many of them referring directly to Merthyr Tydfil, for the use of local historians in the South Wales Valleys; and more sociologically orientated is *The South Wales Valleys: A Contemporary Socio-Economic Bibliography* (Tŷ Toronto, Aberfan, 1974) arranged under subjects, and subject and author indexed, with several additional appendices on further source material and its location. It is especially thorough in its sections on Planning, Community Studies, Environment and Geography. A list of local history titles held in Merthyr Central Library is contained in an admirable *Historical Gazetteer of the Borough of Merthyr Tydfil* (1976) compiled by the Afon Taf History Research Group, Afon Taf High School. This list is also available at the Central Library itself.

Printed Works

Despite the lapse of time, Charles Wilkins's *The History of Merthyr Tydfil* (Merthyr, 1st ed. 1867, 2nd ed. 1908) still remains the most detailed and standard account of the town's history, although the book has been out of print for many years. The story is traced from before Roman times, the martyrdom of Tydfil through to the time of the Industrial Revolution and the beginnings of modern Merthyr down to the turn of the century, 1900. The Merthyr Teachers' Association (NUT) commissioned a splendid shorter history, chiefly for use in the Borough's schools, *The Story of Merthyr Tydfil: An Introductory History of the County Borough of Merthyr* (Cardiff, 1932), likewise out of print and difficult to obtain today, except for reference use in the town's libraries. There are long term plans from the present teachers' organisations in Merthyr to produce a future volume to replace and update this first NUT *History*. Upon the 50th anniversary of Merthyr attaining Borough status, in 1955, a comprehensive review of the half century was produced in *Fifty Years a Borough 1905-1955* (Merthyr, 1956) by the then Chief Librarian, Margaret S. Taylor. Other short studies have followed: an economic geographical study by D. G. R. Belshaw, *The Changing Economic Geography of the Merthyr Valley* (Merthyr, 1956); four lectures given to the WEA 1964-65 have been collected together as *Merthyr Politics: The Making of A Working-Class Tradition*, ed. Glanmor Williams (Cardiff, 1966); and two booklets published by Merthyr Corporation in 1972, Barry Brunt's *The Contemporary Economic Problems in Merthyr Tydfil*, and Eric Willis's *An Analysis of Industrial Change Within the County Borough of Merthyr Tydfil 1939-1969*. These last two bring the story almost up to date, and these works together represent the main books on Merthyr's history.

Several contemporary books and guides, tours and pamphlets are worth consulting, besides the well known works such as Borrow's *Wild Wales* (1862). Specifically on Merthyr town are:
T. E. Clarke's *A Guide To Merthyr Tydfil* (1848); Edwin F. Roberts's *A Visit To The Ironworks & Environs of Merthyr Tydfil in 1852* (1853); H. A. Bruce's lecture published as *Merthyr Tydfil in 1852* (Merthyr, 1852); William Edmunds's (Gwilym Glyn Taf) *Traethawd Ar Hanes Plwf Merthyr* (Aberdâr, 1864). One of the Borough's former MPs Charles H. James wrote his reminiscences in *What I Remember About Myself and Old Merthyr*: written in 1881 (Merthyr 1892-94). As Merthyr applied for the second time officially for incorporation in 1897, a full summary of this application was recorded by John G. E. Astle in his *Illustrated Report of the Merthyr Tydfil Incorporation*

143

Inquiry, 1897 (1897). By the beginning of the 20th century Merthyr was becoming a stronghold of the Independent Labour Party (ILP). The Borough had elected Keir Hardie as an ILP Member of Parliament in 1900, and Hardie contributed a foreword, "My Relations with the Merthyr Boroughs" to the ILP sponsored booklet, *The Democrat's Handbook to Merthyr*: Historical, Topographical, Political, and Illustrated (Cardiff, c.1912) which contained a selection of articles on aspects of local history by several well known public figures in the town.

Merthyr town in its prime at the turn of the century was considered to be a place eminently worthy of visit. Civic pride in the town was manifested in several lavishly illustrated guide-books notably: *Merthyr and Aberdare Illustrated* No. 13 of Burrow's "Royal" Handbooks written by Charles Wilkins (c.1903) including 50 photographs of the Merthyr vicinity and two maps; and the smaller *"Borough" Pocket Guide To Merthyr Tydfil*, specially compiled by H. W. Southey, including 14 illustrations and a Street Plan and two maps (Cheltenham, c.1909). Both these guides were in Cardiff Central Library at W.848.1. Arthur Trystan Edwards's *Merthyr, Rhondda and The Valleys* (1958) in The Regional Book Series is a recent tour of the district. Today's modern counterparts are the numerous travel books and guides to Wales, many of which include a section on the South Wales Valleys and Merthyr town. As from 1977 Merthyr has at last been allocated a mention in the columns of the Wales Tourist Board's *Guide to South Wales*.

For the work of several modern historians on Merthyr over the past 15 years, see the several articles, notably by Professors Gwyn A. Williams and Iuean G. Jones in back numbers of the *Welsh History Review, Morgannwg*: (The Transactions of the Glamorgan History Society), and *The Glamorgan Historian*, as listed in the Library's *Guide To Local History*; the four articles in *Merthyr Politics* noted above, and volumes I and II of the *Merthyr Historian*.

District Histories

"Merthyr Tydfil" for the purposes of this Note normally includes all those districts comprising the Borough of Merthyr Tydfil. There are however several local histories written on the constituent parts of the Borough. In the South D. H. Gwynne Davies's *Historical Survey of Treharris & District* (Merthyr nd.) covers the lower part of the Borough; parts of Pentrebach are covered in Margaret S. Taylor's article on the Plymouth Ironworks in the *Glamorgan Historian* III, and similarly for Penydarren in an article on the Penydarren Works in the *Glamorgan Historian* V. The northern part of the Borough has been covered in greater detail. The Rev. J. Hathren Davies's pamphlet *The History of Dowlais* trans. Tom Lewis (Mab y Mynydd) (nd. c.1891) is the standard account on Dowlais town still. Two less well known works also cover Dowlais: Henry Murton *Recollections of Dowlais 1808-1812* (1874) is a handwritten account found in (C)ardiff (C)entral (L)ibrary, Ref. CCLMs.1.543 in the Research Room, and Henry Allgood *Notes*

On Dowlais (1910) including 8 photographs, Ref. CCL. Ms.4.683. Allgood paid two visits to Dowlais on a fact finding mission as an agent for Frederick Guest, in March 1910. Guest was contesting the East Dorset Parliamentary seat, and had sent Allgood to Dowlais to counter accusations being made by his election opponents about the Guest family's relationship with Dowlais in the past. Further reminiscences of Dowlais are found in *The Diaries of Lady Charlotte Guest* (1950) and *Lady Charlotte Schreiber: Extracts From Her Journal 1853-1891* (1953) both edited by the Earl of Bessborough. The Dowlais Iron Company Works have been extensively researched in several publications and articles listed in the *Local History Guide*, and mentioned below; and recently R. L. Lee's *The Town That Died* (1975) is a personalised account of the author's early years in Horse Street, Dowlais.

Slightly further afield, for Vaynor Parish neighbouring Merthyr, see the Rev. J. E. Jenkins's *Vaynor: Its History & Guide* (Merthyr, 1897) a mine of information on local history and Welsh customs, gossip &c probably only part factual. Neighbouring Bedlinog, once in the Merthyr Poor Law Union has been dealt with by local author, Walter Hadyn Davies's several books, and an article in the *Glamorgan Historian* XI; Gellideg by F. J. Pedler's *History of the Hamlet of Gellideg* (1930).

There are short pieces often quite detailed to be found on the several main districts of Merthyr in the volumes of Directories on South Wales—Kellys and Worralls, from the 1860s onwards, although there is a danger that these notes tend to remain unaltered through several volumes of the Directory per decade without any immediate account taken of changes between those dates. The numerous histories of local chapels provided useful historical background to the respective districts where the particular chapel is located. Local newspapers such as the *Merthyr Express*, the *Western Mail* and the former *South Wales Daily News* have often produced worthy articles on different districts in the Valleys including Merthyr and its "suburbs". Full references to these can be obtained from the present author.

Primary Sources

These so-called "Primary sources" are the bread and butter of historians. The town's industrial past has ensured a mass of manuscript source material, a lot of which has fortunately survived in bulk. Iron making being the most important single venture in the town for a century, 1750-1850, the two main collections of documents cover this aspect of history.

At the National Library of Wales, Aberystwyth, are the Cyfarthfa Papers. A two volume Schedule to the collection is published. Also see John P. Addis's *The Crawshay Dynasty: A Study in Industrial Organisation & Development, 1765-1867* (Cardiff, 1957), and on the Crawshay family itself see Margaret S. Taylor's *The Crawshays of Cyfarthfa Castle* (1968). At the Office of the Glamorgan Archive Service, Cardiff, the vast Dowlais Iron Company collection is now housed consisting of several thousands of letters, maps and plans, reports, ledgers &c. The bound volumes of Company Letters, except for two volumes of "outgoing correspondence", are all in the nature of "incoming" letters to the Company. Unfortunately, the bulk of this material remains uncatalogued, although there are current plans for some indexing work to begin in the near future supervised from Cardiff University. The former Glamorgan Record Office prepared *A Selective Index to the Dowlais Iron Company*, 1782-1860, classified under several subject headings: Business, Markets; Politics; Welfare; &c and this List has been published as *Iron In The Making : The Dowlais Iron Company Letters* ed. M. Elsas (Cardiff, 1960).

The Dowlais Collection has been extensively used by John A. Owen, the present Works Manager of Dowlais BSC Works, in his eminently readable booklet *A Short History of the Dowlais Iron Works 1759-1936* (Merthyr 1973), which has been recently republished with lavish illustrations from the Dowlais photographic collection as *The History Of The Dowlais Iron Works 1759-1970* (Risca, 1977). See also the several articles in the *Merthyr Historian* I & II. Also worth consultation in this respect are the standard texts on the coal and iron industries, which contain substantial chapters and sections on Merthyr Tydfil as the birthplace of the modern iron industry in Wales by such authorities as Wilkins, Lloyd, Page Arnot &c.

There is a little material relating to the Plymouth and Penydarren Companies at the Glamorgan Archive Office.

Religion

Religion has played an important part in the history of the town ever since the date of the original martyrdom of Saintess Tydfil after which Merthyr Tydfil takes its name. A comprehensive list of several church and chapel histories of the area is to be found in the *Local Guide*. Two recent histories, of St. John's Church and the Parish of Dowlais, and St. John's Church, Penydarren have appeared in the last year. Unfortunately, St. David's, the main church in Merthyr is not yet served by its own published history. There is a wealth of chapel histories, written in Welsh and English; it is probable indeed, that nearly every chapel in Merthyr has had something written about itself at some time in the past.

The actual church and chapel records are scattered in different places. Sometimes the local church has still retained its records, the registers of baptisms, marriages and deaths, and old parish magazines, photographs &c. St. David's Church, Merthyr has copies of its old records although the originals are lodged at the National Library of Wales, Aberystwyth. Diocesan policy today is for the church records to be sent where possible to the Glamorgan Archives Office, Cardiff, and the parish records held there, for example, those of St. John's Church, Dowlais are now being transcribed and indexed. The large collection of the records of the Church Commissioners are held at Aberystwyth. For details of the Religious Census of 1851 see I. G.

Jones & D. Williams, *The Religious Census of 1851: A Calendar of the Returns Relating to Wales*, Vol. 1. South Wales (Cardiff, 1976) under "Merthyr Tydfil District" pp.163-190. Individual chapel records are less centralised, and their survival often depended on the attitude of the chapel in question, whether it looked after its documents or transferred them for safe keeping if the chapel closed. The different denominations adopt different policies towards collecting these records: there are several national historical societies for the major sects, but many records have been lost over the years, or known to have been destroyed. Enquiries to the local chapel first are advisable.

Architecture

The study of this subject necessarily involves the collection and use of illustrative material—old paintings and photographs, and Merthyr town has been fortunate in the survival of several old prints and photographs from the late 19th century onwards. A collection of paintings by the Merthyr artist, Penry Williams hangs in the Cyfarthfa Castle Museum. A selection of old photographs collected and edited into a volume is *Old Aberdare & Merthyr Tydfil in Photographs* (1976). Two issues of the *Merthyr Express* on the subject of "Old Merthyr" in Photographs were printed recently, taken from the paper's photographic files. Back numbers of the paper, sometimes weekly contained old prints sent by readers of views of Merthyr town, cricket teams, group photographs of school class forms in the 1920s &c.

Also available, at the Cardiff Central Library is a volume of *Sixty Three Views of Merthyr and District*, photographs by Martin J. Ridley, Bournemouth (Merthyr, c.1905). This is a loose bound single volume with two prints displayed on each page, found at Ref. W.948.1. The majority of the prints are of Merthyr town itself and only the last five or so cover Penydarren and Dowlais. There are also excellent photographs used as illustration in the two Handbooks of Merthyr mentioned above.

On the actual architecture, the works of John B. Hilling should be consulted. See for example his *Cardiff and the Valleys* (1973) and an article in *The Glamorgan Historian* VIII. Trystan Edwards's *Merthyr, Rhondda & the Valleys* (1958) contains a commentary on aspects of Merthyr's buildings as well. A unique study on a particular aspect of architectural history relating to Merthyr is Anthony Jones's *A Thesis and Survey of the Nonconformist Chapel Architecture in Merthyr Tydfil, Glam.* (Merthyr, 1962) a pioneering work illustrating and classifying the different chapel types to be found in Merthyr. Several lecture papers delivered to the Merthyr Tydfil Civic Society also cover aspects of this wide field of architectural history as related to Merthyr in particular. At the beginning of 1977, Merthyr Borough Council Planning Department produced a Consultative Report, *Conservation in Merthyr Tydfil* (1976), a classified checklist on buildings of historical interest considered to be of architectural importance, and many of them thought to be worth preserving as such for this purpose.

147

Education

Most records on the several schools of Merthyr are now with the Glamorgan Archives Office, Cardiff. Refs. E/SB & E/MT. There is a collection of Merthyr Tydfil School Board's minutes and reports for the late 19th century onwards, and details of the separate schools under the Board; Merthyr Education Committee Minutes, correspondence &c run for the 20th century, and Merthyr's School Log Books for the different schools within the Borough begin in the 1870s. See also John Fletcher's study, *A Technical Triumph: One Hundred Years Of Public Further Education in Merthyr Tydfil, 1873-1973* (Merthyr, 1974) and several articles of Leslie Evans, listed in the Library's *Local Guide*, including one on the Dowlais Schools of Sir John and Lady Guest.

Transport

One of the processes of industrialisation which was felt strongest in Merthyr was the rapid change and improvement in all forms of transport from the end of the 18th century. Merthyr Tydfil was the birthplace of the modern steam powered railway locomotive.

Several articles on the different aspects of this subject of transport have appeared in the *Merthyr Historian* I, and there are details in Wilkins and the Merthyr teachers' *History*. Not many records have survived on the subject of Merthyr's system of roadways outside the standard general works on the town, and on the history of Transport, though the actual physical evidence is sometimes still visible today about Merthyr. On the subject of the Glamorganshire Canal, see the several works on canals by Charles Hadfield; some records of the Canal Company are held at the Glamorgan Archives Office, Ref. D/D Xky, 1793. On the bigger subject of railways, see the Oakwood Library of Railway History's two splendid booklets, one on *The Taff Vale Railway* (2nd Ed. 1950) and *The Brecon & Merthyr Railway* (1957), both works by D. S. M. Barrie, and both still in print. Some of the Taff Vale Railway Company's records are held at Cardiff Ref. D/D Tho.1066- and more extensively in London at the Public Record Office, Kew. See also the standard work on the Great Western Railway Company in several volumes by Macdermot.

Public Health

As the first town of the Industrial Revolution in Wales, the living conditions in Merthyr by the mid 19th century were by any standard deplorable in the extreme, and several contemporary reports speak of the total lack of rudimentary sanitation for the houses and streets, no adequate water supply, gross overcrowding of houses &c. In 1849 T. W. Rammell conducted an inspection of the town for the London General Board of Health which was subsequently printed as a *Report to the General Board of Health on a Preliminary Inquiry into the Sewerage, Drainage and Supply of Water, and the Sanitary Condition of the Inhabitants of the Town of Merthyr Tydfil . . .* (1850). The

148

Report ran to 71pp. one of the longest produced for a Welsh town and included a map of the town and a plan of a part of Caedraw. It is a detailed picture of Merthyr town centre and some of its worst quarters in the mid 19th century. The need for remedial action was slowly apparent especially after the publication of this report, and a temporary officer of Health was appointed, William Kay from Bristol. His first report survives, a *Report on the Sanitary Condition of Merthyr Tydfil* . . . (Merthyr, 1855) of 80pp. Kay in turn was followed some years later by Merthyr's first permanently appointed Medical Officer of Health, T. J. Dyke, and his profoundly detailed reports have survived from 1866. See especially his First Report for 1865 and the Second for 1866. Other more specialised and technically orientated reports and surveys have survived, on such subjects as the incidence of fevers in the town, the water supply and reservoirs of Merthyr &c.

At the Glamorgan Archives Office on temporary loan are the several volumes of the Merthyr Tydfil Local Board of Health Minute Books, (Ref. L/B MT) 1850-1894, 7 volumes with gaps; and the Merthyr Board of Guardian's Collection (Ref. U/M) of 56 volumes, 1836-1930 with gaps, containing miscellaneous registers, reports &c.

The present author's researches for the University of Wales will be published shortly, *A Collection of Documents Relating to Aspects of Public Health in Nineteenth Century Wales* (provisional title) University of Wales Press, Cardiff, forthcoming 1978/79, which contains substantial sections on Merthyr; and see also the articles by Dr. Joseph Gross in this issue of the *Merthyr Historian*.

Miscellaneous
Some subjects not included in the above headings are
MUSIC: see David Morgans's *Music & Musicians of Merthyr and District* (Merthyr 1922); and on the town's most famous musician and composer, Joseph Parry see Owain T. Edwards's *Joseph Parry 1841-1903* (Cardiff, 1970) and a recent pamphlet, *Dr. Joseph Parry* (1977) on sale at Merthyr libraries.
SPORT: apart from various old and current team photographs from the local press, see the *Centenary Brochure* of Merthyr Rugby Football Club, Centenary Year 1876-1976.

Official Publications
CENTRAL: On a national level, it would have been almost inconceivable that the several Royal Commissions and Select Committees of central government at Westminster would overlook evidence from Merthyr Tydfil as the main industrial town in Wales for much of the 19th century. A wide range of subjects are covered in this material. Reports of the Royal Commissions, published in British Parliamentary Papers (PP) frequently contain substantial references to Merthyr. A brief selection of some of the best known ones are: the Report on Employment of Women and Children in Mines (1842); the Second Report on Large Towns and Populous Districts (1845); Report of Inquiry into the

State of Education in Wales (1847) — this was the cause for the infamous issue of "the Treason of the Blue Books" (Brad Y Llyfrau Gleision), though the Dowlais Schools emerged relatively favourably from the report; and the Report on Merthyr Tydfil (1935) which recommended, amongst other things, that Merthyr town be moved to a coastal site. The several detailed reports on the coalmining industry for the late 19th and early 20th centuries contain several sections of evidence relating to Merthyr.

LOCAL: On a local level, in the Merthyr Central Library are the several Minute Books, ledgers &c of the proceedings of former Council meetings held in Merthyr. The volumes of the Council Minutes date from 1894- which include the several constituent committees; and separate volumes of Minutes for the Education Committee; Waterworks Committee, &c. A full list is held at the Central Library.

For those with more time, the main local press which has covered the Merthyr area in the past are: the *Cardiff and Merthyr Guardian*, 1832-1860s, held at Cardiff Central Library; *Merthyr Telegraph* 1855-1881, held at the National Library of Wales, Aberystwyth; the *Merthyr Express* 1874 onwards at the Glamorgan Archive Office, and from 1914 onwards as well at Cardiff Library; and the *South Wales Daily News* for the later part of the 19th century and the *Western Mail* 1869 onwards contain items of interest on Merthyr. Several shortrun papers, notably the *Merthyr Pioneer* for the early 20th century, and several papers which appeared and disappeared as quickly again in the 1850s and 60s are available in London, and at Aberystwyth.

A measure of "lighter" reading is afforded by several modern novels with Merthyr town, partly fictional and partly fact used as a backcloth. For example, see Alexander Cordell's *The Fire People* (1972) which concerns the Merthyr Riots of 1831, and the role of Dic Penderyn; as does Rhydwen Williams's *The Angry Vineyard* (1975). Jack Jones's *Off To Philadelphia In The Morning* (1947) is supposed to be a partly biographical novel about Dr. Joseph Parry of Merthyr, and filming for television in 1976 used Merthyr as the locale for some of the scenes. Several other novels by Jones, partly autobiographical, use Merthyr as their setting, e.g. *Unfinished Journey* (1938). Mervyn Jones's *Life on the Dole* (1972) is set in the Merthyr of 1947.

This has not been an exhaustive list; many titles have been omitted here for reasons of space. No mention has been made either of several pieces of research going on at this moment at the University Colleges of Wales both by individual researchers and by sponsored team work where Merthyr is being used as the area for study. It is hoped that some of this work will become more widely available in time.

Outside Merthyr town, the Cardiff Central Library in the Hayes; the Glamorgan Archives Office at Mid-Glamorgan County Hall, Cathays Park, Cardiff; the National Museum of Wales Cardiff, and the National Library of Wales Aberystwyth, all contain sizeable holdings of material directly relating to Merthyr. Only some of the more important items have been mentioned in this article. At the South

Wales Miners' Library, Swansea, there are several collections of personal libraries and papers concerning well known Merthyr citizens; the S. O. Davies Library is housed there, and the J. S. Williams (Dowlais) Papers, to mention just two items.

The South Wales Press today—the *Western Mail*, the *South Wales Echo*, and the local *Merthyr Express* regularly contain features of historical interest relating to Merthyr and district, as well as book reviews, dates of lectures &c. The flourishing Merthyr Tydfil Historical Society holds a full programme of lectures, short local tours, and including this present volume, has published two collections of essays on local history. The study of local history in the Valleys with Merthyr as a main participant has recently been co-ordinated with the formation of a newsletter and information service by the Extra-Mural Department of University College Cardiff, and by the work of the Standing Conference on the History of the South Wales Valleys.

There is no substitute, however, for the study of local history at its source, here in Merthyr Tydfil, and it is hoped opportunity can be taken to visit and examine the many remnants of Merthyr's rich historical heritage, and to support those individuals and organisations working for the preservation of the many monuments to Merthyr's past which still survive in the town today. A visit to Cyfarthfa Castle Museum would be very worthwhile in this respect.